Teacher Resource Copymasters

HOUGHTON MIFFLIN **Math Steps**

![logo] **HOUGHTON MIFFLIN**

Boston • Atlanta • Dallas • Denver • Geneva, Illinois • Palo Alto • Princeton

Printed in the U.S.A.

ISBN: 0-395-98307-X

23456789-B-05 04 03 02 01 00

Contents

Assessments 1

The assessment copymasters give you valuable information about your students' prior knowledge, progress, and understanding of new mathematical content.

From the beginning of the year through the end of the year, you can assess students' understanding of mathematical skills, concepts, and vocabulary. Both free-response and multiple-choice tests are provided.

The results of these tests can help you assess whether students have the necessary prerequisite skills and knowledge in order to be successful with this year's materials, whether students are progressing adequately, and whether students have achieved the goals of the mathematics curriculum.

Reteach Worksheets 53

Reteach Worksheets meet the needs of students who require reinforcement of topics or concepts. The step-by-step instruction on each worksheet supports students through the learning process. The Teacher Note at the bottom of each page tells you when to use the Worksheet.

Some Reteach Worksheets review prerequisite skills or concepts for a unit. Students can use these before they begin a unit.

Most Reteach Worksheets support lessons in a unit. In the Student Book, there is a Quick Check feature that appears at the end of many lessons. The Quick Check reviews the lessons you have just covered. If students have difficulty with any of the concepts or skills on the Quick Check, they can use the Reteach Worksheets that correspond to the items. References to Reteach Worksheets appear in the Teacher Edition in both the Annotated Student Book pages and in the Lesson Support.

Extension Worksheets

Extension Worksheets cover a variety of mathematical content. They give students an opportunity to extend the topic they are learning or they introduce students to new topics.

The Extension Worksheets are organized by unit. The Teacher Note at the bottom of each page tells you when to use the Worksheet. References to Extension Worksheets appear in the Lesson Support in the Teacher Edition.

Teaching Resources

Teaching Resources are copymasters for frequently used teaching aids and for Family Projects. You may use the teaching aids during the presentation of a lesson or reproduce them for students to use individually. Family Projects provide suggestions for students and their families for working together on the skills and objectives in each unit.

Answer Keys

Answer Keys include answers for all of the assessments, as well as the Reteach Worksheets and Extension Worksheets.

Assessments

NOTES

Assessment Overview

At the Beginning of the Year

- **Beginning of the Year Inventory**

  Before your students start Unit 1, you may give them the Beginning of the Year Inventory. This pretest shows whether students possess the necessary prerequisite skills and knowledge to be successful with this year's mathematics.

  You can also use the Inventory as a placement test for students who transfer to your school during the schoolyear.

  The Inventory uses free-response format to test objectives that cover skills, concepts, problem solving, and vocabulary.

Before Each Unit

- **Unit Pretest**

  Assessing prior knowledge helps you build effective lessons using what students already know. You will quickly learn which skills, concepts, and vocabulary your students need to review before they begin a new unit.

  By using the results of the Unit Pretests, you can prepare your students to be confident and successful with the mathematics in the new unit.

During Each Unit

- **Quick Checks in the Student Book**

  Monitor and assess students' progress at regular intervals. The Quick Check reviews the lessons you have just covered.

  References to the Reteach Worksheets and the Skills Tutorial appear in the Teacher Edition in both the Annotated Student Book pages and in the Lesson Support.

After Each Unit

- **Unit Posttest**

  Each Unit Posttest is an additional tool you may use to assess students' mathematical understanding and application of the work in that unit.

  The Unit Posttests are formatted like the Unit Reviews in the Student Book and cover all unit objectives.

At Midyear

- **Midyear Test**

  The Midyear Test covers objectives from Units 1 through 6 in the Student Book. Test results will show which skills or concepts you need to review with students.

  This test is in standardized format to provide your students with valuable experience in taking standardized tests. Students will mark their answers on the answer sheet provided (see Teaching Resource 2) by filling in the space for their answer choice.

At the End of the Year

- **Final Test**

  The Final Test covers objectives from Units 7 through 11 in the Student Book, as well as key objectives from each unit in the first half of the book.

  You can use this summative test to reinforce the topics taught throughout the year and to assess what students have mastered.

  The Final Test is in standardized format to provide your students with more test-taking practice. Students will mark their answers on the answer sheet provided (see Teaching Resource 2) by filling in the space for their answer choice.

Name _____

Compare. Write <, >, or =.

1. $^-3$ ◯ 0   **2.** $^-8$ ◯ 3   **3.** $^-7$ ◯ $^-2$

Graph the integers $^-4$, 3, $^-1$, 2 on this number line.

4.

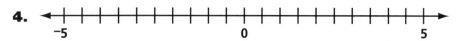

$^-5$ 0   5

Find the volume and the surface area of the prism.

5. $V =$ _____   **6.** $SA =$ _____

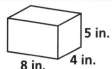

5 in.
8 in.   4 in.

Multiply or divide.

7.   5.38
    × 3.6

8.   10.07
    × 0.6

9. $5.3\overline{)17.49}$

Write the reciprocal.

10. $2\frac{3}{4}$ _____   **11.** $3\frac{1}{3}$ _____   **12.** $5\frac{9}{10}$ _____

Write the factors and the common factors.

13. Factors of **18**: _____ Factors of **32**: _____

Common factors of **18** and **32**: _____

Write *prime* or *composite*. Write each composite as a product of a pair of factors other than itself and 1.

14. 41 _____   **15.** 25 _____   **16.** 23 _____

Write an algebraic expression for the word expression. Let *n* represent the variable.

17. 7 multiplied by a number

_____

18. The product of a number and 58

_____

Use properties to complete the equation.

19. $3 \times 9 =$ _____ $\times 3$ **20.** $0 \times m =$ _____   **21.** $5(2 \times 7) = 5 \times ($_____$)$

22. $3 \times 19 = 3 \times (9 +$ _____$) = (3 \times$ _____$) + ($_____ $\times 10)$

Add or subtract.

23.   5.8
        − 0.4

24.   7.02
        + 1.9

25.   640.2
        −   3.06

26.   67.009
        + 5.22

Write each sum or difference.

27. ⁻2 − 9 = _____

28. 7 + (⁻5) = _____

29. 1 − 5 = _____

30. ⁻3 + (⁻5) = _____

31. 8 − (⁻1) = _____

32. ⁻3 + 7 = _____

Write the opposite of the integer.

33. ⁻19 _____

34. 21_____

35. ⁻7 _____

Use the coordinate grid.
Write the ordered pair for each point.

36. Point *A* _____

37. Point *B* _____

**Use a ruler to measure the segment to the
nearest inch and to the nearest centimeter.**

M |———————————————————————————————| *N*

38. _____ in.

39. _____ cm

Complete each equation.

40. 60 in. = _____ ft

41. 6 km = _____ m

42. 4 pt = _____ c

43. 9,000 mL = _____ L

44. 23 kg = _____ g

45. 208 oz = _____ lb

Multiply or divide.

46.   0.9
        ×   9

47.   0.56
        ×   24

48.   0.86
        × 100

49. 9)‾32.4

50. 5)‾3.7

51. 35)‾0.7

52. 100)‾30.8

Use exponents to write the prime factorization.

53. 50 _____

54. 20 _____

55. 36 _____

Name _____

Write as a decimal and as a fraction in simplest form.

56. 30% _____

57. 25% _____

58. 66% _____

Write the fraction or decimal as a percent.

59. $\frac{1}{4}$ _____

60. 0.02 _____

61. $\frac{5}{8}$ _____

Solve.

Results of
Class Election

62. 25% of 16 _____

63. 20% of 38 _____

64. 10% of 145 _____

65. 38% of 250 _____

66. There were **80** students who voted in the
class election. Use the circle graph to find
the number of students who voted for Ann. _____

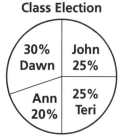

30%
Dawn | John
25%

Ann
20% | 25%
Teri

Use properties to complete the equation.

67. $\frac{1}{5} \times \frac{3}{4} = \frac{3}{4} \times$ _____

68. $\frac{2}{3} + \left(\frac{7}{8} + \frac{3}{5}\right) = \left(\text{\_\_\_\_\_} + \frac{7}{8}\right) + \frac{3}{5}$

Use the data in the table to answer the question.

Ages of Students in the Computer Club	
Males	32, 29, 32, 42, 45, 34, 37, 28, 49, 26
Females	38, 36, 48, 46, 25, 37, 45, 23, 30, 42

69. Are there more males or females in the age range **30–39** years?

_____

70. What is the mean age of the female members? _____

71. What is the mode of the ages of the male members? _____

72. What is the median age of all the members? _____

Find the perimeter and area.

73.

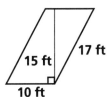

15 ft
17 ft
10 ft

P = _____

A = _____

74.

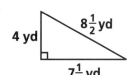

4 yd
$8\frac{1}{2}$ yd
$7\frac{1}{2}$ yd

P = _____

A = _____

Name _____

Write the product in simplest form.

75. $2\frac{3}{4} \times \frac{1}{2} =$ _____

76. $4\frac{4}{5} \times 5 =$ _____

77. $2\frac{1}{4} \times 1\frac{5}{6} =$ _____

Compare. Write <, >, or =

78. 3,746 ◯ 3,764

79. 421,202 ◯ 471,202

Divide.

80. $8\overline{)291}$

81. $42\overline{)221}$

82. $30\overline{)8,907}$

Use the data below to complete the graph.

83.

City	Police Cars	Fire Trucks
Edgar	34	43
Fulton	25	8
Bendo	40	15

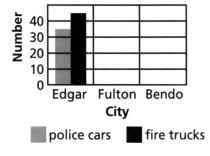

Emergency Vehicles

police cars ■ fire trucks

Use the data below to complete the line plot.

84. Ages of Children at the Park on Sunday
3, 12, 12, 14, 7, 9, 13, 18, 19, 5, 5, 8, 6, 11, 3

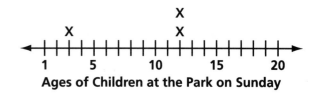

Ages of Children at the Park on Sunday

Use inverse operations to complete the equation.

85. $8 \times y = 48$

$y =$ _____ ÷ _____

$y =$ _____

86. $a \div 2 = 9$

$a =$ _____ × _____

$a =$ _____

Find the product.

87. $20 \times 481 =$ _____

88. $82 \times 700 =$ _____

89. $2,000 \times 304 =$ _____

Write an equation to solve the problem. Then solve.

90. Sally's collection of **17** CDs includes **5** new CDs she got for her birthday. How many CDs did she have before that? _____

8 Beginning of the Year Inventory (6)

Write *acute*, *right*, or *obtuse*.

91. 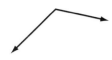 _____

92.  _____

Draw the angle.

93. 105° _____

94. 70° _____

**Draw a number line to represent the 10-mile drive
Elizabeth is making. Then solve.**

95. Elizabeth stopped after $2\frac{5}{8}$ miles to buy gas.

How much farther does she have to drive? _____

Add or subtract. Write the answer in simplest form.

96. $\begin{array}{r} \frac{3}{10} \\ + \frac{4}{10} \\ \hline \end{array}$

97. $\begin{array}{r} 3\frac{5}{12} \\ + 2\frac{1}{12} \\ \hline \end{array}$

98. $\begin{array}{r} 4 \\ - 2\frac{3}{5} \\ \hline \end{array}$

99. $\begin{array}{r} 7 \\ - \frac{9}{10} \\ \hline \end{array}$

Solve the equation for *n*.

100. $13 + n = 28$ _____

101. $n - 15 = 4$ _____

**Make a table of ordered pairs for the equation. Then
graph the equation on the grid.**

102. $y = {}^-2x + 1$

x	y

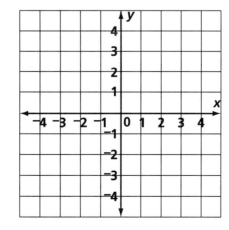

Write each fraction or mixed number as a decimal. Write each decimal as a fraction or mixed number.

103. $\dfrac{8}{100}$ _____

104. $3\dfrac{46}{100}$ _____

105. 0.06 _____

106. 1.075 _____

Add or subtract. Write the answer in simplest form.

107.
$$\begin{aligned}&\dfrac{1}{4}\\ +&\dfrac{5}{12}\\ \hline\end{aligned}$$

108.
$$\begin{aligned}&\dfrac{13}{16}\\ -&\dfrac{1}{4}\\ \hline\end{aligned}$$

109.
$$\begin{aligned}&2\dfrac{1}{4}\\ +&2\dfrac{2}{3}\\ \hline\end{aligned}$$

110.
$$\begin{aligned}&6\dfrac{3}{5}\\ -&2\dfrac{7}{10}\\ \hline\end{aligned}$$

Write the place value of the underlined digit in each number.

111. 11.2$\underline{5}$ _____

112. 0.$\underline{1}$6 _____

113. 476.$\underline{8}$ _____

Compare. Write <, >, or =.

114. 5.1 ◯ 5.10

115. 11.5 ◯ 11.55

116. 378.360 ◯ 378.306

Write the numbers in order from greatest to least.

117. 0.16, 1.6, 0.016, 0.106 _____

Use the order of operations to evaluate the expression.

118. $63 \div (3 + f)$ for $f = 4$ _____

119. $d \times (4 + 7)$ for $d = 2$ _____

Complete.

120. Round **5,824,654** to the nearest million. _____

121. Write three million, sixty thousand, four hundred in standard form. _____

122. Write **5,028** in word form. _____

123. What percent of the grid at the right is shaded? _____

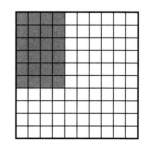

Divide. Write the quotient in simplest form.

124. $6 \div \dfrac{1}{6} =$ _____

125. $\dfrac{3}{8} \div \dfrac{1}{2} =$ _____

126. $\dfrac{2}{5} \div 3 =$ _____

Multiply.

127. $\begin{array}{r} 54 \\ \times\ 3 \\ \hline \end{array}$

128. $\begin{array}{r} 604 \\ \times\ \ 3 \\ \hline \end{array}$

129. $\begin{array}{r} 1{,}033 \\ \times\ \ \ 6 \\ \hline \end{array}$

130. $\begin{array}{r} 693 \\ \times\ 25 \\ \hline \end{array}$

The double-line graph shows the temperatures one morning in two cities. Use the graph to solve.

131. At what time was the

temperature in the

two cities the same? _____

132. In which city did the temperature

increase all morning? _____

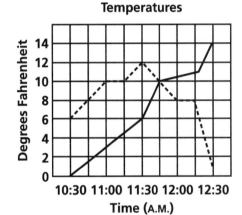

Draw and label the figure.

133. Ray *MN*

134. Line segment *AB*

135. Line *RT*

Multiply. Write the product in simplest form.

136. $\dfrac{2}{5} \times \dfrac{2}{3} =$ _____

137. $\dfrac{5}{6} \times 24 =$ _____

138. $\dfrac{1}{2} \times \dfrac{4}{7} =$ _____

Write the product or quotient.

139. $^-12 \div 4 =$

_____

140. $^-7 \times ^-3 =$

_____

141. $^-9 \div ^-9 =$

_____

142. $20 \div ^-5 =$

_____

Use the graph to solve the problem.

143. During which month was the

greatest amount of money saved? _____

144. How did the amount of money

saved change from April to May? _____

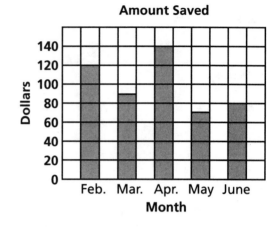

Amount Saved

Add or subtract.

145.   297
          + 526

146.   7,244
          − 3,894

147.   6,000
          −   857

148.   31,007
            68,000
          + 8,525

Are the pair of figures congruent? Write *yes* or *no*.

149. 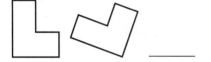 _____

150. 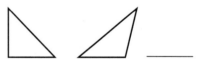 _____

Draw all the lines of symmetry for the figure.

151.

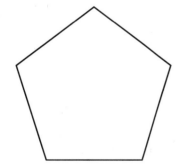

Write each number. (1A)

1. Write three thousand forty in standard form. _____

2. Write **3,027,409** in expanded form. _____

3. Write **90,342** in word form. _____

_____

Add, subtract, multiply, or divide. (1B)

4.   739
     + 264

5.   2,607
     ×   46

6.   12,023
     − 4,652

7. $203\overline{)5,628}$

Evaluate each expression for $n = 2$. (1C)

8. $26 + 8 \div n$ _____

9. $3 + (7 - n) \times 4$ _____

10. $n \times 9 - 16 \div n$ _____

Solve each equation. (1D)

11. $m - 8 = 17$ _____

12. $p \div 5 = 25$ _____

13. $h \times 3 = 18$ _____

14. $\dfrac{a}{2} = 14$ _____

15. $y + 42 = 97$ _____

16. $r - 13 = 120$ _____

Solve. Use the table.

17. Find the mean, median, mode, and range of the data. (1E)

Mean _____   Median _____

Mode _____   Range _____

18. How would the measures above change if Mark were not included in the table? Write *increase*, *decrease*, or *same*. (1E)

Mean _____   Median _____

Mode _____   Range _____

Ages of Students in the Computer Club	
Morgan	16
Jana	18
Mark	9
Angie	19
Bert	15

19. José joins the computer club. The average age of José, Mark, and Bert is **14** years. What equation could you write to find Jose's age? (1F)

_____

Write each number. (1A)

1. Write nine thousand twenty in standard form. _____

2. Write **6,810,062** in expanded form. _____

3. Write **31,065** in word form. _____

_____

Add, subtract, multiply, or divide. (1B)

4. 536
    + 983

5. 4,029
    ×   53

6. 18,907
    −   6,288

7. $421\overline{)7{,}891}$

Evaluate each expression for $n = 5$. (1C)

8. $32 - 20 \div n$ _____

9. $8 + (n - 2) \times 3$ _____

10. $3 \times n + 15 \div n$ _____

Solve each equation. (1D)

11. $d - 11 = 42$ _____

12. $w \div 4 = 20$ _____

13. $g \times 7 = 77$ _____

14. $\dfrac{m}{8} = 32$ _____

15. $b + 18 = 73$ _____

16. $m - 45 = 60$ _____

Solve. Use the table.

17. Find the mean, median, mode, and range of the data. (1E)

Ages of Workers at Gift Shop	
Harriet	32
Arturo	34
Belle	28
Ellen	53
Sidney	37

Mean _____ Median _____

Mode _____ Range _____

18. How would the mean, median, mode, and range change if Ellen were not included in the table? (1E)

Mean _____ Median _____

Mode _____ Range _____

19. A new worker joins the gift shop. The average of hers, Harriet's, and Ellen's ages is **43** years. What equation could you write to find the age of the new worker? (1F)

_____

Write the standard form for each number. (2A)

1. Forty-seven thousandths _____   **2.** 80 + 3 + 0.6 + 0.002 _____

Compare. Write >, <, or =. (2B)

3. 0.7 $\bigcirc$ 0.46 _____   **4.** 8.20 $\bigcirc$ 8.2 _____   **5.** 0.05 $\bigcirc$ 0.23 _____

Round 482.165 to the given place. (2B)

6. Nearest whole   **7.** Nearest   **8.** Nearest
     number _____   tenth _____   hundredth _____

Write each group in order from greatest to least. (2B)

9. 3.04, 30.4, 0.34 _____   **10.** 11.02, 10.12, 11.20 _____

Add, subtract, multiply, or divide. (2C)

11. $\begin{array}{r} 0.462 \\ + 2.185 \end{array}$ **12.** $\begin{array}{r} 8.5 \\ - 1.32 \end{array}$ **13.** $\begin{array}{r} 71.02 \\ + 51.4 \end{array}$ **14.** $\begin{array}{r} \$208.87 \\ - \$\ 86.65 \end{array}$ **15.** $\begin{array}{r} 8.2 \\ + 9.013 \end{array}$

16. $\begin{array}{r} 3.06 \\ \times \quad 8 \end{array}$ **17.** $\begin{array}{r} 18.4 \\ \times 0.23 \end{array}$ **18.** $7\overline{)3.36}$ **19.** $14\overline{)294.42}$ **20.** $0.8\overline{)0.0376}$

Evaluate each expression when $a = 0.2$ and $b = 0.65$. (2D)

21. $b - a$ **22.** $a \times b$ **23.** $9 \div a$ **24.** $0.7 + (2 \div b)$

_____   _____   _____   _____

Solve each equation. (2E)

25. $n \times 9 = 16.2$ **26.** $c \div 0.5 = 11.6$ **27.** $123.7 + d = 197.79$

_____   _____   _____

Solve. (2F)

28. To the nearest tenth, a number in hundredths rounds to **6.1**.
The digit in the hundredths place is one-third of the ones digit
and one more than the tenths digit. What is the number?   _____

29. Each centerpiece for a graduation party will have **15** flowers.
How many centerpieces can be made from **240** flowers?   _____

Write the standard form for each number. (2A)

1. One hundred five thousandths _____   **2.** 200 + 30 + 0.04 + 0.007 _____

Compare. Write >, <, or =. (2B)

3. 0.4 ◯ 0.25 _____   **4.** 0.16 ◯ 0.160 _____   **5.** 3.04 ◯ 3.41 _____

Round 93.528 to the given place. (2B)

6. Nearest whole number _____   **7.** Nearest tenth _____   **8.** Nearest hundredth _____

Write each group in order from greatest to least. (2B)

9. 27.3, 2.73, 2.37 _____   **10.** 0.16, 0.016, 0.106 _____

Add, subtract, multiply, or divide. (2C)

11.   0.173
        + 6.199

12.   7.4
        − 3.71

13.   43.06
        + 14.5

14. $143.19
        − $ 72.68

15.   6.3
        + 0.145

16.   7.05
        ×   6

17.   23.1
        × 0.62

18. 8)5.92

19. 23)415.38

20. 0.4)0.0388

Evaluate each expression when $a = 0.2$ and $b = 0.03$. (2D)

21. $b + a$

22. $0.1 + b$

23. $14 \div a$

24. $8 - (6 \div b)$

_____   _____   _____   _____

Solve each equation. (2E)

25. $n \times 6 = 14.4$ **26.** $g \div 0.4 = 2.6$ **27.** $96.23 + m = 204.63$

_____   _____   _____

Solve. (2F)

28. A company packs games in cartons. Each carton can hold up to **24** games. What is the minimum number of cartons that are needed to pack **400** games?   _____

29. Sam bought **45** muffins. How many dozens did he order?   _____

Name _____

Write whether each number is divisible by 2, 3, 4, 5, 6, 9, or 10. (3A)

1. 252 is divisible by: _____

2. 180 is divisible by: _____

Simplify each expression. (3B)

3. $4^2 - 1 \times 6$ _____

4. $20(7 - 3)^2$ _____

**Write _P_ or _C_ to indicate whether the number is prime or composite.
If it is composite, write the prime factorization in exponent form. (3C)**

5. 30 _____

6. 17 _____

7. 64 _____

Write the GCF and LCM of each pair. (3D)

8. 9 and 12

9. 10 and 15

_____ _____

Write two equivalent fractions for each. (3E)

10. $\frac{4}{10}$ _____

11. $\frac{9}{15}$ _____

Write each as a fraction or mixed number in simplest form. (3E)

12. 0.26 _____

13. $\frac{22}{6}$ _____

Compare. Write >, <, or =. (3F)

14. 2.8 $\bigcirc$ $2\frac{4}{5}$

15. $\frac{5}{6}$ $\bigcirc$ 0.85

16. $\frac{43}{10}$ $\bigcirc$ 0.43

Write these numbers in order from least to greatest. (3F)

17. 0.85, $\frac{2}{3}$, $\frac{4}{5}$, 0.09, 0.75 _____

18. 3.6, $\frac{10}{3}$, $\frac{12}{5}$, 2.75, 3.13 _____

Solve. Use the graph for items 19 and 20. (3G)

19. Which city has more than twice as many police cars as Arkata?

_____

20. Next year, Vineland plans to buy **15** more police cars. After they do, how will their number compare with that of Farmington?

_____

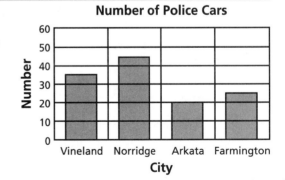

Number of Police Cars

21. Bob, Juan, and Alice are standing in line to buy food. How many different ways can they stand in line if Alice is always last in line?

_____

Write whether each number is divisible by 2, 3, 4, 5, 6, 9, or 10. (3A)

1. 408 is divisible by: _____

2. 240 is divisible by: _____

Simplify each expression. (3B)

3. $7^2 - 3 \times 8$ _____

4. $8(9 - 6)^2$ _____

Write P or C to indicate whether the number is prime or composite.
If it is composite, write the prime factorization in exponent form. (3C)

5. 27 _____

6. 56 _____

7. 31 _____

Write the GCF and LCM of each pair. (3D)

8. 9 and 16

9. 36 and 48

_____   _____

Write two equivalent fractions for each. (3D)

10. $\frac{12}{18}$ _____

11. $\frac{20}{35}$ _____

Write each as a fraction or mixed number in simplest form. (3E)

12. 1.4 _____

13. $\frac{30}{8}$ _____

Compare. Write >, <, or =. (3F)

14. 3.3 $\bigcirc$ $3\frac{1}{3}$

15. 0.88 $\bigcirc$ $\frac{7}{8}$

16. 1.35 $\bigcirc$ $\frac{135}{100}$

Write these numbers in order from least to greatest. (3F)

17. 0.6, $\frac{7}{12}$, $\frac{2}{3}$, 0.8, 0.5 _____

18. 1.6, $\frac{9}{5}$, $\frac{12}{7}$, 1.77, 1.45 _____

Solve. Use the graph for items 19 and 20. (3G)

19. Which city has fewer than half as many firefighters as Howard?

_____

20. If 12 firefighters leave Elkville, will Elkville have more or fewer than Oakton?

_____

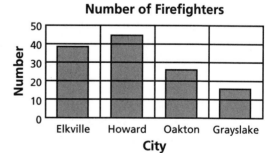

21. Midori and 3 friends are standing in line. How many different ways can they stand if Midori is first?

_____

Write each sum, difference, product, or quotient in simplest form. (4A, 4C)

1. $3\frac{1}{8}$
$-\ \frac{1}{4}$

2. $\frac{3}{4}$
$+\ \frac{1}{5}$

3. $4\frac{2}{3}$
$+\ \frac{5}{8}$

4. $8\frac{1}{5}$
$-\ 2\frac{5}{6}$

5. $\frac{3}{4}\times\frac{4}{7}$ _____

6. $\frac{7}{8}\div\frac{3}{4}$ _____

7. $2\frac{2}{3}\div 8$ _____

8. $4\times 3\frac{1}{6}$ _____

Solve. Write your answer in simplest form. (4B)

9. $\frac{4}{5}$ of $28 =$ _____

10. $\frac{3}{4}$ of $3\frac{1}{2} =$ _____

11. $\frac{1}{12}$ of $90 =$ _____

Solve for n. Write your answer in simplest form. (4D)

12. $n+\frac{4}{9}=3$ $n =$ _____

13. $n\times\frac{5}{6}=\frac{1}{6}$ $n =$ _____

14. $n\div\frac{7}{8}=24$ $n =$ _____

15. $n-\frac{7}{12}=\frac{5}{12}$ $n =$ _____

16. $n\times 2\frac{2}{5}=4$ $n =$ _____

17. $n\div\frac{7}{8}=\frac{2}{5}$ $n =$ _____

18. $n-\frac{4}{9}=\frac{1}{3}$ $n =$ _____

19. $n+\frac{2}{3}=3\frac{1}{2}$ $n =$ _____

Solve.

20. Suppose you are making a pictograph to display the data in the table. One symbol on the pictograph would represent how many hours of practice? Explain your choice. (4E)

_____

_____

Hours Practicing Soccer Last Month	
Bernelli	15
Wong	20
Hansen	5
Mills	25

21. Without overlapping, what is the maximum number of

2 × 3 rectangles that can be drawn on a **5 × 8** grid? (4F) _____

Write each sum, difference, product, or quotient in simplest form. (4A, 4C)

1. $2\frac{1}{6}$
$-\ \frac{1}{3}$

2. $\frac{1}{8}$
$+\ \frac{5}{6}$

3. $3\frac{3}{4}$
$+\ \frac{4}{5}$

4. $6\frac{1}{10}$
$-\ 1\frac{2}{3}$

5. $\frac{3}{8} \times \frac{8}{9}$ _____

6. $\frac{5}{6} \div \frac{2}{3}$ _____

7. $1\frac{1}{5} \div 12$ _____

8. $8 \times 2\frac{1}{10}$ _____

Solve. Write your answer in simplest form. (4B)

9. $\frac{7}{9}$ of $27 =$ _____

10. $\frac{7}{8}$ of $4\frac{1}{3} =$ _____

11. $\frac{1}{9}$ of $57 =$ _____

Solve for n. Write your answer in simplest form. (4D)

12. $n + \frac{3}{4} = 6$ $n =$ _____

13. $n \times \frac{4}{5} = \frac{1}{5}$ $n =$ _____

14. $n \div \frac{5}{12} = 60$ $n =$ _____

15. $n - \frac{1}{6} = \frac{5}{6}$ $n =$ _____

16. $n \times 3\frac{1}{8} = 10$ $n =$ _____

17. $n \div \frac{5}{9} = \frac{3}{4}$ $n =$ _____

18. $n - \frac{3}{5} = \frac{7}{10}$ $n =$ _____

19. $n + \frac{1}{4} = 2\frac{1}{5}$ $n =$ _____

Solve.

20. Suppose you are making a pictograph to display the data in the table. One symbol on the pictograph would represent how many dollars? Explain your choice. (4E)

_____

_____

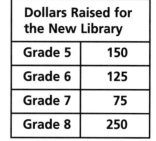

Dollars Raised for the New Library	
Grade 5	150
Grade 6	125
Grade 7	75
Grade 8	250

21. Without overlapping, what is the maximum number of

3 × 4 rectangles that can be drawn on a **7 × 12** grid? (4F) _____

Measure segment *MN* to each unit of measure. (5A)

```
M                                   N
|———————————————————————————|
```

1. Nearest half-inch _____

2. Nearest centimeter _____

Complete. (5B)

3. 2 mi = _____ ft

4. 18 in. = _____ ft

5. 1.7 km = _____ cm

Compare. Write <, >, or = (5B)

6. 1 min 15 s ◯ 65 s

7. 20 min ◯ $\frac{2}{3}$ h

8. 1 h 20 min ◯ 80 min

Circle the greater measure. (5B)

9. 300 mL or 3 L

10. 1.8 kg or 118 g

11. $2\frac{1}{2}$ qt or 7 pt

Circle the temperature that is most likely. (5C)

12. Package of frozen food

0°C or 50°C

13. A snowy day

100°F or 20°F

Solve. (5C, 5D)

14.
$$\begin{array}{r} 2\text{ ft }\ 8\text{ in.} \\ +\ 1\text{ ft } 10\text{ in.} \\ \hline \end{array}$$

15.
$$\begin{array}{r} 2\text{ wk } 1\text{ day } 6\text{ h} \\ \times\ 5 \\ \hline \end{array}$$

16.
$$\begin{array}{r} 4\text{ lb } 6\text{ oz} \\ -\ 1\text{ lb } 8\text{ oz} \\ \hline \end{array}$$

Solve.

17. On another sheet of paper, make a line graph of the data in the table. (5E)

18. Did the hiker walk without stopping for the entire trip? Explain. (5E)

_____

_____

19. At a cross country race, Enos ran 6 miles in 25 minutes. What was his speed in miles per hour? (5F) _____

Distance Traveled	
Time	Total Miles Hiked
10:30	0
11:30	6
11:45	10
12:15	10
2:30	14

Measure segment AB to each unit of measure (5A)

A ├────────────────────────────────┤ B

1. Nearest half-inch _____

2. Nearest centimeter _____

Complete. (5B)

3. $\frac{1}{2}$ mi = _____ ft

4. 3,500 cm = _____ m

5. 22 ft = _____ yd

Compare. Write <, >, or = (5B)

6. 2 min 10 s ◯ 100 s

7. 40 min ◯ $\frac{3}{4}$ h

8. 2 h 50 min ◯ 175 min

Circle the greater measure. (5B)

9. 6,000 mL or 60 L

10. 30 oz or 2 lb

11. 3.6 L or 3,000 mL

Circle the temperature that is most likely. (5C)

12. A hot summer day

30°F or 90°F

13. Cup of hot chocolate

0°C or 90°C

Solve. (5C, 5D)

14.   5 ft 3 in.
   + 4 ft 8 in.

15. 1 wk 3 days 2 h
   _____ × 10

16.   8 lb 2 oz
   − 3 lb 6 oz

Solve. (5E, 5F)

17. On another sheet of paper, make a line graph of the data in the table. (5E)

18. Did the driver travel without stopping for the entire trip? Explain. (5E)

_____

_____

19. Teish drove 44 miles in $\frac{2}{3}$ hour. At that rate how far can she drive in 5 hours? (5F) _____

Distance Traveled	
Time	Total Miles Driven
8:30	0
9:00	60
9:45	80
10:15	80
10:30	140

Write each ratio in three ways. (6A)

1. 3 teachers to 25 students _____

2. 14 chairs to 3 tables _____

Find each missing term. (6B)

3. $\frac{2}{3} = \frac{m}{18}$

4. $\frac{4}{5} = \frac{c}{15}$

5. $\frac{8}{3} = \frac{h}{30}$

6. $\frac{7}{12} = \frac{r}{30}$

7. $\frac{6}{d} = \frac{20}{15}$

_____ | _____ | _____ | _____ | _____

8. 25 pages in 2 hours = p pages in $4\frac{1}{2}$ hours $p =$ _____

Solve. (6C, 6D)

9. If 4 light bulbs cost $1.76, what is the cost of 6 light bulbs? _____

10. A car travels 40 miles in 1 hour. At that rate, how far will it travel in 30 minutes?

_____

11. If 1 inch on a map represents 50 miles, then 1.5 inches represents _____ miles.

12. If 4 feet on a model represents $\frac{1}{2}$ inch, then _____ feet represents 1 inch.

Write each fraction as a percent and each percent as a fraction. (6E)

13. $\frac{2}{3}$ _____

14. $\frac{1}{8}$ _____

15. 20% _____

16. 35% _____

Write each decimal as a percent and each percent as a decimal. (6E)

17. 42% _____

18. 80% _____

19. 0.3 _____

20. 0.075 _____

Solve. (6F, 6G)

21. 4 is what percent of $1\frac{1}{3}$? _____

22. 42 is 60% of what number? _____

23. Use the information in the table to make a graph on another sheet of paper.

Amount Saved

Month	Feb.	Mar.	Apr.	May	June
Dollars	120	90	140	70	80

24. What percent of the money saved during the 5-month period was saved in April? _____

Write each ratio in three ways. (6A)

1. **4** cars to **17** people _____

2. **9** shirts to **2** jackets _____

Find each missing term. (6B)

3. $\dfrac{3}{4} = \dfrac{b}{12}$ | **4.** $\dfrac{6}{5} = \dfrac{w}{25}$ | **5.** $\dfrac{2}{9} = \dfrac{m}{36}$ | **6.** $\dfrac{10}{8} = \dfrac{c}{50}$ | **7.** $\dfrac{4}{10} = \dfrac{15}{z}$

_____   _____   _____   _____   _____

8. **20** inches in **8** days = h inches in $2\dfrac{1}{2}$ days $h =$ _____

Solve. (6C, 6D)

9. If **24** cookies cost **$3.60,** what is the cost of **40** cookies? _____

10. A bicyclist covers **20** miles in **1** hour. At that rate, how far will she travel

in **45** minutes? _____

11. If **1** inch on a map represents **60** miles, then **2.5** inches represent _____ miles.

12. If **3** feet on a model represent $\dfrac{1}{8}$ inch, then _____ feet represent 1 inch.

Write each fraction as a percent and each percent as a fraction. (6E)

13. $\dfrac{7}{8}$ _____   **14.** $\dfrac{1}{6}$ _____   **15.** **60%** _____   **16.** **85%** _____

Write each decimal as a percent and each percent as a decimal. (6E)

17. **37%** _____   **18.** **10%** _____   **19.** **0.06** _____   **20.** **0.125** _____

Solve. (6F, 6G)

21. **9** is what percent of $2\dfrac{1}{4}$? _____

22. **34** is **40%** of what number? _____

23. Use the information in the table to make a graph on another sheet of paper.

New Club Memberships

Month	July	Aug.	Sept.	Oct.	Nov.
Number	23	32	13	37	20

24. What percent of the total new members joined in November? _____

Draw and label a figure to illustrate the description. (7A)

1. Line segment *MN*

2. Line *WX*

3. Ray *CD*

4. △*PQR*

5. Diameter $\overline{GH}$

6. Acute angle *DEF*

7. $\overleftrightarrow{MN} \perp \overleftrightarrow{BC}$

8. $\overleftrightarrow{GH} \parallel \overleftrightarrow{PQ}$

9. $\overleftrightarrow{XY}$ intersecting $\overleftrightarrow{CD}$ at *R*

Write the name of each figure. (7B)

10.

_____

11.

_____

12.

_____

13.

_____

14.

_____

15.

_____

Measure, then classify each angle. (7B)

16.
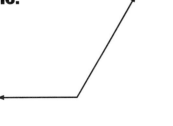
_____ , _____

17.
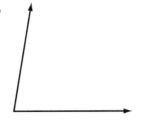
_____ , _____

18.
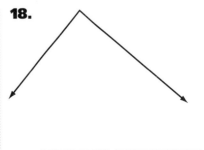
_____ , _____

JKLM ~ WXYZ. Use these figures to answer problems 19–22. (7C, 7E)

19. Find the length of side **YZ.** _____

20. Find the measure of ∠**WXY.** _____

21. ∠*JML* measures 50°.
Find the measure of ∠**WZY.** _____

22. What is the measure of
the supplement of ∠**MLK?** _____

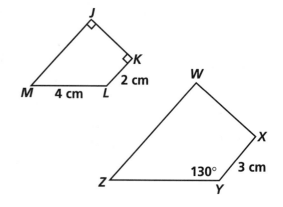

---

23. Draw an angle that measures 85°. (7B)

24. Construct a segment congruent to $\overline{PQ}$. (7A)

---

25. Construct an acute scalene triangle.
Label the vertex of the largest angle **Q**. (7D)

△KLP is isosceles. Find the measure of each angle. (7F, 7G)

26. ∠*LKP* = _____

27. ∠*MKN* = _____

28. ∠*MKL* = _____

29. ∠*LPK* = _____

30. ∠*NKP* = _____

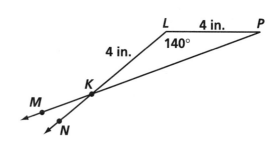

Solve. (7A)

31. The midpoints of three sides of a triangle
are joined with line segments. What is the
total number of triangles in the figures?   _____

Draw and label a figure to illustrate the description. (7A)

1. Line *BC*

2. Ray *ST*

3. Line segment *GH*

4. △*EFG*

5. Radius $\overline{XY}$

6. Obtuse angle *RST*

7. $\overleftrightarrow{AB} \parallel \overleftrightarrow{CD}$

8. $\overleftrightarrow{NP} \perp \overleftrightarrow{EF}$

9. $\overleftrightarrow{ED}$ intersecting $\overleftrightarrow{WV}$ at *A*

Write the name of each figure. (7D)

10.
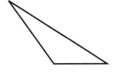
_____

11.

_____

12.

_____

13.

_____

14.

_____

15.

_____

Measure, then classify each angle. (7B)

16.

_____, _____

17.
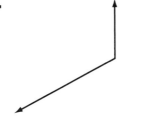
_____, _____

18.
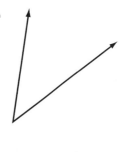
_____, _____

DEFG ~ UVXY. Use these figures to answer problems 19–22. (7C, 7E)

19. Find the length of side **UY.** _____

20. Find the measure of ∠**VXY.** _____

21. ∠**DEF** measures **60°.**
Find the measure of ∠**UVX.** _____

22. What is the measure of
the complement of ∠**UVX?** _____

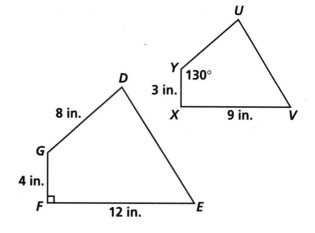

23. Draw an angle that measures **110°.** (7B) | **24.** Construct a segment congruent to $\overline{AB}$. (7A)

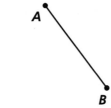

25. Construct a right isosceles triangle.
Label the vertex of the right angle **K.** (7D)

△DEF is isosceles. Find the measure of each angle. (7F, 7G)

26. ∠**DEG =** _____

27. ∠**EDF =** _____

28. ∠**FEH =** _____

29. ∠**DFE =** _____

30. ∠**GEH =** _____

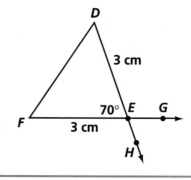

Solve. (7A)

31. A square has two diagonals that break it
up into four small triangles. What is the
total number of triangles in the figure?   _____

Find the perimeter of each polygon. (8A)

1.

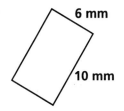

6 mm

10 mm

P = _____

2.

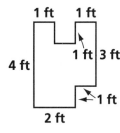

1 ft 1 ft

1 ft | 3 ft

4 ft

1 ft

2 ft

P = _____

Find the circumference of each circle. Use $C = \pi d$ and **3.14** for π. (8B)

3.

7 in.

C = _____

4.

1.5 cm

C = _____

Find the area of each figure. (8C)

5.

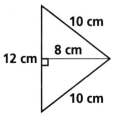

10 cm

8 cm

12 cm

10 cm

A = _____

6.

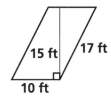

15 ft   17 ft

10 ft

A = _____

7.

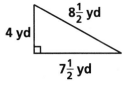

$8\frac{1}{2}$ yd

4 yd

$7\frac{1}{2}$ yd

A = _____

8.

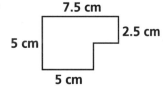

7.5 cm

2.5 cm

5 cm

5 cm

A = _____

Find the volume of each figure. (8E)

9.

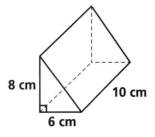

8 cm   10 cm

6 cm

V = _____

10.

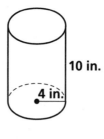

10 in.

4 in.

V ≈ _____

Find the surface area for each prism. (8E)

11.

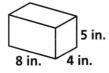

5 in.

8 in.   4 in.

SA = _____

12.

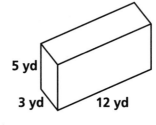

5 yd

3 yd   12 yd

SA = _____

Solve. (8D, 8F)

13. Larry wants to enlarge a cube with edges of **3** cm so that its volume will be **8** times larger. How long must each edge of the enlarged cube be?

_____

14. A cube was shrunk so that its edges now measure 8 in., one half of their original size. How did the surface area of the cube change?

_____

15. You have a **9**-inch by **14**-inch sheet of paper. You cut the largest possible circle out of this paper. What is the area of this circle? What formula did you use?

_____

Find the perimeter of the polygon. (8A)

1.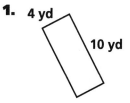

P = _____

2.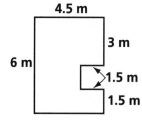

P = _____

Find the circumference of each circle. Use $c = \pi d$ and 3.14 for π. (8B)

3.

C = _____

4.

C = _____

Find the area of each figure. (8C)

5.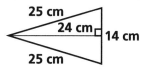

A = _____

6.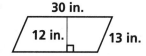

A = _____

7.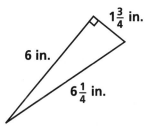

A = _____

8.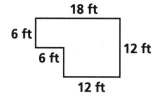

A = _____

Find the volume of each figure. (8E)

9.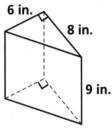

6 in.

8 in.

9 in.

$V =$ _____

10.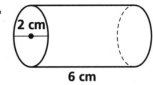

2 cm

6 cm

$V \approx$ _____

Find the surface area of each prism. (8E)

11.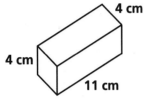

4 cm

4 cm

11 cm

$SA =$ _____

12.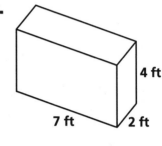

4 ft

7 ft

2 ft

$SA =$ _____

Solve. (8D, 8F)

13. Ruth wants to enlarge a cube with edges of **2** in. so that its volume will be **64** times larger. How long must each edge of the enlarged cube be?

_____

14. A cube was shrunk so that its edges now measure **4** cm, one third of their original size. How did the surface area of the cube change?

_____

15. You have a square that is **10** inches on each side. You want to cut the largest isosceles triangle from it that you can. What is the triangle's area? What formula did you use?

_____

Solve. Use the graph. (9A)

1. Which restaurant increased their number of customers steadily from March to June? _____

2. During which month did Sally's Cafe have more customers than Tony's Diner? _____

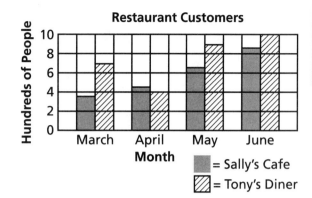

Solve. Use the line plot. (9B)

3. Which measure—the mean, median, or mode—best describes the data?

Explain. _____

_____

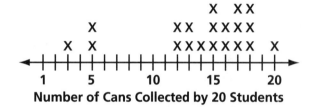

Number of Cans Collected by 20 Students

Solve.

4. Marcia wants to learn whether the students in her school prefer a new library or a new gymnasium. She plans to survey the first **50** people she meets leaving a basketball game. Would this be a representative sample of the students in the school? Explain. (9C)

_____

5. A **1–6** number cube is tossed twice. What is the probability of getting two fives? (9F)

_____

6. The experiment in exercise 5 is repeated 100 times. About how many times would you predict that two **4**'s would be tossed?

_____

7. Art has **4** pairs of shoes—white, black, brown, and tan. He has **2** jackets—black and brown. What is the probability he could choose at random the black jacket and the black shoes? (9E)

_____

8. Kiko bought some CDs on sale. She spent **$32** for **3** CDs. What were the prices of the **3** CDs she bought? (9G)

_____

Cost of Music CDs		
Yellow Tag	Red Tag	White Tag
$18	$12	$8

9. Write **3** different mixed numbers that have a mean of $2\frac{1}{3}$.

_____

Solve. Use the graph. (9A)

1. Which town increased its population steadily from **1985** to **2000**?

_____

2. During which year did Westlake have more people than Archer?

_____

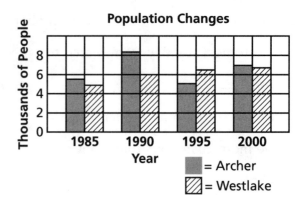

Population Changes

Thousands of People

= Archer

= Westlake

Solve. Use the line plot. (9B)

3. Which measure—the mean, median, or mode—best describes the data?

Explain. _____

_____

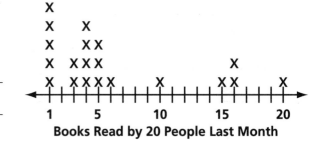

Books Read by 20 People Last Month

Solve.

4. Peter wants to learn whether the students in his school want more bike racks. He plans to survey **50** students getting off the buses in the morning. Would this be a representative sample of the students in the school?

Explain. (9D) _____

5. A **1–6** number cube is tossed twice. What is the probability of NOT getting two threes? (9F)   _____

6. The experiment in exercise **5** is repeated **100** times. About how many times would you predict that you do NOT get two **3's**?   _____

7. Laura has **5** scarves—red, yellow, blue, white, and black. She has **3** sweaters—red, blue, and white. What is the probability she could choose at random the blue scarf and the blue sweater? (9F)   _____

8. Sarno bought some fish for his aquarium. He spent **$56** for **3** fish at the prices shown in the table. What were the sizes of the **3** fish he bought? (9G)

Cost of Fish		
Small	Medium	Large
$11	$16	$24

_____

9. Write **4** different numbers that have a mean of $6\frac{1}{2}$. (9G) _____

Compare. Write >, <, or =. (10A)

1. $\frac{9}{2}$ ◯ 4

2. $^-2\frac{1}{5}$ ◯ 1

3. $^-\frac{6}{12}$ ◯ $^-\frac{1}{2}$

4. 2 ◯ $^-\frac{2}{1}$

---

5. On the number line below, plot point **A** at $^-$**1**, point **B** at $\frac{5}{2}$, and point **C** at $^-\frac{1}{2}$.

Add, subtract, multiply, or divide. (10B, 10C)

6. $^-4 + 9$ _____

7. $^-3 - (^-7)$ _____

8. $3 \cdot (^-6)$ _____

9. $^-12 \div ^-2$ _____

Simplify each expression. (10D)

10. $^-20 - 24 \div 4$ _____

11. $^-9 + (^-3)^2$ _____

12. $10 - 6 \cdot (^-5)$ _____

Solve for n. (10E)

13. $n - 2 = ^-5$

14. $n + (^-3) = 8$

15. $n - (^-1) = 13$

$n =$ _____

$n =$ _____

$n =$ _____

Solve. (10F)

16. The temperature was $^-$**5°C** early this morning. Since that time, it increased **10°C**. To find the temperature now, would you add or subtract? Explain.

_____

17. Suki is **4** years older than her sister Florie. The sum of their ages is **10** years. What equation could be used to find Suki's age? How old is Suki?

_____

Compare. Write <, >, or = . (10A)

1. $\frac{11}{4}$ ◯ 3

2. $^{-}1\frac{3}{4}$ ◯ 0

3. $^{-}\frac{1}{3}$ ◯ $^{-}\frac{4}{12}$

4. $\frac{5}{1}$ ◯ $^{-}5$

5. On the number line below, plot point **A** at $^{-}3$, point **B** at $^{-}\frac{1}{2}$, and point **C** at $^{-}\frac{7}{2}$.

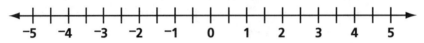

Add, subtract, multiply, or divide. (10B, 10C)

6. $^{-}1 + 6$ _____

7. $^{-}6 - (^{-}2)$ _____

8. $5 \cdot (^{-}4)$ _____

9. $^{-}18 \div ^{-}3$ _____

Simplify each expression. (10D)

10. $^{-}18 - 35 \div 7$ _____

11. $^{-}15 + (^{-}4)^2$ _____

12. $8 - 9 \cdot 2$ _____

Solve for n. (10E)

13. $n - 4 = ^{-}12$

14. $n + (^{-}5) = 9$

15. $n - (^{-}2) = 6$

$n =$ _____

$n =$ _____

$n =$ _____

Solve. (10F)

16. The temperature was $^{-}8°C$ early this morning. Since that time, it decreased 5°C. To find the temperature now, would you add or subtract $^{-}5°C$? Explain.

_____

17. Kevin is **2** years younger than his friend Paula. The sum of their ages is **18** years. What equation could be used to find Kevin's age? How old is Kevin?

_____

Complete a table of values and write ordered pairs for the equation. Then graph the equation. (11A)

1. $y = x - 2$

x	y	Ordered Pairs
		(,)
		(,)
		(,)
		(,)
		(,)

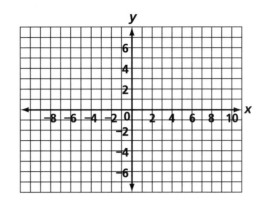

Write the letter that names each number on the number line. (11B)

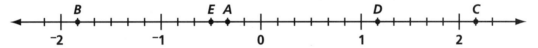

2. $^-0.5$ _____   **3.** $2\frac{1}{6}$ _____   **4.** $^-1.9$ _____   **5.** $1\frac{1}{6}$ _____   **6.** $-\frac{1}{3}$ _____

Order the group of numbers from least to greatest. (11C)

7. $2.5, 2\frac{3}{8}, 2\frac{1}{4}, 2.3$ _____

8. $\frac{7}{8}, \frac{5}{6}, 0.6, 0.9$ _____

Evaluate the expression for $x = \frac{1}{2}$, $y = \frac{2}{5}$, **and** $z = 5$. (11D)

9. $3x + 5y \cdot (^-2z)$ _____

10. $(x + y) \div 2z$ _____

Follow these steps to create a symmetrical design. (11E)

11. • Use the *x*-axis as a line of symmetry and graph the reflection of points *A* and *B*. Label the first point *F* and the second point *E*.

• Use the *y*-axis as a line of symmetry and graph the reflection of point *A* and the reflection of point *B*. Label these points *H* and *G*.

• Use the *x*-axis as a line of symmetry and graph the reflection of points *H* and *G*. Label these points *C* and *D*.

• Connect points *A*, *B*, *C*, *D*, and *E*, *F*, *G*, *H*.

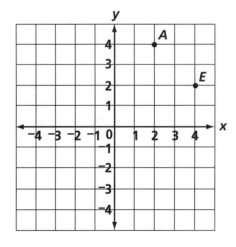

Complete a table of values and write ordered pairs for the equation. Then graph the equation. (11A)

1. $y = x + 3$

x	y	Ordered Pairs
		(,)
		(,)
		(,)
		(,)
		(,)

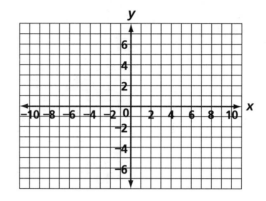

Write the letter that names each number on the number line. (11B)

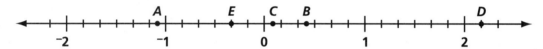

2. $\dfrac{-1}{3}$ _____

3. $2\dfrac{1}{6}$ _____

4. 0.4 _____

5. $^-1\dfrac{1}{12}$ _____

6. $\dfrac{1}{12}$ _____

Order the group of numbers from least to greatest. (11C)

7. $\dfrac{1}{10}$, 0.15, $\dfrac{1}{12}$, 0.08 _____

8. $3\dfrac{1}{6}$, 3.1, 3.3, $3\dfrac{1}{3}$ _____

Evaluate the expression for $x = \dfrac{1}{3}$, $y = \dfrac{3}{10}$, **and** $z = 2$. (11D)

9. $3xy + \dfrac{1}{5}z$ _____

10. $10y \div \dfrac{1}{3}(^-z)$ _____

Follow these steps to create a symmetrical design. (11E)

11.
- Use the x-axis as a line of symmetry and graph the reflection of points *A* and *E*. Label the first point *B* and the second point *F*.

- Use the y-axis as a line of symmetry and graph the reflection of point *A* and the reflection of point *E*. Label these points *D* and *H*.

- Use the x-axis as a line of symmetry and graph the reflection of points *D* and *H*. Label these points *C* and *G*.

- Connect points *A, B, C, D*, and *E, F, G, H*.

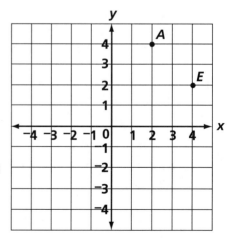

1 Which number is divisible by both 3 and 4?

    A 15   **C** 24

    B 16   **D** 45

2 Which inequality is true?

    F $0.27 > 0.08$

    H $0.72 < 0.08$

    G $0.27 < 0.08$

    J $0.72 > 0.8$

3 What is the prime factorization of 36?

    A $2^2 \cdot 3^2$ **C** $2^2 \cdot 9$

    B $2^3 \cdot 3^2$ **D** $3^2 \cdot 4$

4 What is the least common multiple of 6 and 10?

    F 16   **H** 60

    G 30   **J** 120

5 Which expression gives the best estimate for the answer to this problem?

Petra bought 19 yards of fabric for $5.67 per yard. How much did she spend?

    A $20 \times \$6$ **C** $\$5.50 \div 20$

    B $15 \times \$6$ **D** $\$5.70 \div 20$

6 Which decimal equals $\frac{3}{25}$?

    F 0.6   **H** 0.15

    G 0.12   **J** 0.2

7 Which inequality is true?

    A $\frac{2}{3} > 0.6$

    B $\frac{9}{16} > 0.6$

    C $\frac{5}{6} > 0.9$

    D $\frac{7}{8} > 0.88$

8 What is the median of this set of test scores?

85, 70, 75, 70, 70, 90, 65

    F 25   **H** 75

    G 70   **J** 87.5

9 Which mixed number equals $\frac{13}{4}$?

    A $3\frac{1}{4}$ **C** $3\frac{3}{4}$

    B $1\frac{1}{2}$ **D** $4\frac{1}{3}$

10 In which year was the number of machines sold about twice the number sold in 1850?

    F 1870   **H** 1890

    G 1880   **J** 1910

11 What is the value of this expression for $p = 0.6$?

$$4p - (0.2 + p)$$

A 3.2   C 1.4

B 1.6   D 1.04

12 Each circle on a pictograph represents 10 people. Which of these represents 25 people?

F ⬭⬭◖   H ⬭⬭⬭◖

G ⬭⬭⬭   J ⬭⬭⬭⬭⬭

13 What is the greatest common factor of 15 and 21?

A 1   C 5

B 3   D 7

14 What is the solution of this equation?

$$4 \times n = 6.4$$

F 25.6   H 2.56

G 16   J 1.6

15 A company packs candles in boxes. Each box holds 18 candles. How many boxes are needed to pack 200 candles?

A 8   C 11

B 10   D 12

16 What is the solution of this equation?

$$G \times 2\frac{1}{3} = \frac{7}{12}$$

F $1\frac{13}{36}$ H $\frac{1}{4}$

G $1\frac{1}{3}$ J $\frac{1}{3}$

17 What is the value of $8^2 - 3 \times 2^3$?

A 37   C 488

B 40   D 549

18 Which fraction equals $\frac{10}{15}$?

F $\frac{2}{5}$ H $\frac{3}{5}$

G $\frac{2}{3}$ J $\frac{5}{3}$

19 Which of these is between 80 and 90 seconds?

A 1 min 30 s   C 1 min 15 s

B 1 min 25 s   D 1 min 10 s

20 Which number is prime?

F 24   H 35

G 27   J 43

21 Greg folds a square in half to get two rectangles. He folds the rectangles in half along a diagonal. Which figure shows Greg's square after it is unfolded?

A   C

B   D

22 Which is the expanded form of 3.084?

F $3 + 0.08 + 0.004$

G $3 + 0.08 + 0.04$

H $3 + 0.8 + 0.004$

J $3 + 0.8 + 0.04$

23 Which measure could be the length of segment *CD*?

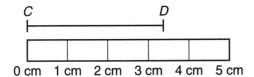

0 cm   1 cm   2 cm   3 cm   4 cm   5 cm

A 44 mm

B 38 mm

C 34 mm

D 24 mm

24 How does the mean of the data in this table change if Harriet is not included?

Ages of Students in the Dance Class	
Geraldine	28
Keisha	16
Harriet	35
Anna	20
Carlota	13

F It increases by 3.15.

G It decreases by 3.15.

H It decreases by 35.

J It stays the same.

25 25 is what percent of 60?

A 24%

B $41\frac{2}{3}$ %

C 240%

D 416%

26 Which of these could be the temperature of a nice spring day?

F 5°F   **H** 55°F

G 15°F   **J** 105°F

27 6 is 15% of what number?

A 4   **C** 40

B $6\frac{2}{3}$ **D** $66\frac{2}{3}$

28 2 lb 3 oz − 10 oz =

F 1 lb 13 oz

G 1 lb 9 oz

H 1 lb 6 oz

J 1 lb 3 oz

29 This graph shows a car trip Jake made one afternoon. When did Jake stop to go shopping?

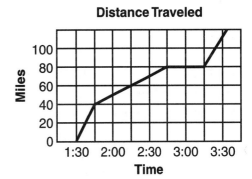

A 2:30 P.M. to 3:15 P.M.

B 2:30 P.M. to 3:30 P.M.

C 2:45 P.M. to 3:15 P.M.

D He did not stop during the trip.

30 What is the value of *n* in this proportion?

$$\frac{5}{2} = \frac{n}{12}$$

F $4\frac{4}{5}$ **H** 15

G $8\frac{1}{3}$ **J** 30

---

31 Which equation can be used to solve this problem?

Tim rented a canoe. He paid $15 per hour and a deposit of $45. How much did it cost to rent the canoe for 4 hours?

A $(4 \times 45) + 15 = H$

B $(4 \times 15) + 45 = H$

C $15 \times (4 + 45) = H$

D $4 \times (15 + 45) = H$

---

32 If $\frac{1}{2}$ inch on a map represents 300 miles, how many miles are represented by 3 inches?

F 1,800 mi   **H** 600 mi

G 900 mi   **J** 150 mi

---

33 What is the solution of this equation?

$$h - 73 = 21$$

A 42   **C** 84

B 52   **D** 94

---

34 What is the value of this expression for *a* = 6?

$$36 + a \div 2$$

F 21   **H** 38

G 24   **J** 39

---

35 Ben paid $14 for 5 notebooks. How much would he pay for 8 notebooks?

A $1.40   **C** $22.40

B $2.80   **D** $28.00

---

36 Which is the standard form for twenty-four thousand, three hundred six?

F 24,603   **H** 24,306

G 24,360   **J** 20,436

---

37 During which two consecutive months did the attendance drop below 15 people?

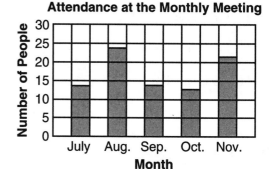

Attendance at the Monthly Meeting

A July and August

B August and September

C September and October

D October and November

38 $427 + 129 =$

F 556 H 456 K 298

G 546 J 446

39 Which list is in order from greatest to least?

A $\frac{3}{16}, \frac{1}{10}, \frac{5}{8}, \frac{5}{6}, \frac{2}{3}$

B $\frac{5}{6}, \frac{2}{3}, \frac{5}{8}, \frac{3}{16}, \frac{1}{10}$

C $\frac{5}{8}, \frac{5}{6}, \frac{3}{16}, \frac{2}{3}, \frac{1}{10}$

D $\frac{2}{3}, \frac{5}{6}, \frac{5}{8}, \frac{3}{16}, \frac{1}{10}$

E NH

40 $15,261 \div 241 =$

F 63 R 7 H 64 R 237 K NH

G 63 R 78 J 643 R 8

41 Which percent equals 0.045?

A 45%

B 40.5%

C 4.5%

D 0.45%

E 0.045%

42 $\frac{8}{9} - \frac{1}{4} =$

F $1\frac{2}{5}$

G $1\frac{5}{36}$

H $\frac{11}{18}$

J $\frac{23}{36}$

K NH

43 Which fraction is equal to $62\frac{1}{2}\%$?

A $\frac{5}{6}$ C $\frac{5}{16}$ E NH

B $\frac{5}{8}$ D $\frac{2}{3}$

44 2.3 km = _____ m

F 0.0023 H 230 K 23,000

G 23 J 2,300

45 $0.45 + 1.7 =$

A 0.62 C 2.15 E NH

B 1.53 D 4.67

46 350 g = _____ kg

F 3,500 H 3.5 K 0.035

G 350 J 0.35

47 $42 \times 856 =$

A 5,136

B 35,952

C 36,330

D 51,360

E NH

48 $\frac{2}{5} \times 1\frac{1}{4} =$

F $\frac{1}{10}$

G $\frac{8}{25}$

H $\frac{1}{2}$

J $\frac{7}{9}$

K $1\frac{13}{20}$

49 14 qt = _____ pt

A $3\frac{1}{2}$ C 28   E NH

B 7   D 56

50 $\frac{5}{6}$ of 27 =

F 15   H 23   K $67\frac{1}{2}$

G $22\frac{1}{2}$ J $32\frac{2}{5}$

51 6 × 7.03 =

A 428.1   C 42.18   E 0.42

B 42.81   D 4.218

52 $14 \div \frac{2}{7} =$

F 4

G 28

H 56

J 98

K NH

53 Which list is in order from least to greatest?

A 0.008, 0.018, 0.108, 0.801

B 0.008, 0.108, 0.018, 0.801

C 0.801, 0.018, 0.108, 0.008

D 0.801, 0.108, 0.018, 0.008

E NH

54 Gina bought 7.26 gallons of gas for her car. What is 7.26 rounded to the nearest tenth?

F 7   H 7.3   K 7.26

G 7.2   J 7.25

55 3.08 − 0.46 =

A 1.62   C 3.34   E NH

B 2.62   D 3.54

56 $3\frac{1}{5} + \frac{7}{10} =$

F $2\frac{1}{2}$ H $3\frac{8}{15}$ K $3\frac{9}{10}$

G $3\frac{3}{10}$ J $3\frac{4}{5}$

57 Which ratio is equivalent to the ratio 18 to 24?

A 4:3   C 3:2   E NH

B 3:4   D 2:3

58 13 ft = _____ yd

F $4\frac{3}{4}$ H $4\frac{1}{3}$ K 4

G $4\frac{2}{3}$ J $4\frac{1}{4}$

59 44,035 − 2,861 =

A 41,274   C 1,674   E NH

B 41,174   D 1,574

60 0.2236 ÷ 4.3 =

F 52   H 0.52   K 0.0052

G 5.2   J 0.052

1 A theater owner wants to predict the success of a new cartoon movie for young children. The movie features talking butterflies. The owner will ask 50 people if they would go to see such a movie. Which is the best group of 50 people to use for this survey?

A 50 people at a shopping mall

B 50 parents of young children

C 50 people who collect butterflies

D 50 people at a local restaurant

2 What is the value of this expression for $g = 5$?

$$42 - g \times 3$$

F $^-27$ **H** 37

G 27   **J** 111

3 Which shape does NOT always have opposite sides that are parallel?

A Parallelogram

B Quadrilateral

C Rhombus

D Rectangle

4 Which term describes this angle?

F Acute   **H** Right

G Obtuse   **J** Scalene

5 Which equation is shown on this graph?

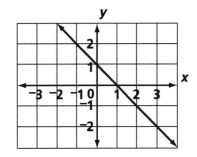

A $y = 1 - x$

B $y = x - 1$

C $y = x + 1$

D $y = x - 2$

6 What is the solution to this equation?

$$n + (^-15) = {}^-20$$

F $^-35$ **H** 5

G $^-5$ **J** 35

7 What is the greatest common factor of 18 and 30?

A 3   **C** 6

B 5   **D** 9

8 Betty is putting a wallpaper border around all 4 sides of a room that measures 15 ft by 20 ft. How much wallpaper does she need?

F 70 ft

G 70 ft²

H 300 ft

J 300 ft²

9 Which angle is greater than 90°?

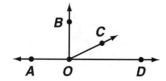

A ∠*AOB*

B ∠*AOC*

C ∠*BOC*

D ∠*BOD*

10 Gerta estimates her probability of winning a prize in a contest at 1 out of 2,000. What is the probability that Gerta will NOT win a prize in the contest?

F 1,999 out of 2,000

G 1 out of 200

H 1 to 2,000

J 2,000 to 1

11 What is the surface area of this figure?

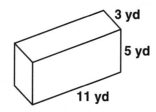

A 19 yd²

B 103 yd²

C 165 yd²

D 206 yd²

12 1.5 is 30% of what number?

F 0.45   H 4.5

G 0.5   J 5

13 Which inequality is true?

A ⁻3 < 1   C ⁻3 > ⁻1

B ⁻3 < ⁻8   D ⁻3 > 0

14 Based on the pattern in this table, what is the measure of ∠*C* in triangle 4?

Triangle	∠*A*	∠*B*	∠*C*
1	40°	30°	110°
2	20°	60°	100°
3	50°	80°	50°
4	90°	45°	

F 40°   H 50°

G 45°   J 100°

15 Which of these ordered pairs is a solution to the equation $y = 3x + 1$?

A (2, 5)   C (⁻2, ⁻5)

B (5, 2)   D (⁻5, ⁻2)

16 Jan is 2 years older than her friend Tina. The sum of their ages is 22. Which equation can be used to find Jan's age (*n*)?

F $n + (n + 2) = 22$

G $n + (n - 2) = 22$

H $n - (n - 2) = 22$

J $n - (n + 2) = 22$

17 What is the volume of this figure?

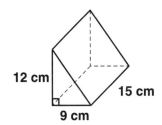

12 cm   15 cm   9 cm

A 36 cm³

B 810 cm³

C 910 cm³

D 1,620 cm³

18 What is the prime factorization of 75?

F $2^5 \cdot 3$

G $2^3 \cdot 5$

H $3 \cdot 5^2$

J $3 \cdot 25$

19 Paula bought 3 items at a bookstore and spent $5.00. The prices of different items are shown in the table.

Harry's Discount Books	
newspapers	$1.00
magazines	$1.50
all books	$2.00

What did Paula buy at the store?

A Two books

B Three books and a newspaper

C Two magazines and a book

D Two newspapers and a book

20 What is the value of the expression

$3(x - 2y)$ for $x = -\frac{3}{4}$ and $y = \frac{1}{2}$?

F $5\frac{1}{4}$

G $\frac{3}{4}$

H $-\frac{3}{4}$

J $-5\frac{1}{4}$

21 Which two terms describe this pair of lines?

A Intersecting and perpendicular

B Intersecting but not perpendicular

C Parallel and not intersecting

D Parallel and intersecting

22 40 in. = _____ ft

F $3\frac{1}{3}$

G $3\frac{1}{2}$

H $13\frac{1}{3}$

J 120

23 If you graph these two equations on a grid, in what point will the two lines intersect?

$y = 2x + 5$ $y = -4x - 1$

A $(-1, -3)$

B $(-1, 3)$

C $(1, -3)$

D $(3, -1)$

24 **What is the perimeter of this polygon?**

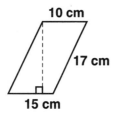

F 27 cm

G 42 cm

H 54 cm

J 69 cm

25 **Which polygons are congruent?**

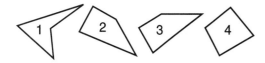

A 1 and 2

B 2 and 3

C 2 and 4

D 3 and 4

26 **A number from 1–10 is chosen at random and a coin is tossed. What is the probability of getting heads and an even number?**

F $\frac{1}{10}$

G $\frac{1}{4}$

H $\frac{1}{2}$

J $\frac{3}{4}$

27 **How did the number of students at Trenton School change from 1997 to 1999?**

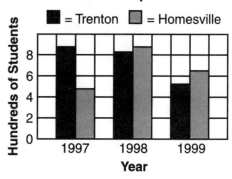

A Increased and then decreased

B Decreased and then increased

C Steadily increased

D Steadily decreased

28 **What is the median of this set of test scores?**

82, 87, 70, 94, 65, 80, 94, 78

F 29

G 70

H 81

J 94

29 **Which list is in order from least to greatest?**

A $-\frac{9}{10}$, -0.67, $-\frac{3}{8}$, 0.25, $\frac{2}{5}$

B $-\frac{9}{10}$, -0.67, 0.25, $-\frac{3}{8}$, $\frac{2}{5}$

C 0.25, $\frac{2}{5}$, $-\frac{3}{8}$, -0.67, $-\frac{9}{10}$

D $\frac{2}{5}$, 0.25, $-\frac{3}{8}$, -0.67, $-\frac{9}{10}$

30 How does the mean of the data in this table change if the 36-foot tree is not included?

Heights of Trees (feet)
18, 23, 15, 36, 19

F It increases by 3.45.

G It decreases by 3.45.

H It decreases by 7.2.

J It stays the same.

31 These triangles are similar. What is the length of side *QR*?

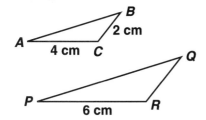

A 2 cm

B 3 cm

C 8 cm

D 12 cm

32 What is the circumference of a circle with a diameter of 10 ft?

F 15.7 ft

G 31.4 ft

H 78.5 ft

J 314 ft

33 What is the solution of this equation?

$$3 \cdot n = 23.4$$

A 0.78   **C** 70.2

B 7.8   **D** 78

34 A coin and a cube numbered 1–6 are used in an experiment. How many different outcomes are possible?

F 2

G 6

H 8

J 12

35 What is the area of this triangle?

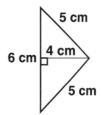

A 12 cm²

B 15 cm²

C 24 cm²

D 30 cm²

36 What is the area of a circle with a diameter of 8 cm?

F 12.56 cm²

G 25.12 cm²

H 50.24 cm²

J 200.96 cm²

37 A librarian wants to find out what kinds of books she should order. Which of these survey questions is the best to use?

A Do you prefer history books or mysteries?

B Do you use an encyclopedia at the library?

C What types of books have you checked out in the last 6 months?

D What types of books have you bought in the last 6 months?

38 Which polygons are similar?

F 1 and 2

G 1 and 3

H 2 and 3

J 3 and 4

39 Which list is in order from greatest to least?

A ⁻8, ⁻1, 0, 2, 6

B ⁻8, 6, 2, ⁻1, 0

C 6, 2, ⁻1, 0, ⁻8

D 6, 2, 0, ⁻1, ⁻8

40 What is the volume of this figure?

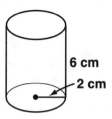

6 cm

2 cm

F 301.44 cm³

G 150.72 cm³

H 75.36 cm³

J 37.68 cm³

41 Which is the expanded form for 12.03?

A 10 + 2 + 0.003

B 10 + 2 + 0.03

C 10 + 2 + 0.3

D 12 + 0.03

42 A person picks a number at random from the numbers 20–30. What is the probability that the chosen number will be odd?

F $\frac{1}{2}$

G $\frac{5}{6}$

H $\frac{5}{11}$

J $\frac{6}{11}$

43 Which inequality is true?

A $-\frac{2}{3} > {}^{-}0.9$

B $-\frac{2}{3} < {}^{-}0.9$

C $-\frac{2}{3} > {}^{-}0.6$

D $-\frac{2}{3} < {}^{-}0.7$

44 Simplify the expression.
$$8 \cdot (^-2)$$

F $-\frac{1}{4}$ H $^-4$ K $^-18$

G 4   J $^-16$

45 6.2 kg = _____ g

A 0.0062   C 62   E NH

B 0.62   D 620

46 Choose the best name for this figure.

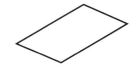

F Parallelogram

G Quadrilateral

H Rhombus

J Rectangle

K Square

47 Which pair of angles is complementary?

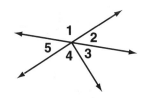

A 1 and 2

B 1 and 4

C 2 and 3

D 2 and 4

E NH

48 Simplify the expression.
$$^-18 \div (^-6)$$

F $^-3$ H 12   K 144

G 3   J 108

49 Simplify the expression.
$$\frac{3}{8} \times 1\frac{1}{2}$$

A $\frac{1}{4}$ C $\frac{9}{16}$ E $2\frac{1}{16}$

B $\frac{5}{8}$ D $1\frac{7}{9}$

50 What number is located at point *M*?

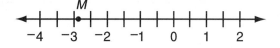

F $^-3\frac{1}{6}$ H $^-2\frac{1}{2}$ K $^-2\frac{1}{4}$

G $^-2\frac{5}{6}$ J $^-2\frac{1}{3}$

51 Simplify the expression.
$$^-3 + (^-12)$$

A $^-15$ C 9   E NH

B $^-9$ D 15

52 Choose the best name for this figure.

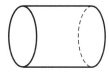

F Cone   H Prism   K NH

G Cylinder   J Pyramid

53 Which pair of angles is supplementary?

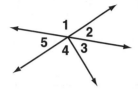

A 1 and 2   C 2 and 3   E 4 and 3

B 5 and 3   D 4 and 5

54 Simplify the expression.
$$^-1 - (^-7)$$

F $^-8$ H 6   K 9

G $^-6$ J 8

55 What number is located at point *R*?

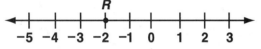

A $^-3$ C $^-1$ E NH

B $^-2$ D 2

56 Choose the best name for this figure.

F Square prism

G Square pyramid

H Triangular prism

J Triangular pyramid

K NH

57 Find $\frac{2}{9}$ of 36.

A 4

B 8

C 9

D 18

E 21

58 Choose the best name for this figure.

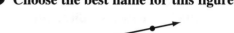

F Ray *PQ*

G Ray *QP*

H Line *PQ*

J Line segment *PQ*

K NH

59 What is the value of *n* in this proportion?
$$\frac{5}{6} = \frac{n}{18}$$

A $1\frac{2}{3}$ C 16   E 30

B 15   D $21\frac{3}{5}$

60 Simplify the expression.
$$^-4 + 8 \cdot (^-2)$$

F $^-20$ H 12   K 24

G 8   J 20

Reteach Worksheets

NOTES

In a numeral, groups of three digits are called **periods**.

Standard Form: Separate periods by commas. Start at the right.

8,632,749

Word Form: Use the period names.

eight million,
six hundred thirty-two thousand,
seven hundred forty-nine

Expanded Form: Write a sum, using the standard form for the value represented by each digit.

8,000,000 + 600,000 + 30,000 + 2,000 + 700 + 40 + 9

Place-Value Chart

Millions Period			Thousands Period			Ones Period		
Hundred Millions	Ten Millions	Millions	Hundred Thousands	Ten Thousands	Thousands	Hundreds	Tens	Ones
		8	6	3	2	7	4	9

This 6 is in the hundred thousands place. So, it means 6 × 100,000 or 600,000.

Complete.

1. In **608,415**, the 8 means 8 × _____ , or _____ .

2. In **35,463,708**, the 5 means 5 × _____ , or _____ .

3. The word form of **11,596,400** is eleven _____ , five hundred ninety-six

   _____ , _____ .

4. The word form of **7,604,110** is _____ , _____ , _____ .

5. **38,942** = 30,000 + _____ + 900 + _____ + 2

6. **457,516** = _____ + 50,000 + _____ + _____ + 10 + 6

7. **2,803,699** = _____ + _____ + 3,000 + _____ + 90 + 9

8. **849,672** = _____ + _____ + _____ + _____ + _____ + __

Write the number in expanded form.

9. **249,568** = _____

10. **7,822,631** = _____

Write the number in standard form.

11. **3 × 10,000** = _____

12. **2 × 1,000,000** = _____

13. **9,000,000 + 200,000 + 30,000 + 5,000 + 600 + 30 + 4** = _____

Teacher Note: Use before Unit 1, Lesson 1. **(6)**

Comparing and Ordering
Whole Numbers

As the number of places in a whole number
increases, the number becomes greater.

1,725 > 725

When two numbers are in the same period,
compare the digits of that period.

6,597,438 < 19,896,392

Millions Period			Thousands Period			Hundreds Period		
Hundreds	Tens	Ones	Hundreds	Tens	Ones	Hundreds	Tens	Ones
						1	7	2	5

Look at the millions period: 6 < 19.

Complete. Write > (greater than) or < (less than) in each circle.

1. Since **8,653** is in the thousands period and **1,145,000** is in the _____ period,

then **8,653** ◯ **1,145,000**.

2. Both **15,693** and **9,857** are in the _____ period. **15 > 9**. So, **15,693** ◯ **9,857**.

3. Both numbers **72,895,653** and **72,654,132** are equal in the _____ period. To

compare, look at the thousands period: **895 >** _____. So, **72,895,653** ◯ **72,654,132**.

Compare the numbers. Write > or < in each circle.

4. 6,548 ◯ 9,874

5. 29,678 ◯ 9,840

6. 98,632 ◯ 104,098

7. 9,397,436 ◯ 2,986,128

8. 1,687,000 ◯ 1,593,000

9. 2,397,436 ◯ 2,399,128

Use these four numbers: 98,567,890   103,786,562   15,905,786   72,865,132

10. Of the four numbers, **15,905,786** is the least and _____ is the greatest.

11. In order from least to greatest, the four numbers are

15,905,786   _____   _____   _____.

Order the numbers from least to greatest.

12. 9,854   6,873   16,498   9,964   _____

13. 125,687   125,786   125,493   125,567   _____

14. 5,693,127   9,593,127   7,693,721   1,569,721 _____

Teacher Note: Use before Unit 1, Lesson 1. (6)

In **scientific notation,**
a number is written as
a product of two factors.

$$7,000,000 = 7 \times 10^6$$

The first factor is at least 1 but less than 10.	The second factor is a power of 10.

Complete.

1. *Powers of 10* have as many zero digits as indicated by the exponent.

So, $10 = 10^1$ $100 = 10^2$ $1,000 = 10^{\underline{}}$

$10,000 = 10^{\underline{}}$ $100,000 = 10^{\underline{}}$ $1,000,000 = 10^{\underline{}}$

2. $8,000 = 8 \times 1,000$. So, in scientific notation, $8,000 = 8 \times 10^{\underline{}}$.

3. In scientific notation, $3,000,000 = \underline{} \times 10^{\underline{}}$.

Write the number in scientific notation.

4. $4,000 = 4 \times 10^{\underline{}}$

5. $9,000 = \underline{}$

6. $30,000 = \underline{}$

7. $60,000 = \underline{}$

8. $500,000 = \underline{}$

9. $5,000,000 = \underline{}$

10. $200,000 = \underline{}$

11. $3,000,000 = \underline{}$

12. $100,000 = \underline{}$

Complete.

13. To change a number from scientific notation to standard form, the

power of **10** tells how many zeros to write. For 9×10^5, you need to

write _____ zeros. First, write **9 0 0 0 0 0** and then insert the

comma. So, in standard form, $9 \times 10^5 = $ _____.

Write the number in standard form.

14. $4 \times 10^2 = \underline{}$

15. $9 \times 10^4 = \underline{}$

16. $7 \times 10^3 = \underline{}$

17. $6 \times 10^3 = \underline{}$

18. $3 \times 10^5 = \underline{}$

19. $2 \times 10^6 = \underline{}$

20. $2 \times 10^5 = \underline{}$

21. $1 \times 10^2 = \underline{}$

22. $8 \times 10 = \underline{}$

Teacher Note: Use before Unit 1, Lesson 1. **(6)**

Name _____

Every numeral is separated into groups of three digits, called **periods.**

Standard Form: Use commas to separate periods.

14,264,576,912

Word Form: Use period names.

fourteen billion,
two hundred sixty-four million,
five hundred seventy-six thousand,
nine hundred twelve

Expanded Form: Write a sum using the standard form for the value represented by each digit.

Place-Value Chart

Billions Period			Millions Period			Thousands Period			Ones Period		
Hundred Billions	Ten Billions	Billions	Hundred Millions	Ten Millions	Millions	Hundred Thousands	Ten Thousands	Thousands	Hundreds	Tens	Ones
1	4	2	6	4	5	7	6	9	1	2

This 2 is in the hundred-millions place. So, it means 2 × 100,000,000 or 200,000,000.

10,000,000,000 + 4,000,000,000 + 200,000,000 + 60,000,000 + 4,000,000 + 500,000 + 70,000 + 6,000 + 900 + 10 + 2

Complete.

1. In **135,589,502,708**, the **3** means 3 × _____, or _____.

2. The word form for **2,110,402,400** is two _____, one hundred ten _____,

four hundred two _____, four _____.

3. In word form, the number **16,358,762,108** is sixteen billion, _____

_____, _____.

4. In word form, the number **717,298,321,004** is _____

_____, _____.

5. In standard form, twelve billion, six hundred ten million,

one hundred forty-two thousand, five hundred six is _____.

6. **32,348,178,651** = _____ + 2,000,000,000 + _____ + 40,000,000 +

_____ + 100,000 + _____ + 8,000 + 600 + _____ + 1

7. **64,512,329,783** = _____ + _____ + _____

+ _____ + _____ + _____ + _____

+ _____ + _____ + _____ + _____

Teacher Note: Use after Quick Check, page 8, to reteach Unit 1, Lesson 1. **(6)**

There are **3** important properties of addition:

1. **Commutative**
   $4 + 6 = 6 + 4$ ◄── Different order, same result

2. **Associative**
   $(4 + 6) + 3 = 4 + (6 + 3)$ ◄── Different grouping, same result

3. **Zero**
   $7 + 0 = 7$ ◄── Zero plus any number
   equals that number

Use the properties to do mental math
and evaluate expressions.

$42 + h + 58$ for $n = 17$	$42 + 17 + 58$ by substitution	$42 + 58 + 17$ by commutative property	$100 + 17$	117

Which is different, the order or the grouping?

1. $(3 + 8) + 7 = 7 + (3 + 8)$

_____

2. $(6 + 13) + 1 = 6 + (13 + 1)$

_____

Complete the statement.

3. $5 + \underline{} = 9 + 5$

4. $64 + \underline{} = 64$

5. $1 + (2 + 7) = (\underline{} + 2) + 7$

Use the properties and mental math to find the sum.

6. $130 + 49 + 70$

$130 + 70 + \underline{} = \underline{}$

7. $13 + 62 + 37 + 38$

$13 + \underline{} + 62 + \underline{} = \underline{}$

8. $240 + 18 + 60$

_____

9. $24 + 92 + 6 + 8$

_____

Evaluate for $n = 17$.

10. $469 + n$

_____

11. $9 + n$

_____

12. $n + 7$

_____

13. $n + 199$

_____

14. $(5 + 3) + n$

_____

15. $(n + 8) + 9$

_____

Teacher Note: Use after Quick Check, page 8, to reteach Unit 1, Lesson 3. **(6)**

Use inverse operations to solve an equation.

Addition Equation	**Subtraction Equation**

Addition Equation

$x + 4 = 9$

$x + 4 - 4 = 9 - 4$ Subtract **4**
from each side.

$x = 5$ This is the solution.

Subtraction Equation

$x - 4 = 9$

$x - 4 + 4 = 9 + 4$ Add **4**
to each side.

$x = 13$ This is the solution.

To check, substitute the solution into the original equation.
Is the new equation true?

$x + 4 = 9$
$5 + 4 = 9$

$x - 4 = 9$
$13 - 4 = 9$

Since **5 + 4 = 9**, the solution checks.

Since **13 − 4 = 9**, the solution checks.

Which operation would you use to solve the equation?

1. $k + 8 = 15$ **2.** $x - 3 = 18$ **3.** $6 + y = 13$ **4.** $5 = z + 6$

_____   _____   _____   _____

Solve and check.

5. $m + 5 = 9$

$m + 5 - 5 = 9 -$ ____

$m =$ ____

Check: _____ $+ 5 = 9$

6. $w - 2 = 41$

$w - 2$ ____ $= 41$ ____

$w =$ ____

Check: _____

7. $q + 7 = 32$

_____

$q =$ ____

Check: _____

8. $p + 12 = 40$

Check: _____

9. $x - 8 = 15$

Check: _____

10. $18 = y + 3$

Check: _____

Replace _n_ with 10. Complete.

11. $n + 2 = 12$

____ $+ 2 = 12$

Is **10** a solution? _____

12. $n - 3 = 7$

_____

Is **10** a solution? _____

13. $7 - n = 13$

_____

Is **10** a solution? _____

Teacher Note: Use after Quick Check, page 17, to reteach Unit 1, Lesson 4. **(6)**

Name _____

Here are some important multiplication properties.

1. **Commutative**
$4 \times 6 = 6 \times 4$ ← Different order, same result

2. **Associative**
$(4 \times 6) \times 3 = 4 \times (6 \times 3)$ ← Different grouping, same result

3. **Identity**
$7 \times 1 = 7$ ← Any number times 1 is that number.

4. **Zero**
$7 \times 0 = 0$ ← Any number times zero is zero.

Use the properties to make mental math easier.

$25 \times 17 \times 4 = 25 \times 4 \times 17$
by the commutative
property
> $25 \times 4 \times 17 =$
100×17
> $1,700$

Which is different, the order or the grouping?

1. $3 \times 8 \times 7 = 8 \times 3 \times 7$

_____

2. $9 \times (11 \times 1) = (9 \times 11) \times 1$

_____

Complete the statement.

3. $7 \times \underline{\quad} = 9 \times 7$

4. $74 \times \underline{\quad} = 74$

5. $4 \times (3 \times 7) = (\underline{\quad} \times 3) \times 7$

Complete. Name the property used.

6. $\underline{\quad} \times 130 = 0$

_____

7. $\underline{\quad} \times 4 = 4 \times 11$

_____

8. $(5 \times 9) \times 2 = 5 \times (9 \times \underline{\quad})$

_____

9. $6 \times \underline{\quad} = 14 \times 6$

_____

10. $\underline{\quad} \times 1 \times 4 = 0$

_____

11. $(\underline{\quad} \times 3) \times 8 = 5 \times (3 \times 8)$

_____

Use the properties and mental math.

12. $5 \times 49 \times 2$

$5 \times 2 \times \underline{\quad} = \underline{\quad}$

13. $50 \times 76 \times 2$

_____

14. $62 \times 78 \times 137 \times 0$

_____

Teacher Note: Use after Quick Check, page 17, to reteach Unit 1, Lesson 6. **(6)**

61

Operations in an expression need to be performed in a standard order.

Order of Operations
1. Work within parentheses.   2. Multiply and divide.   3. Add and subtract.

$$8 + 2 \times (4 + 3) - 6$$

Simplify within parentheses first. $8 + 2 \times \ \ (7) \ \ - 6$

Next multiply and divide from left to right. $8 \ + \ 14 \ \ - 6$

Then add and subtract from left to right. $22 \ \ \ \ \ - 6 = 16$

List the signs for the operations in the order shown in the expression. Then list the signs in the order they must be done.

1. $7 \times 8 + 3$

_____

_____

2. $2 + 5 \times 6$

_____

_____

3. $43 - 16 \div 2$

_____

_____

Complete the calculation.

4. $25 \times 4 + 8$

_____ $+ 8$

_____

5. $8 + 10 \times 10$

$8 +$ _____

_____

6. $450 - 200 \div 2$

$450 -$ _____

_____

7. $5 \times 7 + 8 \times 2$

_____ $+ 8 \times 2$

_____

8. $27 - 18 \div 3 + 9$

$27 -$ _____ $+ 9$

_____

9. $26 - 3 \times (4 + 2)$

$26 - 3 \times$ _____

_____

Use the order of operations to evaluate the expression.

10. $56 - (7 + 9)$

_____

11. $19 + 3 \times (6 + 4)$

_____

12. $72 \div 12 \times 3$

_____

13. $16 \times 5 + 20 \times 4$

_____

14. $100 \div 5 + 90 \div 6$

_____

15. $(6 + 8) \div (3 + 4) \times 7$

_____

Teacher Note: Use after Quick Check, page 23, to reteach Unit 1, Lesson 8. **(6)**

The mean, median, or mode can be used to describe a set of data.

Jorge's grades for 6 tests were **70, 86, 84, 74, 82,** and **84.**

To find the **mean,** or average:

Find the sum of the items in the data set. $70 + 86 + 84 + 74 + 82 + 84 = 480$

Divide the sum by the number of items. $480 \div 6 = 80$ ◄── | **80 is the mean.** |

To find the **median:**

Arrange the data from least to greatest.   **70, 74, 82, 84, 84, 86**

Find the middle number. If there are two middle numbers, find their mean.

| **83 is the median,**
halfway between 82 and 84. |

To find the **mode:**

Find the number that occurs most often.   **84** is the mode.

Use these temperatures: 84°F, 70°F, 69°F, 74°F, 74°F, 83°F, 71°F.

1. Add the temperatures.   _____

Divide the sum by **7.**   _____

What statistical number have you found for the data?   _____

2. Arrange the temperatures from coldest to warmest.   _____

Find the middle one.   _____

What statistical number have you found for the data?   _____

3. Find the temperature that occurs most often.   _____

What statistical number have you found for the data?   _____

Use these test scores: 92, 93, 92, 95, 95, 75, 93, 93. Find:

4. the mode *(most)*

_____

5. the median *(middle)*

_____

6. the mean *(average)*

_____

Use this data about the number of cars in a parking lot:
111, 114, 107, 123, 126, 123, 113, 119, 118, 116. Find:

7. the median _____

8. the mode _____

9. the mean _____

Teacher Note: Use after Quick Check, page 32, to reteach Unit 1, Lesson 10. **(6)**

Use inverse operations to solve an equation.

Multiplication Equation	**Division Equation**
$3n = 24$	$\frac{n}{3} = 24$
$\frac{3n}{3} = \frac{24}{3}$ Divide each side by 3.	$3 \cdot \frac{n}{3} = 24 \cdot 3$ Multiply each side by 3.
$n = 8$ This is the solution.	$n = 72$ This is the solution.

To check, substitute into the original equation.

$3n = 24$	$\frac{n}{3} = 24$
$3 \times 8 = 24$ ✔	$\frac{72}{3} = 24$ ✔

Name the operation needed to solve the equation.

1. $4m = 64$ **2.** $\frac{m}{4} = 64$ **3.** $81 = 9t$ **4.** $81 = \frac{t}{9}$

_____ _____ _____ _____

Solve and check.

5. $4a = 64$

$\frac{4a}{4} = $ _____

$a = $ _____

Check: $4 \times $ ___ $= 64$

6. $\frac{b}{5} = 25$

$5 \cdot \frac{b}{5} = 25 \cdot$ ___

$b = $ ___

Check: _____

7. $6y = 72$

$y = $ _____

Check: _____

8. $\frac{t}{6} = 72$

$t = $ _____

Check: _____

---

9. $144 = 12w$

$w = $ _____

Check: _____

10. $50 = \frac{x}{25}$

$x = $ _____

Check: _____

11. $17q = 136$

$q = $ _____

Check: _____

12. $\frac{m}{16} = 64$

$m = $ _____

Check: _____

---

13. $240 = \frac{s}{15}$

$s = $ _____

Check: _____

14. $8z = 168$

$z = $ _____

Check: _____

15. $12t = 1,716$

$t = $ _____

Check: _____

16. $\frac{f}{21} = 231$

$f = $ _____

Check: _____

Teacher Note: Use after Quick Check, page 32, to reteach Unit 1, Lesson 11. **(6)**

A place-value chart can be extended to include place values less than **1**.

Standard Form: A **decimal point** separates the ones and tenths places.

673.28

Word Form: Read the decimal point as *and*.

six hundred seventy-three
and twenty-eight hundredths

Expanded Form: Write a sum, using the standard form for the value represented by each digit.

600 + 70 + 3 + 0.2 + 0.08

Hundreds	Tens	Ones		Tenths	Hundredths
6	7	3	.	2	8

This 8 is in the hundredths place. So, it means 8 × 0.01 or 0.08.

Complete.

1. In **38.91**, the **9** means 9 × _____, or _____ .

2. In **562.37**, the **7** means 7 × _____, or _____ .

3. The word form of **16.7** is sixteen and seven _____ .

4. The word form of **927.41** is nine hundred twenty-seven and forty-one _____ .

5. The word form of **593.72** is _____ .

6. **57.63** = 50 + _____ + 0.6 + _____

7. **186.39** = 100 + _____ + _____ + _____ + 0.09

8. **439.72** = _____ + _____ + _____ + _____ + _____

Write the number in expanded form.

9. **798.3** = _____

10. **8,962.74** = _____

Write the number in standard form.

11. **4 × 0.1** = _____

12. **7 × 0.01 ×** _____

....

13. **600 + 30 + 4 + 0.8 + 0.02** = _____

14. **9 × 1000 + 4 × 100 + 8 × 10 + 3 × 1 + 6 × 0.1 + 4 × 0.01** = _____

Teacher Note: Use before Unit 2, Lesson 1. **(6)**

You can compare decimal numbers by using what you know about whole numbers.

Same Number of Decimal Places

tenths: **0.8 > 0.5** since **8 > 5**

hundredths: **0.83 > 0.79** since **83 > 79**

Different Numbers of Decimal Places

Compare **0.2** and **0.16**.

Think: | Compare: | Think: | So,
0.2 = 0.20 | 0.20 and 0.16 | 20 > 16 | 0.2 > 0.16

Complete the statements.

1. The decimal number **0.7** is read as *seven tenths,* and **0.9** is read as _____.

Since **7 < 9**, then **0.7** is _____ than **0.9**.

2. **0.93** is read as *ninety-three hundredths* and **0.71** is read as _____.

Since **93** is _____ than **71**, then **0.93** is _____ than **0.71**.

3. The decimal number **0.6** is read as *six tenths* and **0.68** as _____.

The decimal number **0.6** can be written with two decimal places as _____.

Now it can be compared to **68** hundredths. **60** hundredths is _____ than **68**

hundredths. So, **0.6** is _____ than **0.68**.

Compare the two numbers. Write > (greater than) or < (less than) in each circle.

4. 0.4 ◯ 0.8	**5.** 7.5 ◯ 7.1	**6.** 0.86 ◯ 0.94	**7.** 4.32 ◯ 4.79
8. 0.4 ◯ 0.83	**9.** 0.74 ◯ 0.5	**10.** 3.9 ◯ 3.87	**11.** 7.86 ◯ 7.9
12. 4.6 ◯ 4.78	**13.** 8.01 ◯ 8.1	**14.** 6.3 ◯ 6.03	**15.** 19.4 ◯ 19.87

Complete.

16. Of the numbers **0.6, 0.1, 0.3,** and **0.59,** the least is _____ and the greatest is _____.

17. Order **7.6, 7.32, 7.01,** and **7.1** from greatest to least. _____, _____, _____, _____

Teacher Note: Use before Unit 2, Lesson 1. **(6)**

Multiply 9.7 by 32.

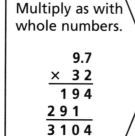

Multiply as with whole numbers.

```
    9.7
 ×  3 2
  1 9 4
  2 9 1
  3 1 0 4
```

Insert a decimal point in the product.

```
    9.7
 ×  3 2
  1 9 4
  2 9 1
  3 1 0.4
```

Use the same number of decimal places as in the decimal factor. Start at the right.

How many decimal places will be in the product?

1. 7.8
  × 9 _____

2. 1 3.3
  × 2 6 _____

3. 2.9 4
  × 8 _____

4. 1.6 1 8
  × 4 7 _____

5. 1 3 7
  × 6.1 _____

6. 2.9
  × 4.3 _____

7. 4 8 3
  × 0.2 9 _____

8. 1 6 4 9
  × 0.4 3 2 _____

Insert the decimal place in the product.

9.
```
    3 5.1
 ×    4 9
  3 1 5 9
1 4 0 4
1 7 1 9 9
```

10.
```
      5 8 4
 ×    3 6.8
    4 6 7 2
  3 5 0 4
1 7 5 2
2 1 4 9 1 2
```

11.
```
      8 9 6
 ×    3.5 8
    7 1 6 8
  4 4 8 0
2 6 8 8
3 2 0 7 6 8
```

12.
```
      4 2 0
 ×  0.7 3 9
    3 7 8 0
  1 2 6 0
2 9 4 0
3 1 0 3 8 0
```

Find the product.

13.
```
    1 6.4
 ×    3 2
    3 2 8
  4 9 2
```

14. 6 8 2
  × 1.1

15. 7.4 8
  × 5 6

16. 9 5 4
  × 0.2 4

17. 3.4 6
  × 4 5 2

18. 9 2 6
  × 1.5 8

19. 0.5 8 4
  × 3 9

20. 9 5 9
  × 0.0 1 6

Teacher Note: Use after Quick Check, page 53, to reteach Unit 2, Lesson 4. **(6)**

Divide: **9.44 ÷ 4**

Insert a decimal point in the quotient directly above the point in the dividend.

$$4\overline{)9.44}$$

Divide as with whole numbers.

$$\begin{array}{r} 2.36 \\ 4\overline{)9.44} \\ -8 \\ \hline 14 \\ -12 \\ \hline 24 \\ -24 \\ \hline 0 \end{array}$$

Insert the decimal point in the quotient.

1. $8\overline{)9.94}$ → 123

2. $7\overline{)7.35}$ → 105

3. $4\overline{)11.48}$ → 287

4. $3\overline{)88.8}$ → 296

How many digits will be before the decimal point in the quotient?

5. $6\overline{)8.28}$ _____

6. $7\overline{)9.576}$ _____

7. $3\overline{)75.3}$ _____

8. $8\overline{)84.96}$ _____

Divide. Multiply to check.

9. $4\overline{)9.84}$

10. $7\overline{)78.05}$

11. $3\overline{)7.371}$

12. $4\overline{)74.892}$

How many digits will be before the decimal point in the quotient?

13. $25\overline{)32.5}$

14. $12\overline{)38.16}$

15. $24\overline{)50.976}$

16. $30\overline{)153.69}$

_____

_____

_____

_____

Divide. Multiply to check.

17. $41\overline{)57.4}$

18. $17\overline{)53.04}$

19. $43\overline{)96.148}$

20. $40\overline{)257.52}$

Teacher Note: Use after Quick Check, page 53, to reteach Unit 2, Lesson 7. **(6)**

Using **10** or **100** as a multiplier moves the decimal point to the right.

| Think:

 4.74 × 10

 = 4.74 1 zero
       1 place | Write:

 4.74 × 10 = 47.4 | Think:

 4.74 × 100

 = 4.74 2 zeros
       2 places | Write:

 4.74 × 100 = 474. |

Using **10** or **100** as a divisor moves the decimal point to the left.

| Think:

 4.74 ÷ 10

 = 4.74 1 zero
       1 place | Write:

 4.74 ÷ 10 = 0.474 | Think:

 4.74 ÷ 100

 = 04.74 2 zeros
       2 places | Write:

 4.74 ÷ 100 = 0.0474 |

Complete.

1. To multiply **6.34** by **10,** move the decimal point one place to the _____ .

2. To multiply **97.32** by **100,** move the decimal point _____ places to the _____ .

3. To multiply **78.4** by **1,000,** move the decimal point **3** places to the _____ .

Multiply mentally.

4. 7.6 × 10 = _____   **5.** 3.58 × 10 = _____   **6.** 6.924 × 10 = _____

7. 19.367 × 100 = _____   **8.** 27.35 × 100 = _____   **9.** 65.1 × 100 = _____

10. 8.253 × 1000 = _____   **11.** 14.67 × 1000 = _____   **12.** 9.1 × 1000 = _____

Complete.

13. To divide **9.31** by **10,** move the decimal point one place to the _____ .

14. To divide **54.12** by **1,000,** move the decimal point _____ places to the _____ .

Divide mentally.

15. 48.1 ÷ 10 = _____   **16.** 83.32 ÷ 10 = _____   **17.** 37.944 ÷ 10 = _____

18. 41.3 ÷ 100 = _____   **19.** 2.54 ÷ 100 = _____   **20.** 0.47 ÷ 100 = _____

21. 1,359.4 ÷ 1000 = _____   **22.** 38.9 ÷ 1000 = _____   **23.** 1.8 ÷ 1000 = _____

As with whole numbers, use inverse operations to solve equations with decimals.

Addition Equation
Use subtraction to solve.

$$x + 4.1 = 9.7$$
$$x + 4.1 - 4.1 = 9.7 - 4.1$$
$$x = 5.6$$

Subtraction Equation
Use addition to solve.

$$x - 4.1 = 9.7$$
$$x - 4.1 + 4.1 = 9.7 + 4.1$$
$$x = 13.8$$

Multiplication Equation
Use division to solve.

$$3.1n = 24.8$$
$$\frac{3.1n}{3.1} = \frac{24.8}{3.1}$$
$$n = 8$$

Division Equation
Use multiplication to solve.

$$\frac{n}{3.1} = 24.8$$
$$3.1 \times \frac{n}{3.1} = 24.8 \times 3.1$$
$$n = 76.88$$

Name the type of equation and the operation needed to solve.

1. $p - 4.2 = 8.1$

2. $m + 1.3 = 7.9$

3. $4.2k = 25.2$

4. $\frac{w}{3.1} = 9.3$

Complete the solution and check.

5. $p + 4.7 = 9.6$

$p + 4.7 - 4.7 = 9.6$ _____

$p =$ _____

Check: _____ $+ 4.7 = 9.6$

6. $y - 2.3 = 6.9$

$y - 2.3$ _____ $= 6.9$ _____

$y =$ _____

Check: _____

7. $4.4 + t = 7.8$

4.4 _____ $+ t = 7.8$ _____

$t =$ _____

Check: _____

Solve and check.

8. $6.3 = w - 7.4$

9. $14.8 = \frac{x}{7.4}$

10. $5.9 + k = 6.11$

11. $28.8 = 3.6t$

Teacher Note: Use after Quick Check, page 62, to reteach Unit 2, Lesson 11. **(6)**

A whole number is divisible

by	if its last digit	Example
2	is even	**9,436** is divisible by **2** since **6** is even.
5	is **0** or **5**	**8,670** is divisible by **5** since its last digit is **0**.
10	is **0**	**7,980** is divisible by **10** since its last digit is **0**.

by	if its sum of digits	Example
3	is divisible by **3**	**132** is divisible by **3** since $1 + 3 + 2 = 6$, and **6** is divisible by **3**.
9	is divisible by **9**	**288** is divisible by **9** since $2 + 8 + 8 = 18$, and **18** is divisible by **9**.

by	if it is divisible	Example
6	by both **2** and **3**	**10,404** is divisible by **2** (last digit is even) and by **3** (sum of digits is divisible by **3**). So **10,404** is divisible by **6**.

Is the number divisible by 2? Write *yes* or *no*.

1. 778 _____

2. 887 _____

3. 1,086,956 _____

Is the number divisible by 5? by 10? In each case, write *yes* or *no*.

4. 465 _____ _____

5. 8,790 _____ _____

6. 5,001 _____ _____

Complete.

7. **861** is divisible by **3** since $8 + 6 + 1 =$ _____, which is divisible by _____.

8. **864** is divisible by **9** since $8 + 6 + 4 =$ _____, which is divisible by _____.

9. **6,444** is divisible by **2** since it is even and **6,444** is divisible by **3**

since _____ is divisible by _____. So, **6,444** is divisible by _____.

Of the possible divisors 2, 3, 5, 6, 9, 10, list all that apply to the given number.

10. 5,508

11. 100,440

12. 5,715

_____

_____

_____

Teacher Note: Use after Quick Check, page 72, to reteach Unit 3, Lesson 1. (6)

Name _____

An **exponent** tells
how many times
to use a **base** as a factor.

exponent

$$3^5 = 3 \times 3 \times 3 \times 3 \times 3 = 243$$

base   5 factors

Work with exponents before other operations,
except operations in parentheses.

| Evaluate the exponent term.
Next, multiply.
Then, add. | $3 + 2 \times 4^3$
$3 + 2 \times 4 \times 4 \times 4$
$3 + 2 \times 64$
$3 + 128 = 131$ | Work inside parentheses.
Evaluate exponents.
Multiply. | $(3 + 2) \times 4^3$
5×4^3
$5 \times 4 \times 4 \times 4$
$5 \times 64 = 320$ |

Complete the statement.

1. In 2^4, the exponent, _____, says to use the base, _____, as a factor **4** times.

2. In 5^2, the exponent, _____, says to use the base, _____, as a factor _____ times.

3. In exponent form, $7 \times 7 \times 7$ is written as $7^{\underline{\quad}}$, and $6 \times 6 \times 6 \times 6 \times 6$ as _____.

4. In factored form, 8^4 is written as _____ × _____ × _____ × _____, and

   3^5 as _____ .

Tell which calculation to do first. Show that value.

5. 3×2^4

   $2^4 = 2 \times 2 \times 2 \times 2 =$ _____

6. $7 + 3^5$

   $3^5 =$ _____

7. $2 \times 4 + 4^2$

   _____

Following the order of operations, complete the calculation.

8. 5×2^3

   $5 \times$ _____

   _____ = _____

9. $12 + 3^2$

   $12 +$ _____

   _____ = _____

10. $6^2 - 10$

   _____ $- 10$

   _____ = _____

11. $6 \times 5 + 3^2$

   $6 \times 5 +$ _____

   _____

12. $4 \times 5^3 + 100$

   $4 \times$ _____ $+ 100$

   _____

13. $10 + (7 + 2)^2$

   $10 +$ _____^{2}

   _____

Find the value.

14. $18 + 4^3$

   _____

15. $5 + 2^3 + 8$

   _____

16. $(1 + 6) \times 5^2$

   _____

Teacher Note: Use after Quick Check, page 72, to reteach Unit 3, Lesson 3. **(6)**

Counting numbers other than **1** are either

  prime: only factors are itself or **1,** or
  composite: not prime.

A composite number has only one set of prime factors, which can be found by using a **factor tree.**

All these factor trees of 100 end in the same prime factors but the order of the factors is different.

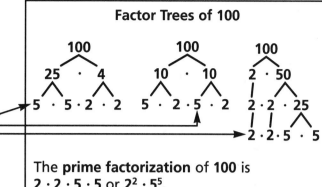

Factor Trees of 100

The **prime factorization** of **100** is $2 \cdot 2 \cdot 5 \cdot 5$ or $2^2 \cdot 5^5$.

Complete the last line in each factor tree for 24.

1.

$2 \cdot 2 \cdot \underline{} \cdot \underline{}$

2.

$3 \cdot 2 \cdot \underline{} \cdot \underline{}$

3.

$2 \cdot 3 \cdot \underline{} \cdot \underline{}$

4. The prime factorization of **24** is _____ · _____ · _____ · _____ or,

using exponents, **2**——·**3**——.

Complete these four factor trees for 36 and write the prime factorization.

5.

$\underline{} \cdot \underline{} \cdot \underline{} \cdot \underline{}$

6.

$\underline{} \cdot \underline{} \cdot \underline{} \cdot \underline{}$

7.

$3 \cdot \underline{} \cdot \underline{} \cdot \underline{}$

8.

$\underline{} \cdot \underline{} \cdot \underline{} \cdot \underline{}$

9. The prime factorization of **36** is _____ or _____.

Complete.

10. Create a factor tree for **200.**

11. Using exponents, the prime factorization of **200** is _____.

Teacher Note: Use after Quick Check, page 78, to reteach Unit 3, Lesson 4. **(6)**

To write a fraction as a decimal, divide the denominator into the numerator.

Terminating Decimal
Find the decimal equal to $\frac{3}{4}$.

$$\begin{array}{r} 0.75 \\ 4\overline{)3.00} \\ -2\,8 \\ \hline 20 \\ -20 \\ \hline 0 \end{array}$$

$\frac{3}{4} = 0.75$

Since the remainder is 0, the division ends.

Repeating Decimal
Find the decimal equal to $\frac{5}{6}$.

$$\begin{array}{r} 0.8333 \\ 6\overline{)5.0000} \\ -4\,8 \\ \hline 20 \\ -18 \\ \hline 20 \\ -18 \\ \hline 20 \\ -18 \\ \hline 20 \\ -18 \\ \hline 2 \end{array}$$

$\frac{5}{6} = 0.8333 \ldots = 0.8\overline{3}$

Use a bar to show which digit(s) repeat.

The remainder 2 keeps repeating. The division never ends.

Complete.

1. To change the fraction $\frac{3}{8}$ to a decimal, divide _____ into _____.

$$\begin{array}{r} 0.375 \\ 8\overline{)3.000} \\ -2\,4 \\ \hline 60 \\ -56 \\ \hline 40 \\ -40 \\ \hline 0 \end{array}$$

2. In the division, what is the last remainder? _____

3. A remainder of **0** shows that the division _____.

So, the decimal equivalent of the fraction $\frac{3}{8}$ ends

and is called a _____ decimal.

4. To change the fraction $\frac{2}{3}$ to a decimal, complete this division:

$$\begin{array}{r} 0.6 \\ 3\overline{)2.000} \\ -1\,8 \end{array}$$

5. What remainder keeps repeating? _____

6. What digit keeps repeating in the quotient? _____

7. To show the repeat in the decimal, use a bar. $\frac{2}{3} = 0.6666 \ldots =$ _____

Change these fractions to terminating decimals.

8. $\frac{1}{4} =$ _____ **9.** $\frac{4}{5} =$ _____ **10.** $\frac{7}{8} =$ _____ **11.** $\frac{3}{16} =$ _____

Change these fractions to repeating decimals. Use a bar to show the repeating digit(s).

12. $\frac{4}{9} =$ _____ **13.** $\frac{7}{15} =$ _____ **14.** $\frac{5}{3} =$ _____

Teacher Note: Use after Quick Check, page 90, to reteach Unit 3, Lesson 12. **(6)**

A **number line** can be used to compare fractions.

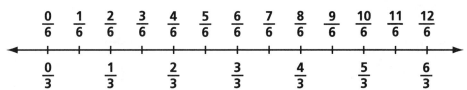

This number line is marked in sixths and in thirds.

On the line, a number to the left of another is the lesser of the two.

$$\frac{5}{6} < \frac{4}{3}$$

On the line, $\frac{5}{6}$ is to the left of $\frac{4}{3}$.

On the line, a number to the right of another is the greater of the two.

$$\frac{5}{3} > \frac{7}{6}$$

On the line, $\frac{5}{3}$ is to the right of $\frac{7}{6}$.

Refer to the number line above. Complete.

1. On the number line, $\frac{7}{6}$ is to the left of $\frac{5}{3}$. So, $\frac{7}{6}$ is the _____ of the two fractions.

2. On the number line, $\frac{2}{3}$ is to the right of $\frac{3}{6}$. So, _____ is the lesser of the two.

3. On the number line, $\frac{6}{3}$ is to the _____ of $\frac{8}{6}$. So, $\frac{8}{6}$ is the _____ of the two.

4. Of the two fractions, $\frac{10}{6}$ and $\frac{6}{3}$, $\frac{6}{3}$ is to the _____ of _____.

So, _____ < _____, which means that _____ > _____.

Refer to the number line below to compare the fractions. Use > or <.

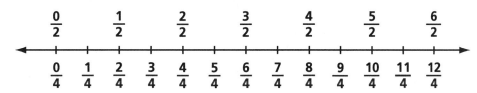

5. $\frac{7}{4} \bigcirc \frac{5}{2}$ **6.** $\frac{4}{2} \bigcirc \frac{5}{4}$ **7.** $\frac{10}{4} \bigcirc \frac{5}{4}$ **8.** $\frac{11}{4} \bigcirc \frac{6}{2}$

9. $\frac{3}{2} \bigcirc \frac{3}{4}$ **10.** $\frac{2}{2} \bigcirc \frac{3}{4}$ **11.** $\frac{5}{2} \bigcirc \frac{3}{2}$ **12.** $\frac{6}{2} \bigcirc \frac{10}{4}$

A fraction can be rounded to one of three
convenient numbers, called **benchmarks**.

$\frac{1}{12}$ is close to $\frac{0}{12}$. So, $\frac{1}{12}$ rounds to 0.

$\frac{9}{16}$ is close to $\frac{8}{16} = \frac{1}{2}$. So, $\frac{9}{16}$ rounds to $\frac{1}{2}$.

$\frac{9}{10}$ is close to $\frac{10}{10} = 1$. So, $\frac{9}{10}$ rounds to **1**.

Benchmarks for Fractions
$0, \frac{1}{2}, 1$

Rounding fractions is helpful in estimating sums or differences of
mixed numbers.

Estimate $19\frac{7}{12} + 3\frac{10}{12}$.

Think:

$\frac{7}{12}$ is close to $\frac{6}{12} = \frac{1}{2}$. So $19\frac{7}{12}$ rounds to $19\frac{1}{2}$.

$\frac{10}{12}$ is close to $\frac{12}{12} = 1$. So $3\frac{10}{12}$ rounds to 4.

Write:

$19\frac{7}{12} + 3\frac{10}{12}$

$\approx 19\frac{1}{2} + 4 = 23\frac{1}{2}$

Complete.

1. $\frac{5}{8}$ is close to $\frac{4}{8} = \frac{1}{2}$. So, $\frac{5}{8}$ rounds to _____ . $\frac{1}{8}$ is close to

$\frac{}{8} = 0$. So, $\frac{1}{8}$ rounds to _____ .

2. $\frac{7}{9}$ is close to $\frac{}{9} = 1$. So, $\frac{7}{9}$ rounds to _____ . $\frac{4}{9}$ rounds to

_____ since **4** is close to half of **9**.

Estimate the sum or difference. Show the benchmarks you used.

3. $16\frac{5}{6} + 3\frac{1}{6}$

$17 +$ _____ = _____

4. $20\frac{9}{11} - 6\frac{5}{11}$

_____ $- 6\frac{1}{2} =$ _____

5. $13\frac{9}{12} - 2\frac{7}{12}$

$14 -$ _____ = _____

6. $28\frac{3}{8} - 3\frac{7}{8}$

_____ $-$ _____ = _____

7. $10\frac{2}{3} + 11\frac{6}{7}$

_____ $+$ _____ = _____

8. $9\frac{5}{9} + 31\frac{7}{15}$

_____ $+$ _____ = _____

9. $\quad 4\frac{7}{12}$ _____

$\quad -2\frac{4}{5}$ $-$ _____

$\qquad$ _____

10. $\quad 15\frac{1}{3}$ _____

$\quad +2\frac{5}{6}$ $+$ _____

$\qquad$ _____

11. $\quad 5\frac{7}{8}$ _____

$\quad -1\frac{2}{3}$ $-$ _____

$\qquad$ _____

Teacher Note: Use before Unit 4, Lesson 1. **(6)**

Multiplying Fractions
Using Area

You can use area diagrams to model multiplication of fractions.

Model $\frac{2}{3} \times \frac{1}{4}$.

Use the first fraction to divide a rectangle horizontally.
Use the second fraction to divide it vertically.

The denominator of $\frac{2}{3}$ tells how many horizontal parts to make.

The numerator of $\frac{2}{3}$ tells how many parts to shade.

The denominator of $\frac{1}{4}$ tells how many vertical parts.

The numerator of $\frac{1}{4}$ tells how many vertical parts to shade.

Count the number of parts with both shadings. 2 of the 12 total parts are shaded twice.

Write:
$\frac{2}{3} \times \frac{1}{4} = \frac{2}{12}$

Simplify:
$\frac{2}{12} = \frac{1}{6}$

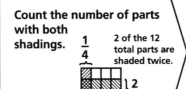

Shade the rectangle to model the product. Complete the result.

1. To model $\frac{1}{2} \times \frac{3}{5}$:

The rectangle is divided into **2** horizontal parts. Shade **1**.

The rectangle is divided into **5** vertical parts. Shade **3**.

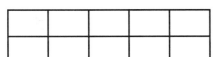

$\frac{1}{2} \times \frac{3}{5} =$ _____

2. To model $\frac{3}{4} \times \frac{1}{2}$:

Divide the rectangle into **4** horizontal parts, and shade **3**.

Divide the rectangle into **2** vertical parts, and shade **1**.

$\frac{3}{4} \times \frac{1}{2} =$ _____

Write the product shown by the model.

3.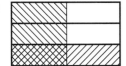

4.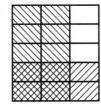

5.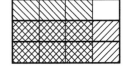

Reteach Worksheets

Teacher Note: Use after Quick Check, page 112, to reteach Unit 4, Lesson 5. **(6)**

Two numbers with a product of **1** are called **reciprocals.**

$$\frac{2}{7} \times \frac{7}{2} = 1 \qquad\qquad \frac{7}{1} \times \frac{1}{7} = 1$$

$\frac{2}{7}$ and $\frac{7}{2}$ are reciprocals. 7 and $\frac{1}{7}$ are reciprocals.

Complete.

1. $\frac{3}{8} \times \frac{8}{3} =$ _____ . So, $\frac{3}{8}$ and $\frac{8}{3}$ are _____ .

2. If two numbers are reciprocals, then their product must equal _____ .

Write the reciprocal of each number.

3. $\frac{5}{7}$ $\frac{7}{\square}$ **4.** $\frac{3}{5}$ $\frac{\square}{3}$ **5.** $\frac{9}{2}$ $\frac{\square}{\square}$ **6.** $\frac{10}{3}$ $\frac{\square}{\square}$

Choose the letter of the item that best completes the statement.

7. $9 \times \frac{1}{9} =$ _____ .   (A) $9\frac{1}{9}$ (B) $\frac{91}{9}$ (C) 0.91   (D) 1

8. Since $9 \times \frac{1}{9} = 1$, 9 and $\frac{1}{9}$ are _____ .

   (A) fractions   (B) primes   (C) reciprocals   (D) divisors

Write the reciprocal of each number.

9. 8 $\frac{1}{\square}$ **10.** $\frac{1}{4}$ $\frac{4}{\square}$ or _____   **11.** 15 $\frac{\square}{\square}$ **12.** $\frac{1}{10}$ $\frac{\square}{\square}$ or _____

Complete.

13. The mixed number $5\frac{2}{3}$ is equivalent to $\frac{3 \times 5 + 2}{7}$, or $\frac{\square}{3}$.

   The reciprocal of $\frac{17}{3}$ is $\frac{\square}{17}$. So, the reciprocal of $5\frac{2}{3}$ is $\frac{\square}{17}$.

Write the reciprocal of each number.

14. $1\frac{1}{5} = \frac{6}{5}$ _____ | **15.** $2\frac{2}{9}$ _____ | **16.** $7\frac{3}{8}$ _____ | **17.** $15\frac{2}{3}$ _____

18. 3 _____ | **19.** $\frac{5}{6}$ _____ | **20.** $\frac{9}{4}$ _____ | **21.** 13 _____

Teacher Note: Use after Quick Check, page 118, to reteach Unit 4, Lesson 9. **(6)**

As with whole numbers, use inverse operations to solve equations
with fractions.

Addition Equation

Use subtraction to solve.

$$x + \frac{1}{5} = \frac{3}{5}$$

$$x + \frac{1}{5} - \frac{1}{5} = \frac{3}{5} - \frac{1}{5} \longleftarrow \boxed{\text{Same denominators, so subtract numerators.}}$$

$$x = \frac{2}{5}$$

Subtraction Equation

Use addition to solve.

$$x - \frac{1}{5} = \frac{3}{4}$$

$$x - \frac{1}{5} + \frac{1}{5} = \frac{3}{4} + \frac{1}{5} \longleftarrow \boxed{\text{Different denominators, so use LCD = 20.}}$$

$$x = \frac{3}{4} \cdot \frac{5}{5} + \frac{1}{5} \cdot \frac{4}{4}$$

$$x = \frac{15}{20} \cdot \frac{4}{20} = \frac{19}{20}$$

Complete the solution.

1.
$$x + \frac{1}{3} = \frac{2}{3}$$

$$x + \frac{1}{3} - \frac{1}{3} = \frac{2}{3} \ _____$$

$$x = _____$$

2.
$$x - \frac{2}{7} = \frac{3}{7}$$

$$x - \frac{2}{7} + \frac{2}{7} = \frac{3}{7} \ _____$$

$$x = _____$$

3.
$$y + \frac{1}{3} = \frac{5}{6}$$

$$y + \frac{1}{3} - \frac{1}{3} = \frac{5}{6} - \frac{1}{3}$$

$$y = \frac{5}{6} - \frac{1}{3}$$

$$y = \frac{5}{6} - \frac{}{6}$$

$$y = _____$$

4.
$$9n = \frac{1}{3}$$

$$\frac{1}{9} \cdot 9n = \frac{1}{3} \cdot \frac{1}{9}$$

$$n = \frac{1}{3} \cdot _____$$

$$n = _____$$

5.
$$k - \frac{1}{3} = \frac{3}{4}$$

$$k - \frac{1}{3} + \frac{1}{3} = \frac{3}{4} + \frac{1}{3}$$

$$k = _____ + _____$$

$$k = _____$$

6.
$$\frac{2}{5}w = \frac{2}{3}$$

$$\frac{5}{2} \cdot \frac{2}{5}w = _____$$

$$w = _____$$

Teacher Note: Use after Quick Check, page 126, to reteach Unit 4, Lesson 14. **(6)**

A metric ruler is marked off in centimeters (cm) and millimeters (mm).
Centimeter is the larger unit, **1 cm = 10 mm.**

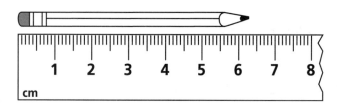

The length of this pencil is between **6** cm and **7** cm. The length is closer to **6** cm.

So to the nearest cm, the pencil is **6** cm long.

More accurately, the length is **6 cm + 3 mm.**

Using only centimeters: **6 cm + 3 mm = 6 cm + 3 × 0.1 cm = 6.3 cm**

Using only millimeters: **6 cm + 3 mm = 6 × 10 mm + 3 mm = 63 mm**

Complete.

1. Since **1 mm = 0.1 cm,**

then **5 mm = 5 × 0.1**

or _____ cm.

2. Since **1 cm = 10 mm**

then **3 cm = 3 × 10**

or _____ mm.

3. 7 mm = _____ cm

4. 7.3 mm = _____ cm

5. 8 cm = _____ mm

6. 8.2 cm = _____ mm

Write the length of segment AB in the units shown.

7. AB = _____ cm + _____ mm

8. AB = _____ cm

9. AB = _____ mm

A ──────────────────────── B

cm 1 2 3 4 5 6 7 8

Write the length of segment PQ in the units shown.

10. in centimeters _____

11. in millimeters _____

12. to the nearest centimeter _____

P ──────── Q

Teacher Note: Use after Quick Check, page 118, to reteach Unit 4, Lesson 9. **(6)**

A customary ruler is marked off in inches (in. and "),
with finer markings at halves, quarters, eighths, and sixteenths.

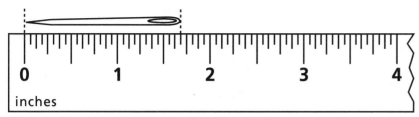

inches

The length of this needle is between **1″** and **2″**.

The length is closer to **2″**. So to the nearest inch, the length is **2″**.

More accurately: to the nearest half inch, $1\frac{1}{2}″$

to the nearest quarter inch, $1\frac{3}{4}″$

to the nearest eighth inch, $1\frac{5}{8}″$

Still more accurately, the length is $1\frac{11}{16}″$.

Complete. Refer to the diagram at the right.

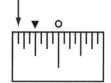

1. This inch is marked off in half inches, in quarter inches,

in _____ inches, and in _____ inches.

2. The symbol ○ is at the _____-inch mark.

3. The symbol ▼ is at the _____-inch mark.

4. The symbol ↓ is at the _____-inch mark.

Write the length of segment $\overline{AB}$.

5. to the nearest eighth inch _____

6. to the nearest sixteenth inch _____

7. to the nearest half inch _____

8. to the nearest inch _____

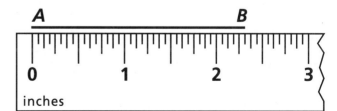

**Write the measure of each line segment
to the nearest sixteenth inch.**

9. C _____ D   **10.** E _____ F   **11.** G _____ H

CD = _____   EF = _____   GH = _____

Teacher Note: Use before Unit 5, Lesson 1. **(6)**

The basic metric unit of length is the **meter** (m).

Often-used shorter units are
the **centimeter** (cm) and the **millimeter** (mm).

1,000 m = 1 km
1 m = 100 cm
1 m = 1,000 mm

A longer unit is the **kilometer** (km).

Complete. Think about reciprocals. Use fractions and decimals.

1. Since **1 km** is _____ times **1 m**, then **1 m** is $\frac{1}{1,000}$ of **1 km**, or **1 m = 0.001** km.

2. Since **1 m** is **100** times **1 cm**, then **1 cm** is _____ of **1 m**, or **1 cm =** _____ m.

3. Since **1 m** is _____ times **1 mm**, then **1 mm** is _____ of **1 m**, or **1 mm =** _____ m.

Complete. Think of balancing an equation.

4. Since **1 km = 1,000 m**, then **6** times **1 km** is **6** times _____ m, or **6 km =** _____ m.

5. 8 km = _____ m   **6.** 70 km = _____ m   **7.** 150 km = _____ m

---

Complete.

8. 1 km = 1,000 m and 1 m = 100 cm.

So, **1 km = (1,000 × 100)** cm, or **1 km =** _____ cm. So **7 km =** _____ cm.

9. 8 km = _____ cm   **10.** 70 km = _____ cm   **11.** 150 km = _____ cm

12. 1 km = 1,000 m and 1 m = 1,000 mm.

So **1 km = (1,000 ×** _____ **)** mm, or **1 km =** _____ mm. So **7 km =** _____ mm.

13. 8 km = _____ mm   **14.** 70 km = _____ mm   **15.** 150 km = _____ mm

16. Since **1 m =** _____ cm, then **9 m =** _____ cm.

17. Since **1 m =** _____ mm, then **9 m =** _____ mm.

18. 8 m = _____ cm   **19.** 80 m = _____ cm   **20.** 150 m = _____ cm

21. 8 m = _____ mm   **22.** 70 m = _____ mm   **23.** 150 m = _____ mm

---

Complete to compare. Write >, <, or =.

24. 3 km = 3,000 m and 3,000 m = 3,000,000 mm. So 3 km ◯ 3,000,000 mm.

25. 50 cm ◯ 500 mm   **26.** 3 km ◯ 3,000 mm   **27.** 2,000 mm ◯ 20 m

28. 5.5 m ◯ 55 cm   **29.** 800 cm ◯ 0.8 m   **30.** 200 m ◯ 20 cm

Teacher Note: Use after Quick Check, page 136, to reteach Unit 5, Lesson 1. **(6)**

The basic metric unit of capacity is the **liter** (L). It is about the same capacity as a quart.

Smaller units include the **centiliter** (cL) and the **milliliter** (mL). A larger unit is the **kiloliter** (kL).

$$1,000 \text{ L} = 1 \text{ kL}$$
$$1 \text{ L} = 100 \text{ cL}$$
$$1 \text{ L} = 1,000 \text{ mL}$$

The basic metric unit of mass is the **gram** (g). A paper clip has a mass of about 1 gram.

One smaller unit is the **milligram** (mg). Larger units are the **kilogram** (kg) and the **metric ton**.

$$1 \text{ metric ton} = 1,000 \text{ kg}$$
$$1 \text{ kg} = 1,000 \text{ g}$$
$$1 \text{ g} = 1,000 \text{ mg}$$

Complete.

1. *Kilo-* means "**1,000.**" So **1 kL =** _____ **L.** Then, **1 L =** _____ **kL,** or **1 L = 0.001 kL.**

2. *Milli-* means "$\frac{1}{1000}$." So **1 mg =** _____ **g** or, using decimals, **1 mg =** _____ **g.**

3. **1** metric ton = _____ **kg** and **1 kg =** _____ **g.** So **1** metric ton = (**1,000** × _____) **g.**

4. **1 cL** is **10** times **1 mL.** So **1 mL** is _____ of **1 cL,** or, using decimals, **1 mL =** _____ **cL.**

Complete. Think of balancing an equation.

5. Since **1 kg = 1,000 g,** then **0.5** times **1 kg** is **0.5** times _____ **g,** or **0.5 kg =** _____ **g.**

6. **0.3 kg =** _____ **g**   **7.** **0.8 kg =** _____ **g**   **8.** **2 kg =** _____ **g**

9. Since **1 L = 100 cL,** then **2.5** times **1 L** is **2.5** times _____ **cL,** or **2.5 L =** _____ **cL.**

10. **1.7 L =** _____ **cL**   **11.** **0.6 L =** _____ **cL**   **12.** **4 L =** _____ **cL**

13. Since **1 g = 1,000 mg,** then **4** times **1 g** is **4** times _____ **mg,** or **4 g =** _____ **mg.**

14. **30 g =** _____ **mg**   **15.** **200 g =** _____ **mg**   **16.** **0.5 g =** _____ **mg**

Compare. Write >, <, or =.

17. **3 L = 300 cL** and **3 L = 3,000 mL.** So **300 cL** ◯ **3,000 mL.**

18. **40 mL** ◯ **4 cL**   **19.** **3 kL** ◯ **3,000 mL**   **20.** **2 mL** ◯ **20 cL**

21. **0.002 kg** ◯ **20 g**   **22.** **3,000 g** ◯ **3 kg**   **23.** **2,000 mg** ◯ **20 g**

Vocabulary

thermometer   an instrument to measure temperature

degree (°)   a unit of measure for temperature

degrees Celsius (°C)   an international unit for measuring temperature, shown on the thermometer at the right

boiling point   100°C   **freezing point**   0°C

A temperature below **0°**, such as
⁻10°C, is read as *10 degrees below 0.*

100°	← water boils
90°	
80°	
70°	
60°	} hot water
50°	
40°	← normal body temperature
30°	
20°	← room temperature
10°	
0°	← water freezes
-10°	
-20°	cold winter temperature
-30°	

Refer to the thermometer shown. Match the items in the columns.

Column A

0°C   __d__

1. 37°C   _____

2. ⁻10°C   _____

3. 24°C   _____

4. 100°C   _____

Column B

a. the boiling point

b. room temperature

c. normal body temperature

d. the freezing point

e. cold winter temperature

Complete. Refer to the thermometer shown.

5. **10°C** is **10** degrees above **0** and **⁻10°C** is **10** degrees _____ **0**.

Between these two temperatures, there are _____ degrees.

6. When the temperature changes from **⁻10°C** to **20°C**, it rises by _____ degrees.

Complete the table. Refer to the thermometer shown.

7.

Temperature	Change	New Temperature
⁻20°C	rise of 10°C	⁻10°C
15°C	rise of 10°C	
⁻15°C	rise of 10°C	
⁻5°C	rise of 10°C	

8.

Temperature	Change	New Temperature
⁻20°C		⁻10°C
15°C		0°C
15°C		⁻10°C
⁻20°C		0°C

Time Zones and
Elapsed Time

A **time zone** is a geographic region that regulates its time in the same way. The continental United States has four time zones. The time in any zone is **1** hour later than in the zone just to the west. The time is **1** hour earlier than in the zone just to the east of it.

| Pacific Standard Time | Mountain Standard Time | Central Standard Time | Eastern Standard Time |

Complete. Refer to the clocks above and the time zone map.

1. Central Standard Time is _____ hour earlier than Eastern Standard Time.

Central Standard Time is **2** hours later than _____ Standard Time.

2. Mountain Standard Time is _____ hours earlier than Eastern Standard Time.

So if it is **4:00** P.M. in western Kansas (KS), then it is _____ P.M. in Ohio (OH).

3. A plane left Seattle, WA, at **3:00** P.M. on a **6**-hour flight to Phoenix, AZ.

When the plane landed in Phoenix, the time in Seattle was **3 + 6**, or _____ P.M.

Since Mountain Standard Time is **1** hour later than Pacific Standard Time,

the plane landed in Phoenix at _____.

4. A plane left New York, NY, at **11:00** A.M. on a **6**-hour flight to San

Francisco, CA. When the plane landed in San Francisco, the time there

was _____.

5. A plane left Bismarck, ND, at **9:00** A.M., Central Standard Time, and landed in Butte, MT,

at **10:00** A.M., Mountain Standard Time. To find the flying time, remember that the

time in Butte is **1** hour earlier than in Bismarck. So subtract **9** from **10** and _____ **1**.

The length of the flight was _____ hours.

6. A plane left Austin, TX, at **8:00** A.M., Central Standard Time, and landed in Detroit, MI,

at **2:00** P.M., Eastern Standard Time. The length of the flight was _____ hours.

Reteach Worksheets

Customary units of length include **inch** (in.),
foot (ft), **yard** (yd), and **mile** (mi). The
abbreviations are used for both singular
and plural measures.

Equivalent Lengths
1 ft = 12 in.
1 yd = 3 ft or **36 in.**
1 mi = 5,280 ft or **1,760 yd**

Complete the statements.

1. Since **1 ft = 12 in.**, **4 × 1 ft = 4 ×** _____ **in.**, or **4 ft =** _____ **in.**

2. To change from feet to inches, multiply by _____.

To change from inches to feet, divide by _____.

3. **18 ft = 18 × 12** or _____ **in.**   **4.** $4\frac{1}{4}$ **ft =** _____ **in.**   **5.** $5\frac{1}{2}$ **ft =** _____ **in.**

6. **84 in. = 84 ÷ 12** or _____ **ft**   **7.** **114 in. =** _____ **ft**   **8.** **819 in. =** _____ **ft**

Complete the statements.

9. Since **1 yd =** _____ **ft**, **7 yd = 7 ×** _____ **ft**, or **7 yd =** _____ **ft.**

10. To change from yards to feet, multiply by _____.

To change from feet to yards, _____.

11. Since **1 yd =** _____ **in.**, **7 yd = 7 ×** _____ **in.**, or **7 yd =** _____ **in.**

12. To change from yards to inches, multiply by _____.

To change from inches to yards, _____.

13. **6 yd = 6 × 3** or _____ **ft**   **14.** **5 yd =** _____ **in.**   **15.** $8\frac{1}{3}$ **yd =** _____ **ft**

16. **57 ft = 57 ÷ 3** or _____ **yd**   **17.** **540 in. =** _____ **yd**   **18.** **45 ft =** _____ **yd**

Complete the statements.

19. Since **1 mi =** _____ **ft**, **4 mi = 4 ×** _____ **ft**, or **4 mi =** _____ **ft.**

20. To change from miles to feet, multiply by _____.

21. Since **1 mi =** _____ **yd**, **4 mi = 4 ×** _____ **yd**, or **4 mi =** _____ **yd.**

22. To change from miles to yards, multiply by _____.

23. **75 mi =** _____ **ft**   **24.** **100 mi =** _____ **yd**

Teacher Note: Use after Quick Check, page 142, to reteach Unit 5, Lesson 6. **(6)**

Customary units of liquid capacity are the
fluid ounce (fl oz), **cup** (c), **pint** (pt), **quart**
(qt), and **gallon** (gal).

Customary units of weight are the **ounce**
(oz), **pound** (lb), and **ton** (T).

> **Equivalent Capacities**
> **1** c = **8** fl oz
> **1** pt = **2** c
> **1** qt = **2** pt
> **1** gal = **4** qt

> **Equivalent Weights**
> **16** ounces (oz) = **1** pound (lb)
> **2,000** lb = **1** ton (T)

Complete these statements.

1. To find the fluid ounces equal to **7** c, multiply **7** times _____ fl oz.

   7 c = _____ fl oz

2. To change a measurement from cups to fluid ounces, multiply by _____.

   To change from fluid ounces to cups, divide by _____.

3. 6 c = _____ fl oz   **4.** $3\frac{1}{2}$ c = _____ fl oz   **5.** 6 fl oz = _____ c

6. To change a measurement from pints to fluid ounces, multiply by _____.

   To change from fluid ounces to pints, divide by _____.

7. To change a measurement from pounds to ounces, multiply by _____.

   To change from ounces to pounds, _____.

Write an equivalent measurement.

8. 6 pt = _____ c   **9.** 10 pt = _____ fl oz   **10.** $8\frac{1}{2}$ c = _____ pt

11. 9 qt = _____ pt   **12.** $10\frac{1}{2}$ pt = _____ qt   **13.** 12 qt = _____ c

14. 28 c = _____ qt   **15.** 3 qt = _____ fl oz   **16.** 64 fl oz = _____ qt

17. 9 gal = _____ qt   **18.** 8 gal = _____ fl oz   **19.** 10 gal = _____ pt

20. 9 lbs = _____ oz   **21.** 96 oz = _____ lb   **22.** $8\frac{1}{2}$ lbs = _____ oz

Complete.

23. To change from tons to pounds, multiply by _____. So 2 T = _____ lb.

24. To change from pounds to tons, _____. So 8,400 lb = _____ T.

25. 3 T = _____ lb   **26.** 6,400 lb = _____ T   **27.** 12,500 lb = _____ T

Teacher Note: Use after Quick Check, page 146, to reteach Unit 5, Lesson 7. **(6)**

This **line graph** shows the normal temperature, in **degrees Fahrenheit** (°F), in Los Angeles, CA, for each month of the year.

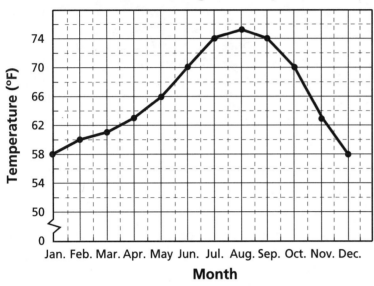

Normal Los Angeles Temperatures

Complete. Refer to the line graph.

1. a. Look for the dot at the highest level. It represents the highest temperature. Trace down to find the month for that dot.

The month with the highest normal temperature is _____.

b. Go back to that highest dot. Trace left to read the temperature for that dot.

The highest normal temperature is _____ °F.

2. a. The months that have the lowest normal temperature are _____.

b. That temperature is about _____ °F.

3. a. June has a normal temperature of _____.

b. Another month with that same normal temperature is _____.

4. a. April (Apr) has a normal temperature of _____.

b. Does any other month have the same normal temperature? _____

If so, which one? _____

5. a. From left to right, the **12** temperatures shown on the graph are

58°F, 60°F, _____°F, _____°F, _____°F, 70°F, _____°F, 75°F, _____°F, _____°F, _____°F, _____°F

b. The mean of these temperatures is _____.

Teacher Note: Use after Quick Check, page 146, to reteach Unit 5, Lesson 8. **(6)**

Percent comes from Latin *per centum,* meaning "per hundred."
The 10 × 10 grid at the right shows *1 whole unit.* Each of the

100 small squares is $\frac{1}{100}$, or **1%**, of the whole **unit square.**

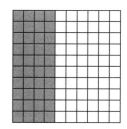

Since there are **100** small squares, the whole unit is **100%**.
Since **40** small squares are shaded, the diagram shows **40%**.

The unit square below represents **300** marchers in a parade.

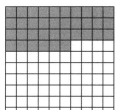

Each small square stands for **1%**, or $\frac{1}{100}$ of the marchers.

$\frac{1}{100}$ × **300 = 3**, so **1%** of **300** marchers is **3** marchers.

36 small squares = **36%** of **300** = **36 × 3 = 108** marchers.

Complete. Refer to the models.

1. The **10 × 10** grid below

has **24** shaded squares

to represent _____%.

2. The **10 × 10** grid below

has _____ shaded squares

to represent _____%.

3. The shaded squares in

the model below

represent _____%.

4. The unit square at the right is divided into fifths.
Shade one of these fifths.

    a. The number of small squares shaded is _____.

    b. _____% of the unit square is shaded.

5. The unit square at the right represents **200** students in a school.

    a. Each small square represents $\frac{1}{100}$ of **200**, or _____ students.

    b. The number of students represented by 4 small squares is _____.

    c. So **4%** of **200** is _____. To find **4%** of **200**, multiply **4** by _____.

Find the percentage.

    6. **39%** of **600** is _____.

    7. **84%** of **700** is _____.

    8. **73%** of **1,400** is _____.

    9. **6%** of **300** is _____.

    10. **11%** of **1,500** is _____.

    11. **99%** of **500** is _____.

Teacher Note: Use before Unit 6 , Lesson 1. **(6)**   **89**

A **ratio** compares numbers in a certain order.

At the right, the ratio of A's to a's is **6** to **4** or $\frac{6}{4}$.

The ratio of a's to A's is **4** to **6** or $\frac{4}{6}$.

In simplest form, $\frac{6}{4} = \frac{6 \div 2}{6 \div 4} = \frac{3}{2}$.

What is the ratio of **3** feet to **4** inches?
To compare measurements,
the units must be the same.

A A A A A A

a a a a

Write feet as inches.	Write the ratio.	Find the simplest form.	
$3 \times 12 = 36$ in.	$\frac{36}{4}$	$\frac{36}{4} = \frac{36 \div 4}{4 \div 4}$	$\frac{9}{1}$

Complete. Refer to this set of symbols:

1. The ratio of ■ to ⬣ is **6** to _____. The ratio of ⬣ to ■ is _____ to _____.

2. Written as fractions, the ratio **6** to **9** is $\frac{6}{9}$ and the ratio **9** to **6** is $\frac{\square}{\square}$.

3. In simpest form, the ratio $\frac{6}{9}$ is $\frac{6 \div 3}{9 \div 3}$, or $\frac{\square}{\square}$.

Write each ratio as a fraction in simplest form.

4. 2 nurses out of **10**

$\frac{2}{10} = \frac{2 \div 2}{2 \div 10} = \frac{\square}{\square}$

5. 3 teachers out of **60**

$\frac{3}{60} = \frac{\square \div \square}{\square \div \square} = \frac{\square}{\square}$

6. 12 sweaters to **8** sweaters

_____

7. 150 passengers to **5** passengers

_____

Compare the measurements by writing a ratio in simplest form.

8. 8 months to **2** years

$\frac{8}{24} = \frac{8 \div 8}{24 \div 8} = \frac{\square}{\square}$

9. 6 yd to **4** ft (1 yd = 3 ft)

_____

10. 4 lb to **20** oz (1 lb = 16 oz)

_____

11. 64 cm to **3** m

_____

Teacher Note: Use before Unit 6, Lesson 1. **(6)**

Use **equal ratios** to solve problems.

José can type **45** words per minute.
At that rate, how many words can he type in **3** minutes?

Step **1** Let *n* stand for the number of words José can type in **3** minutes.

Step **2** Write the rate in ratio form. $\dfrac{45 \text{ words}}{1 \text{ minute}}$

Step **3** Write an equal ratio using the remaining information.

$$\frac{45 \text{ words}}{1 \text{ min}} = \frac{n \text{ words}}{3 \text{ min}}$$

Step **4** Solve.

$$\frac{45}{1} = \frac{n}{3} \rightarrow \frac{45 \times 3}{1 \times 3} = \frac{n}{3} \rightarrow \frac{135}{3} = \frac{n}{3}$$

Step **5** To find *n*, read the numerators of the equal ratios. $135 = n$

So José can type **135** words in **3** minutes.

Complete, using equal ratios to find the missing term.

1. $\dfrac{3}{5} = \dfrac{n}{10}$

$\dfrac{3 \times 2}{5 \times 2} = \dfrac{n}{10}$

$n =$ _____

2. $\dfrac{4}{9} = \dfrac{m}{18}$

$\dfrac{4 \times \Box}{9 \times 2} = \dfrac{m}{18}$

$m =$ _____

3. $\dfrac{7}{8} = \dfrac{a}{24}$

$\dfrac{7 \times \Box}{8 \times \Box} = \dfrac{a}{24}$

$a =$ _____

Complete, using equal ratios to solve the problem.

4. Karen can run **2** miles in **11** minutes.
At that rate, how many miles can she
run in **33** minutes?

Let *n* = the number of miles in **33** min.

$$\frac{2}{11} = \frac{n}{33}$$

$$\frac{2 \times \Box}{11 \times 3} = \frac{n}{33}$$

$n =$ _____

In **33** min, Karen can run _____ miles.

5. Mr. Diaz can make **4** chairs in **7** days.
At that rate, how many chairs can
he make in **35** days?

Let *n* = the number of chairs in **35** days.

$$\frac{4}{\Box} = \frac{\Box}{\Box}$$

$$\frac{\Box \times \Box}{\Box \times \Box} = \frac{\Box}{\Box}$$

$n =$ _____

In **35** days, Mr. Diaz can make _____ chairs.

Teacher Note: Use after Quick Check, page 158, to reteach Unit 6, Lesson 3. **(6)**

In a **scale drawing**, the ratio of any distance in the drawing to the real distance is always the same. The ratio is called the **scale**.

A map is a type of **scale drawing**. The **scale** on the map at the right is

$$1 \text{ cm} = 220 \text{ km.}$$

On the map, the distance between San Francisco and Los Angeles is about **2.5** cm.

About how many kilometers does this represent?

centimeters $\longrightarrow \dfrac{1}{220} = \dfrac{2.5}{d} \longleftarrow$ centimeters
kilometers $\longrightarrow$ $\longleftarrow$ kilometers

$$1 \times d = 220 \times 2.5$$

$$d = 550$$

So the distance between San Francisco and Los Angeles is about **550** km.

California

Sacramento

San Francisco

Los Angeles

km 0   220

San Diego

Complete. Suppose you have a map with a scale of 1 in. = 75 mi.

1. Two cities on this map are **3** in. apart. What is the actual distance between them?

$$\dfrac{\text{in. on map}}{\text{actual mi}} \to \dfrac{1}{75} = \dfrac{3}{d} \leftarrow \dfrac{\text{in. on map}}{\text{actual mi}}$$

$$1 \times d = \underline{} \times \underline{}$$

$$d = \underline{}$$

The actual distance is _____ mi.

2. Two cities on this map are **4.5** in. apart. What is the actual distance between them?

$$\dfrac{1}{75} = \underline{}$$

$$\underline{} \times \underline{} = \underline{} \times \underline{}$$

$$d = \underline{}$$

The actual distance is _____.

3. The actual distance between two cities is **600** mi. How far apart are they on this map?

$$\dfrac{1}{75} = \dfrac{m}{600}$$

$$75 \times m = \underline{} \times \underline{}$$

$$m = \underline{}$$

The map distance is _____ in.

4. The actual distance between two cities is **1,050** mi. How far apart are they on this map?

$$\dfrac{1}{75} = \underline{}$$

$$\underline{} \times \underline{} = \underline{} \times \underline{}$$

$$m = \underline{}$$

The map distance is _____.

Teacher Note: Use after Quick Check, page 158, to reteach Unit 6, Lesson 3. **(6)**

The amount by which a price
is reduced is called a **discount**.

To find the **sale price** (what you pay)
for this box of floppy disks, use
these steps.

Box of Floppy Disks

Regular Price = $27

Discount = 20%

| To find the amount of discount, multiply the regular price by the discount rate. | $27 \times 20\%$ $= \$27 \times .020$ $= \$5.40$ | To find the sale price, subtract the discount from the regular price. | $\begin{array}{r} \$27.00 \\ -\ 5.40 \\ \hline \$21.60 \end{array}$ Sale Price |

Interest can be earned or paid. Use a formula to calculate it.
Interest (I) = Principal (p) × Rate (r) × Time (t)

After **3** years at the rate of
7%, a savings deposit of
$1,500 will earn **$315** in
simple interest.

$I = p \times r \times t$
$p = \$1,500$
$r = 7\% \rightarrow 0.07$
$t = 3$

$\$1,500 \times 0.07 \times 3$

$= \$315$

Interest

Complete, using this situation: The regular price of a TV is $500.

Discount offer is 25%.

1. Amount of
Discount

$= \$500 \times$ _____

$= \$500 \times$ _____

$=$ _____

2. Sale
Price $= \$500 -$ _____

$=$ _____

So the price you pay for the TV is

_____.

Complete to calculate the simple interest.

3. **$700** is invested at **6%** for **4** years.

$I = p \times r \times t$

$= \$700 \times 6\% \times$ _____

$= \$700 \times$ _____ $\times$ _____

The amount of interest earned is _____.

4. **$1,350** is borrowed at **12%** for **2** years.

$I = p \times r \times t$

$=$ _____ $\times$ _____ $\times$ _____

$=$ _____ $\times$ _____ $\times$ _____

The amount of interest owed is _____.

5. **$3,500** is invested at **7.5%** for **7** years. The amount of interest earned is _____.

Teacher Note: Use after Quick Check, page 176, to reteach Unit 6, Lesson 10. **(6)**

You can estimate a percent of a number by using close fractions.

| Estimate 76% of 25. | 76% is close to **75%**. $\frac{75}{100} = \frac{3}{4}$ | $\frac{3}{4} \times 24$ = 18 | 76% of 24 is about **18**. |

In some calculations, you may need to adjust both numbers.

| Estimate 63% of 43. | 63 rounds to **60**. 43 rounds to **40**. | Find **60%** of **40**. 60% = 0.6 0.6 × 40 = 24 | 63% of 43 is about **24**. |

Since both numbers rounded down, the result is an *underestimate*.
The actual percentage is **0.63 × 43 = 27.09**.

Complete.

1. 27% is close to **25%**, which is $\frac{\square}{100}$, or $\frac{1}{4}$. So for **27%**, use the easy fraction $\frac{\square}{\square}$.

2. For **35%**, which is the decimal _____, use the fraction $\frac{1}{\square}$, which is $0.\overline{33}$.

3. 56% is close to **50%**. Use the fraction $\frac{\square}{\square}$.   **4.** For **67%**, use the fraction $\frac{\square}{\square}$.

Complete to estimate each product. Find the actual product.

5. To find **37%** of **29**, use **40%** of **30**.

10% of 30 = _____

40% of 30 = _____

So **37%** of **29** is about _____.

This is an overestimate since both numbers were rounded _____.

The actual product is

0.37 × 29 = _____.

6. To find **23%** of **52**, use **20%** of _____.

10% of _____ = _____

20% of _____ = _____

So **23%** of **52** is about _____.

This is an _____ since

both numbers were rounded _____.

The actual product is _____.

Estimate each product. Is your result an overestimate or an underestimate?

7. 64% of 90   **8.** 26% of $8.43   **9.** 73% of 156

_____   _____   _____

Teacher Note: Use after Quick Check, page 182, to reteach Unit 6, Lesson 14. (6)

A figure has **line symmetry** if you can divide it into two parts that are mirror images of each other.

The figure has one horizontal line of symmetry.

To identify a line of symmetry, think about folding the figure so that the two pieces fit exactly on top of each other.

A figure has **rotational symmetry** if it can be turned around a center point so that it matches up with itself.

The figure will fit on top of itself three times during one full turn.

To identify a figure with rotational symmetry, think about turning the figure so it fits on top of itself at least once before a full turn is made.

Consider the capital letters of the English alphabet, when written as shown.

A B C D E F G H I J K L M
N O P Q R S T U V W X Y Z

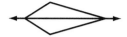

1. B has a horizontal line of symmetry. Name the other letters that have

   a horizontal line of symmetry. _____

2. H has both vertical and horizontal line symmetry. Name the other letters that have

   both vertical and horizontal line symmetry. _____

Draw all possible lines of symmetry.

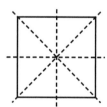

3.

4.

Tell if the figure has rotational symmetry. Write *yes* or *no*.

yes

5.

_____

6.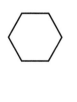

_____

7.

_____

8.

_____

Teacher Note: Use before Unit 7, Lesson 1. **(6)**

Figure	Description	Diagram	Write	Read
point	a location in space	•P	P	point P
line	a collection of points that extend in two opposite directions with no beginning or end	$\overset{\longleftrightarrow}{A \quad B}$	$\overleftrightarrow{AB}$	line AB
segment	part of a line with two endpoints	$A \quad\quad B$	$\overline{AB}$	segment AB
ray	part of a line with one endpoint that goes on without end in one direction	$A \quad B$	$\overrightarrow{AB}$	ray AB

A **plane** is a flat surface extending without end in all directions. **Space** is the set of all points.

Two lines in the same plane can be:

intersecting, (meet in a point)	**perpendicular,** (form square corners)	or	**parallel.** (never meet)

symbol: ⊥   symbol: ∥

Match the word phrase in Column A with the symbols in Column B.

Column A

1. Is parallel to ____e____

2. Segment DE _____

3. Ray DE _____

4. Line DE _____

5. Is perpendicular to _____

Column B

a. $\overline{DE}$

b. $\overrightarrow{DE}$

c. $\overleftrightarrow{DE}$

d. ⊥

e. ∥

Complete. Refer to the diagram at the right.

6. Three rays that have Q as an endpoint are $\overrightarrow{QR}$, $\overrightarrow{QY}$, and _____.

7. Two segments that are part of $\overrightarrow{QR}$ are $\overline{RP}$ and _____.

8. $\overrightarrow{PX} \perp \overrightarrow{QR}$ and also _____ $\perp \overrightarrow{QR}$.

9. The line that intersects $\overrightarrow{QT}$ at T is _____.

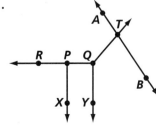

Teacher Note: Use after Quick Check, page 192, to reteach Unit 7, Lesson 1. **(6)**

Angles can be classified by the number of **degrees** they contain.

Acute angle	Right angle	Obtuse angle
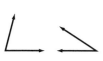		
Less than **90°**	Exactly **90°**	Greater than **90°** and less than **180°**

A **protractor** is a tool used to find the number of degrees in an angle.

There are two scales, each from **0°** to **180°**.

To measure ∠**ABC**:

Step 1 Place the center of the protractor on the vertex of the angle.

Step 2 Align the base of the protractor with $\overrightarrow{BC}$.

Step 3 Read the number where $\overrightarrow{BA}$ crosses the scale. Choose the scale that $\overrightarrow{BC}$ crosses at 0.

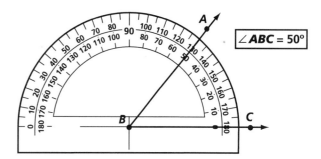

∠**ABC** = 50°

Complete. Refer to the diagram at the right.

1. ∠**ABC** = 20°. Since the measure is less than **90°**, ∠**ABC** is an

_____ angle.

2. ∠**ABF** is an obtuse angle.

∠**ABF** = _____°

3. a. ∠**ABE** = _____°

   b. ∠**ABE** is a _____ angle.

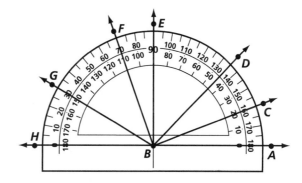

Refer to the diagram. Find the angle measure. Classify the angle as *acute*, *right*, or *obtuse*.

4. ∠**ABG** = _____°

_____

5. ∠**HBG** = 30°

_____

6. ∠**HBF** = _____°

_____

7. ∠**HBE** = _____°

_____

8. ∠**HBD** = _____°

_____

9. ∠**CBD** = _____°

_____

Teacher Note: Use after Quick Check, page 192, to reteach Unit 7, Lesson 2. **(6)**

Angle Pair	Description	Diagram	Relationship
Congruent angles	Two angles with the same measure	50° A 50° B	$\angle A \cong \angle B$
Vertical angles	Angles on opposite sides of the intersection of two lines	a x b y	$x = y$ $a = b$
Supplementary angles	Two angles whose measures have a sum of **180°**	D 140° 40° A B C	$\angle ABD + \angle DBC = 180°$
Complementary angles	Two angles whose measures have the sum of **90°**	A 50° D 40° B C	$\angle ABD + \angle DBC = 90°$

Complete. Refer to the diagram at the right.

1. Since $\overleftrightarrow{AB}$ and $\overleftrightarrow{CD}$ intersect, two pairs of vertical angles are formed.

   One pair is $\angle APC$ and $\angle BPD$. The other is $\angle$ _____ and $\angle$ _____.

2. If $\angle APC = 40°$, then its vertical angle $\angle BPD =$ _____°.

3. $\angle APD = 140°$, then $\angle$ _____ is also **140°**.

4. a. $\angle APC + \angle APD =$ _____°.

   b. So, $\angle APC$ and $\angle APD$ are _____ angles.

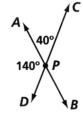

Complete. Refer to the diagram at the right.

5. $\angle ABC = \angle FBE =$ _____°.

6. a. $\angle ABD =$ _____°.

   b. $\angle EBD =$ _____°.

   c. $\angle ABD = \angle EBD =$ _____°.

   d. So $\angle ABD$ and $\angle EBD$ are

   _____ angles.

7. $\angle HBF$ and $\angle$ _____ are complementary.

8. $\angle ABC$ and $\angle EBC$ are _____ angles.

9. $\angle ABG$ and $\angle HBG$ are _____ angles.

10. $\angle ABC$ and $\angle$ _____ are supplementary angles.

Teacher Note: Use after Quick Check, page 192, to reteach Unit 7, Lesson 3. **(6)**

A **circle** is the set of all points on a flat surface that are the same distance from a given point, which is called the **center** of the circle.

Circle O

Radius	**Chord**	**Diameter**	**Central angle**
A segment connecting the center to any point on the circle	A segment whose endpoints are any two points on the circle	A chord that passes through the center	An angle formed by two radii

Radius $\overline{OA}$

Chord $\overline{AB}$

Diameter $\overline{AOB}$

Central $\angle AOB$

Complete. Refer to the diagram at the right.

1. The center of this circle is at O.

So the circle is called _____.

2. The diagram shows two radii, $\overline{OP}$ and _____.

3. a. $PQ = PO +$ _____.

b. So the diameter equals the length of the two _____.

Identify these parts in the circle at the right.

4. Center _____

5. Radii _____, _____, _____, _____

6. Diameters _____, _____

7. Chords _____, _____, _____, _____, _____

8. Central angles _____, _____, _____, _____

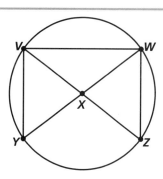

Complete for the circle with center at C.

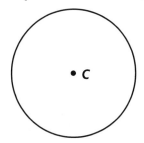

9. Draw two radii, $\overline{CP}$ and $\overline{CQ}$, that do not form a diameter.

10. Draw diameter $\overline{RS}$.

11. What figure is formed by $\overline{CP}$ and $\overline{CQ}$?

_____

Congruence and
Constructions

These steps show how to use a protractor to draw an angle of **35°**.

1. Draw $\overrightarrow{BA}$ for
one side of
the angle.

2. Place the protractor as
you would for
measuring. Make a
mark at **35°**.

3. Label the point you
marked **C**. Draw $\overrightarrow{BC}$,
the other side of the
angle.

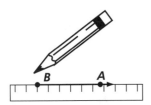

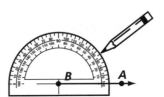

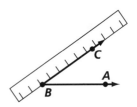

These steps show how to construct a segment congruent to a given segment, $\overline{AB}$.

1. Draw a ray longer
than $\overline{AB}$ with
endpoint **C**.

2. Adjust the radius of the
compass to the length
of $\overline{AB}$.

3. Draw an arc with center
C and radius **AB** that
intersects the ray. Label
the intersection **D**.

Then $\overline{CD} \cong \overline{AB}$.

Use a protractor to draw angles having these measures.

1. $\angle ABC = 60°$

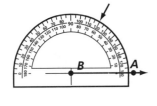

2. $\angle QPR = 90°$

3. $\angle JKL = 120°$

Complete to construct a segment congruent to $\overline{MN}$.

4. **a.** In the space at the right, draw a ray
longer than $\overline{MN}$ with endpoint **P**.

b. Adjust your compass to the length of $\overline{MN}$.

c. Keeping the length of $\overline{MN}$ on your compass,
put the point of the compass on **P** and
draw an arc that intersects the ray.

d. Label the intersection **Q**. $\overline{MN} \cong$ _____

•
P

Teacher Note: Use after Quick Check, page 198, to reteach Unit 7, Lesson 5. **(6)**

A **triangle** is a **3**-sided polygon. Triangle **ABC** can be written as △**ABC**.

Triangles can be classified by the name of the angle with the greatest measure.	**Acute Triangle**	**Right Triangle**	**Obtuse Triangle**

Triangles also can be classified by the number of congruent sides.	**Scalene Triangle** No congruent sides No congruent angles	**Isosceles Triangle** 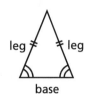 Two congruent sides Two congruent angles	**Equilateral Triangle** Three congruent sides Three congruent angles

Use a protractor to measure each angle of the triangle. Write the measure near the angle. Classify the triangle by its angle sizes.

1.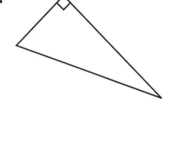

_____

2.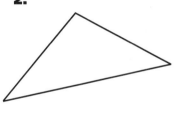

_____

3.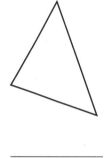

_____

Follow these steps to construct an equilateral triangle with three sides of length d.

4. a. Use your compass to verify that the length of $\overline{AB}$ below is **d**.

d

b. Keep the length **d** on your compass. Put the point of the compass on **A** and draw an arc above the ray.

c. Keep the length **d** on your compass. Put the point of the compass on **B** and draw an arc, intersecting the first arc. Label the intersection **C**.

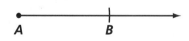
A   B

d. Draw $\overline{AC}$ and $\overline{BC}$. Since sides $\overline{AB}$, $\overline{AC}$, and $\overline{BC}$ are

congruent, △**ABC** is an _____ triangle.

Four-sided polygons, called **quadrilaterals**, are classified by their properties.

1 pair of parallel sides

2 pairs of sides that are parallel and congruent

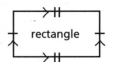

Parallelogram with **4** right angles

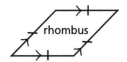

Parallelogram with **4** congruent sides

Parallelogram with **4** right angles and **4** congruent sides

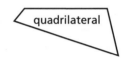

Some quadrilaterals have no congruent or parallel sides and no right angles.

Complete. Refer to quadrilaterals above.

1. a. If a quadrilateral has only one pair of sides parallel, it is a _____.

  b. If a quadrilateral has both pairs of sides parallel, it is a _____.

2. a. Since a rectangle is a parallelogram, both pairs of opposite sides are parallel

     and _____.

  b. In addition, all **4** angles of a rectangle are _____ angles.

3. a. Since a rhombus is a parallelogram, both pairs of opposite sides are

     _____.

  b. In addition, all **4** sides of a rhombus are _____.

4. a. Since a square is a rectangle, all **4** angles are _____.

  b. Since all **4** sides of a square are _____, a square is also a

     _____.

Complete.

5. Since $\angle A + \angle B + \angle C =$ _____,

  then $\angle D = 360° -$ _____ $=$ _____.

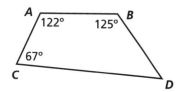

6. $\angle Q =$ _____

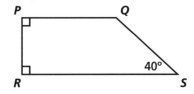

Teacher Note: Use after Quick Check, page 206, to reteach Unit 7, Lesson 7. **(6)**

Similar figures have the same shape.

In similar polygons:
Corresponding angles are congruent.

$\angle A \cong \angle X \qquad \angle B \cong \angle Y \qquad \angle C \cong \angle Z$

Corresponding sides are also in proportion.

$\dfrac{AB}{XY} = \dfrac{AC}{XZ} = \dfrac{BC}{YZ}$

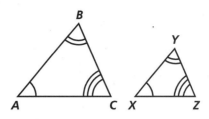

Triangle **ABC** is similar to triangle **X'Y'Z'**.

This is written: $\triangle ABC \sim \triangle XYZ$

Use a proportion to find a missing length in one of two similar figures.

To find **DF** in the similar triangles shown, write a proportion of the corresponding sides.

$$\frac{14}{7} = \frac{10}{DF}$$

$$14(DF) = 7(10)$$

$$\frac{14(DF)}{14} = \frac{70}{14}$$

$$DF = 5$$

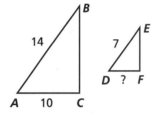

$\triangle ABC \sim \triangle DEF$

Complete. Refer to the diagram.

1. In order, the vertices of $\triangle MNO$ correspond to those of the similar triangle, $\triangle ABC$. So **M** corresponds to **A**,

N corresponds to _____, and **O** corresponds to _____.

2. a. Side $\overline{MN}$ of $\triangle MNO$ corresponds to side _____ of $\triangle ABC$.

b. Side $\overline{NO}$ of $\triangle MNO$ corresponds to side _____ of $\triangle ABC$.

c. Side $\overline{MO}$ corresponds to _____.

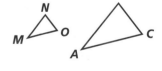

$\triangle MNO \sim \triangle ABC$

Write and solve a proportion to find the length of the side marked "?".

3.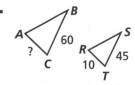

$\triangle JKL \sim \triangle ABC$

$\dfrac{JL}{AC} = \dfrac{JK}{AB}$

_____ = _____

$AB =$ _____

4.

$\triangle ABC \sim \triangle RST$

$AC =$ _____

Reteach 50

Classifying Polygons

The names of polygons are related to the number of sides they have.

Name	Number of Sides	Name	Number of Sides
*tri*angle	3	*hexa*gon	6
*quadri*lateral	4	*hepta*gon	7
*penta*gon	5	*octa*gon	8

A regular polygon has:
- *all* of its sides congruent

    and

- *all* of its angles congruent.

A *square* is a regular polygon.

A *rectangle* is not a regular polygon.

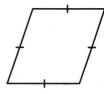

A *rhombus* is not a regular polygon.

Complete.

1. *Penta* means *five*. So a **5**-sided polygon is called a _____.

2. *Hexa* means *six*. So a _____-sided polygon is called a _____.

3. *Octa* means _____. So an _____-sided polygon is called

   an _____.

4. a. In a square, all **4** angles are congruent and all **4** sides _____.

   b. So a square is a _____ polygon.

5. A rectangle is not a regular polygon because its **4** _____ may not be all congruent.

6. A rhombus is not a regular polygon because _____.

7. The only quadrilateral that is a regular polygon is the _____.

Complete the table.

8.

Name of Regular Polygon	Measure of One angle	Number of Angles	Sum of the Angle Measures	Pattern for the Sum
equilateral triangle	60°	3	180°	1 • 180°
square	90°		360°	2 • 180°
regular pentagon	108°			
regular hexagon	120°			
regular heptagon	$128\frac{4}{7}°$			
regular octagon	135°			

104 Teacher Note: Use after Quick Check, page 206, to reteach Unit 7, Lesson 10. **(6)**

Concepts

Measuring Plane Figures

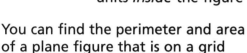

- **Perimeter** the number of units *around* the figure

- **Area** the number of square units *inside* the figure

You can find the perimeter and area of a plane figure that is on a grid by *counting* units.

To count the perimeter, count each unit of length around the outside of the figure.

To count for area, count all the squares inside the figure. Remember to label your answer in square units.

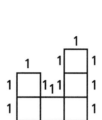

Perimeter = **2 + 3 + 3 + 1 +**
   2 + 1 + 1 + 1
   = 14 units
Area = **2 + 1 + 3**
   = 6 units²

Find: a. the perimeter   b. the area

1.

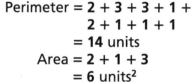

a. _____ units

b. _____ units²

2.

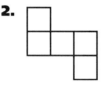

a. _____ units

b. _____ units²

3.

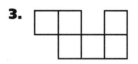

a. _____ units

b. _____ units²

4.

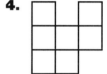

a. _____ units

b. _____ units²

Complete.

5. If ☐ represents one unit², then ▷ represents one-half _____.

6. If two sides of ▷ are **1** unit long, then the longer side is about

1.4 units. What is the perimeter of ▷? about _____ units

Find the area and perimeter.

7.

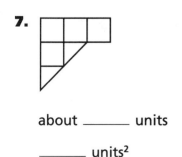

about _____ units

_____ units²

8.

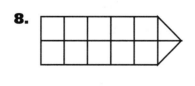

about _____ units

_____ units²

9.

about _____ units

_____ units²

Teacher Note: Use before Unit 8, Lesson 1. **(6)**

Volume is the number of *cubic units* contained within a space figure.

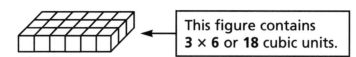 This figure contains **3 × 6** or **18** cubic units.

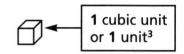 **1 cubic unit or 1 unit³**

To count the number of cubic units in a space figure when some of them are hidden, think of *layers*.

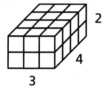

In the figure at the right,
Volume = Layer **1** + Layer **2**
= 3 × 4 + 3 × 4 = **24** units³

Complete. Refer to the diagram at the right.

1. A layer of cubic units fills the bottom of the box.

This first layer contains _____ units³.

2. To fill the box with cubic units, you

need _____ layers in all, each

containing _____ units³.

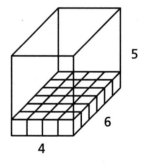

3. So the volume of this box is _____ units³.

Find the volume.

4.

_____ units³

5.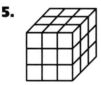

_____ units³

6.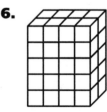

_____ units³

7.

_____ units³

8.

_____ units³

9.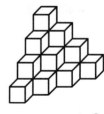

_____ units³

Teacher Note: Use before Unit 8, Lesson 1. **(6)**

Name _____

Perimeter and Area

Plane figures have two measures of size, **perimeter (P)** and **area (A).**

$P = s + s + s + s$
$P = 4s$

$A = s \times s$
$A = s^2$

$P = l + l + w + w$
$P = 2l + 2w$

$A = l \times w$

You can use formulas to find the perimeter and area of squares and rectangles.

$P = 4s$ $A = s^2$ ← Formula
$P = 4(3)$ $A = 3^2$ ← Substitute.
$P = 12$ units $A = 9$ units^2 ← Simplify.

$P = 2l + 2w$ $A = l \times w$ ← Formula
$P = 2(6) + 2(2)$ $A = 6 \cdot 2$ ← Substitute.
$P = 16$ units $A = 12$ units^2 ← Simplify.

Use formulas to find the perimeter and area.

1. 5, 5

$P =$ _____

$A =$ _____

2. 3, 9

$P =$ _____

$A =$ _____

3. 1.3, 1.3

$P =$ _____

$A =$ _____

4. $\frac{1}{2}$, $4\frac{1}{2}$

$P =$ _____

$A =$ _____

Complete.

5. You can think of this figure

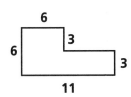

as being composed of square I and rectangle II.

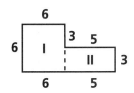

a. The perimeter of the composite figure is

_____ + _____ + _____ + _____ + _____ + _____ + _____ = _____ units.

b. Area of square I = _____ units^2

c. Area of rectangle II = _____ units^2

d. Area of composite figure = area I + area II = ____ + ____ = ____ units^2

6. True or False: Perimeter I + perimeter II = perimeter of complex figure. _____

7. True or False: Area I + area II = area of complex figure. _____

Teacher Note: Use after Quick Check, page 220, to reteach Unit 8, Lesson 1. **(6)**   **107**

The *height* of a figure is measured along a line perpendicular to the base. The height (**h**) and base (**b**) are used to compute the area (**A**).

triangle

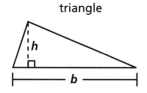

$$A = \frac{1}{2} \cdot b \cdot h$$

parallelogram

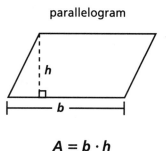

$$A = b \cdot h$$

You can use the formulas to find areas of triangles and parallelograms.

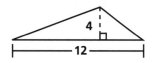

Area formula $\qquad A = \frac{1}{2} \cdot b \cdot h$

Substitute **12** for **b** $\quad A = \frac{1}{2} \cdot 12 \cdot 4$
and **4** for **h**.

$\qquad\qquad\qquad A = 6 \cdot 4 = 24$ units²

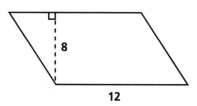

Area formula $\qquad A = b \cdot h$

Substitute **12** for **b** $\quad A = 12 \cdot 8$
and **8** for **h**.

$\qquad\qquad\qquad A = 96$ units²

Complete to find the area.

1.

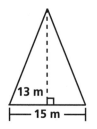

$A = \frac{1}{2} \cdot b \cdot h$

$A = \frac{1}{2} \cdot$ _____ $\cdot$ _____

$A =$ _____ m²

2.

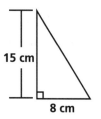

15 cm

8 cm

$A =$ _____ cm²

3.

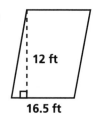

12 ft

16.5 ft

$A = b \cdot a$

$A =$ _____ $\cdot$ _____

$A =$ _____ ft²

4.

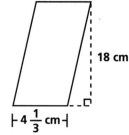

18 cm

$4\frac{1}{3}$ cm

$A =$ _____ cm²

5. True or false: Any two congruent triangles can be joined along

an edge to form a parallelogram. _____

Teacher Note: Use after Quick Check, page 220, to reteach Unit 8, Lesson 2. **(6)**

The distance around a circle is called the **circumference.** It is measured in the same linear unit as the diameter.

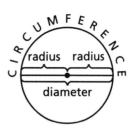

In any circle, the ratio of the circumference (**C**) to the diameter (**d**) is always the same value, about **3.14** or, $\frac{22}{7}$, represented by π.

You can use this relationship to find a formula for the circumference of any circle.

$$\frac{C}{d} = \pi$$

$$d \cdot \frac{C}{d} = \pi \cdot d$$

$$C = \pi \cdot d$$

Sometimes you will know only the radius of the circle. Since a diameter is the length of two radii, **2r = d.** Then, you can rewrite the formula as **C = π · (2r)** or

$$C = 2 \cdot \pi \cdot r.$$

Find the circumference of a circle whose diameter is **10** cm.

$$C = \pi \cdot d$$
$$C \approx 3.14 \cdot 10$$
$$C \approx 31.4 \text{ cm}$$

Find the circumference of a circle whose radius is **7** in.

$$C = 2 \cdot \pi \cdot r$$
$$C \approx 2 \cdot \frac{22}{7} \cdot 7$$
$$C \approx 44 \text{ in.}$$

Complete.

1. The letter π represents the ratio of circumference to _____.

2. A decimal approximation for π is _____. A fraction value is _____.

Complete to find the circumference. Use π ≈ 3.14.

3.

18 in.

4.
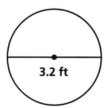
3.2 ft

5.

1.4 cm

6.
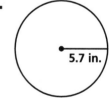
5.7 in.

$C = \pi \cdot d$

$C \approx 3.14 \cdot$ _____

$C \approx$ _____ in.

$C \approx$ _____ ft

$C = 2 \cdot \pi \cdot r$

$C \approx 2 \cdot 3.14 \cdot$ _____

$C \approx$ _____ cm

$C \approx$ _____ in.

Find the circumference of the circle with the given measure. Use $\frac{22}{7}$ for π.

7. **d = 14** ft   C ≈ _____ ft

8. **r = 84** cm   C ≈ _____ cm

Teacher Note: Use after Quick Check, page 220, to reteach Unit 8, Lesson 3. (6)

To find a formula for the area of a circle, divide a circle into
wedges and rearrange them.

1. Divide a circle into congruent parts and rearrange the parts to
   form a figure that is approximately a parallelogram.

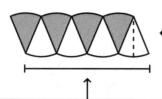

The height of parallelogram
equals the radius of circle, **r.**

By alternating the shading of the parts,
you see that the base of the parallelogram
is half the circumference of the circle, or $\frac{C}{2}$.

2. So, the dimensions of the parallelogram
   are in terms of the measures of the circle.

3. Substitute into the formula for the area
   of a parallelogram.

$$A = b \cdot h$$

$$A = \frac{C}{2} \cdot r \qquad \text{Use } \frac{C}{2} \text{ for } b \text{ and } r \text{ for } h.$$

$$A = \frac{2\pi r}{2} \cdot r \qquad \text{Use } 2\pi r \text{ for } C.$$

$$A = \pi r^2. \qquad \text{Formula for the area of a circle}$$

Use the formula to
find the area of a circle
with radius = **10** in.

$$A = \pi r^2$$

$$A \approx 3.14 \cdot 10^2 \qquad \text{Substitute } \textbf{3.14} \text{ for } \pi \text{ and } \textbf{10} \text{ for } r.$$

$$A \approx 3.14 \cdot 100 \qquad \text{Evaluate } 10^2.$$

$$A \approx 314 \text{ in.}^2 \qquad \text{Multiply.}$$

Complete, to find the area. Use $\pi \approx 3.14$ or $\frac{22}{7}$.

1.

3 cm

$A = \pi r^2$

$A = 3.14 \cdot$ _____

$A =$ _____ cm²

2.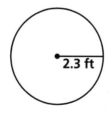

2.3 ft

$A =$ _____ ft²

3.

18 in.

$A =$ _____ in.²

4.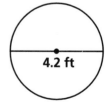

4.2 ft

$A =$ _____ in.²

5. Radius = $1\frac{3}{4}$ in.; area = _____

6. Diameter = **70** m; area = _____

Teacher Note: Use after Quick Check, page 224, to reteach Unit 8, Lesson 4. **(6)**

Space figures are **3**-dimensional. Not all their points are in the same plane.

A **prism** is a space figure with two bases that are congruent. It takes its name from the shape of the bases.

The sides of a prism are its **faces**. The top and bottom faces are the **bases**. The lines at which the faces meet are the **edges**. The corners at which the edges meet are **vertices**.

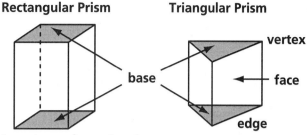

Rectangular Prism   **Triangular Prism**

base   vertex   face   edge

A rectangular prism has **6** faces, **12** edges, and **8** vertices.

When the **6** faces are squares, the prism is a **cube**.

You can form a prism from a pattern, called a **net**.

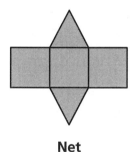

Net   **Fold**   **Prism**

Complete.

1. a. A rectangular prism has _____ faces, all of which are in the shape of a

   _____.

b. The top and bottom faces, called _____, are rectangles that are

   _____.

2. A cube has _____ faces, all of which are in the shape of a _____,

and all of which are _____ to each other.

Name the figure that can be made from each net.

3.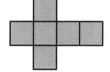

4.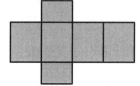

5.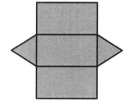

_____   _____   _____

Teacher Note: Use after Quick Check, page 224, to reteach Unit 8, Lesson 5. **(6)**

The surface area (**SA**) of a space figure is the sum of the areas of all its faces.

A cube has **6** congruent square faces.

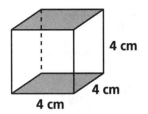

4 cm
4 cm
4 cm

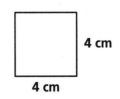

4 cm
4 cm

To find the surface area, find the total area of the six faces.

SA = 6s² or 96 cm²

A rectangular prism has **6** faces. But they may not all be congruent.

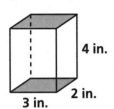

4 in.
2 in.
3 in.

Unfold the prism to examine the **6** faces.

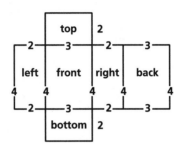

Find the area of each of the **6** faces, and add.

Face	Area	in.²
front	3 × 4	12
back	3 × 4	12
top	3 × 2	6
bottom	3 × 2	6
left	2 × 4	8
right	2 × 4	8
	Total	52

The surface area is **52** in.²

Complete.

1. A cube has _____ faces. They are squares that are all _____.

2. The surface area of a **5 cm** by **5 cm** by **5 cm** cube is 6 × _____ or _____ cm².

3. When unfolded, this prism   looks like this

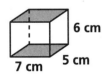

6 cm
7 cm   5 cm

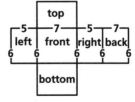

Use the table. Find the **SA**.

Face	Area	cm²
front		
back		
top		
bottom		
left		
right		
	Total	

The surface area is _____ cm².

4.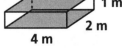

1 m
2 m
4 m

SA = _____ in.²

5.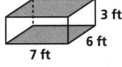

3 ft
6 ft
7 ft

SA = _____ ft²

6. A rectangular prism is **6** in. by $1\frac{1}{2}$ in by **10** in. Its **SA** is _____.

Teacher Note: Use after Quick Check, page 232, to reteach Unit 8, Lesson 6. **(6)**

Name _____

Volume (V) is the number of cubic units contained within a space figure.

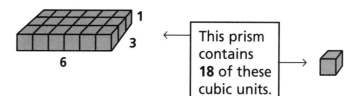

← This prism contains **18** of these cubic units. →

For a prism with more than one layer, the volume **(V)** is the product of the area of the base **(B)** and the height **(h)** of the prism.

$$V = B \cdot h$$

Rectangular Prism

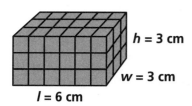

$h = 3$ cm
$w = 3$ cm
$l = 6$ cm

Base is a rectangle.

Use the area formula for a rectangle.

$V = B \cdot h$
$V = (l \cdot w) \cdot h$
$V = 6 \cdot 3 \cdot 3$
$V = 54$ cm³

h and h' (read "h prime") represent different numbers.

Triangular Prism

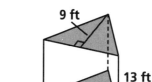

9 ft
13 ft
18 ft

$V = B \cdot h$
$V = \left(\frac{1}{2} \cdot b \cdot h'\right) \cdot h^2$
$V = \frac{1}{2} \cdot 18 \cdot 9 \cdot 13$
$V = 1{,}053$ ft³

Base is a triangle.

Complete.

1. To find the volume of a prism, multiply the area of the

_____ by the _____ of the prism.

2.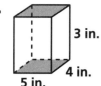

3 in.
4 in.
5 in.

$V = B \cdot h$

$V = \underline{\hspace{1cm}} \cdot h$

$V = \underline{\hspace{1cm}} \cdot \underline{\hspace{1cm}} \cdot \underline{\hspace{1cm}}$

$V = \underline{\hspace{1cm}}$ in.³

3.

4 cm
4 cm
4 cm

$V = \underline{\hspace{1cm}}$ cm³

4.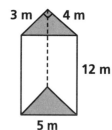

3 m   4 m
12 m
5 m

$V = \underline{\hspace{1cm}}$ m³

5. A rectangular prism is **3** ft by 6 ft by $\frac{2}{3}$ ft.

Its volume is _____.

Teacher Note: Use after Quick Check, page 232, to reteach Unit 8, Lesson 8. **(6)**

Stem-and-leaf plots help organize large data sets to show how often data values occur. They also show the distribution of the data values.

Number of Cashews in Cans of Mixed Nuts

43 39 40 48 41 40 51 43 39 38 39 42

36 38 39 41 40 39 41 43 42 44 45 51

List the stems. Use the leftmost digit of the data items.	Write the ones digit for each item.	Reorder the leaves from least to greatest. Add a key.

stem	leaf
3	
4	
5	

stem	leaf
3	9 9 8 9 6 8 9 9
4	3 0 8 1 0 3
	2 1 0 1 3 2 4 5
5	1 1

stem	leaf
3	6 8 8 9 9 9 9 9
4	0 0 0 1 1 1 2 2
	3 3 3 4 5 8
5	1 1

Key: 3 | 6 represents 36 cashews.

Check to see that the number of leaves is the same as the number of data.

Complete.

1. Use the data below.

95	83	101	95	115
107	98	95	91	108
93	118	92	102	89
87	93	98	96	116
104	117	100	99	105

a. List the unordered data.

stem	leaf
8	
9	
10	
11	

b. Complete the stem-and-leaf plot.

stem	leaf

2. Use the data below.

20	25	28	18	26
20	17	24	24	21
30	26	21	36	18
22	20	20	20	21
24	20	29	20	33

a. List the unordered data.

stem	leaf

b. Complete the stem-and-leaf plot.

stem	leaf

Teacher Note: Use before Unit 9, Lesson 1. **(6)**

Histograms resemble bar graphs that do not have spaces
between their bars. Consumer groups often use histograms to
determine the age group that is most likely to buy their products.

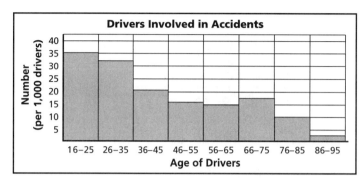

All the **intervals** in a histogram must be equal. In this histogram,
the ages are shown in **10**-year ranges.

Complete. Use the histogram above to answer the questions.

1. Which age group had the highest number of accidents? _____

2. In which age group did **15** of every
1,000 drivers have accidents? _____

3. Why would you expect the age group
86–95 to have the fewest accidents? _____

4. Use the information in the table to complete the histogram.

Number of Movies	
Age Group	Yearly Average
10 and under	16
11–20	36
21–30	40
31–40	29
41–50	23
51–60	12
61–70	7

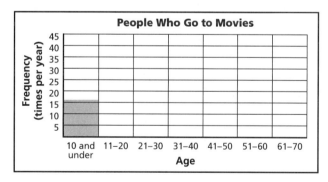

5. Which two age groups attend movies most often? _____

6. A **48**-year-old woman went to see "Today is the Day." How many
other movies is she likely to have seen in the last **12** months? _____

7. A **32**-year-old man went to see "Jungle Beat." How many
other movies is he likely to have seen in the last **12** months? _____

8. One man who went to the movies was **20** years and
8 months old. Which age group does he belong to? _____

Teacher Note: Use before Unit 9, Lesson 1. **(6)**

Name _____

A **line plot** shows the number of times each data value occurs in a
set. Data is organized using a number line and X's.

**Number of Commercials
On TV (per hour)**

27	29	26	28	27
31	29	28	30	29
28	27	32	31	28
29	31	28	33	30
26	30	28	27	29

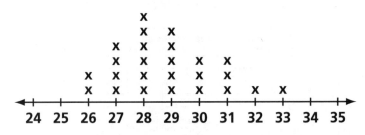

Number of Commercials on TV (per hour)

The most frequent number of commercials per hour is **28**. More
than half the data values are included in the **27–29** range.

Complete.

1. Make a line plot using the given data.

2	3	5	7	5
3	6	3	3	2
1	4	3	5	3

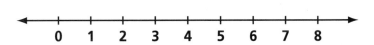

a. What is the most frequent number? _____

b. What range includes most of the data values? _____

2. Make a line plot using the given data.

102	101	103	101	100	102
102	104	102	103	100	101
101	101	101	105	104	102

a. What is the most frequent number? _____

b. What range includes most of the data values? _____

3. Make a line plot using the given data.

9	5	11	6	11	12
10	13	12	7	7	11
11	9	11	6	7	9

a. What is the most frequent number? _____

b. In what range are most of the data clustered? _____

Teacher Note: Use before Unit 9, Lesson 1. **(6)**

Probability is the chance that an event or selected outcome will occur.

Use a ratio to express probability. $P(\text{event}) = \dfrac{\text{Number of ways the event can happen}}{\text{Total number of possible outcomes}}$

What is the probability of spinning red on this spinner?

Find the number of ways you can spin red.	Find the total number of outcomes.	Write a ratio of these two numbers as the probability.
2	4	2:4 or $\frac{2}{4}$ or $\frac{1}{2}$

Probability is always a number from **0** (impossible outcome) to **1** (certain outcome).

Complete.

1. What is the probability of spinning an A on this spinner?

    a. Number of ways you can spin an A _____

    b. Total number of possible outcomes _____

    c. $P(A) =$ _____

2. What is the probability of tossing a **5** on a number cube with sides numbered **1–6**?

    a. Number of ways you can toss a **5** _____

    b. Total number of possible outcomes _____

    c. Write the probability. _____

3. What is the probability of spinning blue on this spinner?

$P(\text{blue}) =$ _____

4. What is the probability of spinning a **6** on this spinner?

$P(6) =$ _____

5. There are **8** blue socks and **4** white socks in a drawer. If you select one sock without looking, what is the probability you would select a blue sock?

_____

6. There are **7** green socks and **11** striped socks in a drawer. If you select one sock without looking, what is the probability you would select a striped sock?

_____

A **double bar graph** is used to compare two sets of data on one graph. This graph compares the number of points scored by two teams. Each weekend game is represented by a different bar.

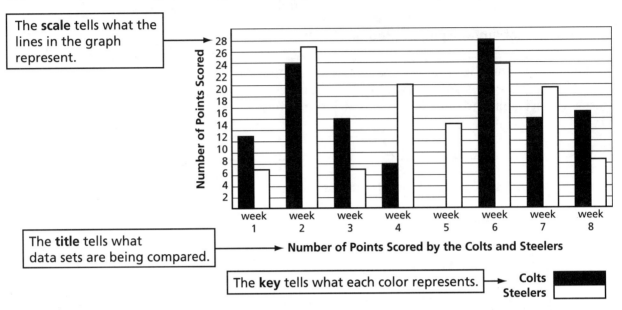

The **scale** tells what the lines in the graph represent.

Number of Points Scored

The **title** tells what data sets are being compared.

Number of Points Scored by the Colts and Steelers

The **key** tells what each color represents.

Colts
Steelers

To read the graph, find the top of the bar. Follow the line to the left and read the number. The first bar on the graph shows that the Colts scored **13** points in Week **1**.

A bar may end between two intervals on the horizontal scale. In that case, estimate the number.

Complete. Refer to the graph above.

1. What interval is used on the scale in this graph? _____

2. Which teams are being compared by this graph? _____

3. What time period is covered by this graph? _____

4. a. Which team scored the most points? _____

   b. During which week did they earn this score? _____

   c. How many points did they score? _____

5. a. During which week did the Steelers score **27** points? _____

   b. How many points were scored by the Colts that week? _____

6. During which week did the Colts score **0** points? _____

7. During which week did the Steelers score **14** more points than the Colts? _____

8. By how many points did the Colts outscore the Steelers in Week **6**? _____

Teacher Note: Use after Quick Check, page 248, to reteach Unit 9, Lesson 1. **(6)**

Name _____

This table and line plot show the number of grams of carbohydrates in different soups.

Grams of Carbohydrates				
19	20	35	18	21
24	22	9	19	33
17	21	24	21	19

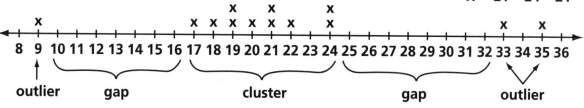

outlier   gap   cluster   gap   outlier

Most of the items in the plot are in a group from **17** to **24**.
This is called a **cluster.** Some intervals on the plot have no points.
These are called **gaps.** Some items have values much less or much
greater than the others. These are called **outliers**.

Find the **mean** or average of the values.

Add all the items.

$9 + 17 + 18 + 19 + 19 + 19 + 20 + 21 +$
$21 + 21 + 22 + 24 + 24 + 33 + 35 = 322$

Divide by the
number of items.

$322 \div 15 = 21.47$

Find the **median,** or middle number, of the values.

—Median

9 17 18 19 19 19 20 21 21 21 22 24 24 33 35

When the data are listed
from least to greatest, the
eighth item is **21.**

For these data, the mean **(21.47)** and the median **(21)** are fairly close.
Either one would be useful for describing the typical item of data.

Complete. Use the line plot to answer the questions.

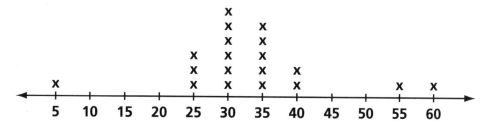

1. Name the outliers, if any. _____

2. What is the range of the values in the cluster? _____

3. What is the mean of all the values? _____

4. What is the mean of the cluster values? _____

5. What is the median of the values? _____

6. Which measure best describes this data? Why? _____

Teacher Note: Use after Quick Check, page 248, to reteach Unit 9, Lesson 2. **(6)**   **119**

When you do a survey, the **population** is the group of people or things you want to study. If the population is very large, you can study a **representative sample,** or part of the population.

Use the results of the sample to make predictions about the population by making a proportion. A representative sample will have answers in the same proportion as the answers of the whole population.

You want to predict how many students will have soup tomorrow in the cafeteria.

Survey question: Will you have soup in the cafeteria tomorrow?
Population: 1,500 students
Representative sample: 150 students (**1** out of every **10** students) entering the cafeteria

Collect the data.

Yes	No
58	92

Write a proportion.

"Yeses" in sample → $\dfrac{58}{150} = \dfrac{n}{1,500}$ ← "Yeses" in population
Size of sample →   ← Size of population

Solve the proportion by cross multiplying.

$$\dfrac{58}{150} = \dfrac{n}{1,500}$$

$1,500 \times 58 = 150 \times n$

$150n = 87,000$

Divide to solve for **n**.

$150n = 87,000$

$n = 87,000 \div 150$

$n = 580$

Write a prediction.

Of **1,500** students, about **580** will have soup in the cafeteria tomorrow.

Complete.

1. In a sample, **8** out of **50** students planned on taking the city bus to the dance. Based on this sample, how many of the **800** students would you predict will take the bus?

$$\dfrac{8}{50} = \dfrac{n}{800}$$

_____ × _____ = _____ × _____

$n =$ _____

_____ students will take the bus.

2. In a sample, **35** of **140** students said they planned to eat the pudding in the cafeteria. Based on this sample, how many of the **1,300** students would you predict would eat the pudding?

_____ $= \dfrac{n}{}$

_____ = _____

_____ = _____

_____ students will eat pudding.

3. In a sample, **95** of **145** students said they planned to vote for Ed for Student Council president. Based on this sample, how many of the **1,200** students will vote for Ed?

_____ students

Teacher Note: Use after Quick Check, page 248, to reteach Unit 9, Lesson 4. **(6)**

A **random sample** for a survey is a part of the population such every person (or object) in the population has an equal chance of being chosen.

In a factory, light bulbs are chosen from the assembly line to test for quality. If the first **10** light bulbs that come off the line are tested, the bulbs are not sampled randomly.

The results of such a survey may be **biased.** That is, they may not be representative of the whole population. For example, the assembly line may not be running smoothly yet and may produce more defective bulbs than later.

People may also be chosen for a survey in a biased way. For example, surveying musical tastes at a rock concert would probably show a bias toward rock music.

Surveying **1** out of **10** or **1** out of **20** is a reasonable sample size for a large population. If your school has **3,000** students, surveying every **20**th student will assure a reasonable sampling of opinion.

Sample size
3,000 ÷ 20 = 150

Complete. Write *random* **or** *not random* **for the sample about students' favorite school subject.**

1. Survey every fifth girl.

_____

2. Survey **1** out of **6** students.

_____

3. Survey students by drawing names out of a hat.

_____

4. Survey students in alphabetical order.

_____

How many of each group would you survey if you sampled 1 out of 10?

5. **841** dancers

841 ÷ 10 = _____

6. **2,188** shoppers

_____

7. **34,612** dog owners

_____

8. **249,179** airline passengers

_____

Tell whether the sample is fair or biased.

9. Survey your friends about a movie _____

10. Survey golfers about favorite golf shoes _____

Teacher Note: Use after Quick Check, page 248, to reteach Unit 9, Lesson 5. **(6)**

Sometimes graphs can be misleading. Always check to see how a graph has been drawn before reaching any conclusions about it.

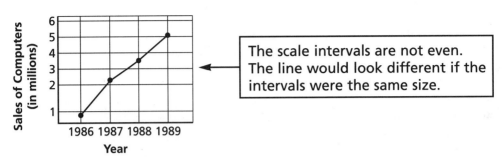

The scale intervals are not even. The line would look different if the intervals were the same size.

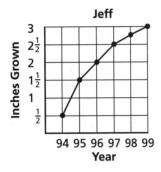

These two graphs use different scales. It looks as if Jeff grew more from **1994** to **1999,** but actually Demont did.

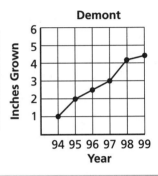

Complete. Tell why each graph is misleading.

1.

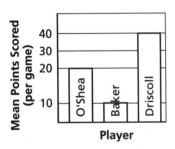

_____

_____

2.

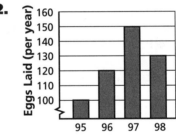

_____

_____

3.

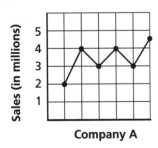 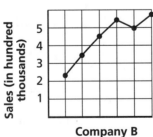

_____

_____

4.

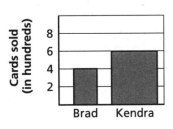

_____

_____

Teacher Note: Use after Quick Check, page 256, to reteach Unit 9, Lesson 8. **(6)**

Name _____

Probability is a measure of how likely something is to happen.
You can represent probability on a number line. It is a number
between **0** and **1**.

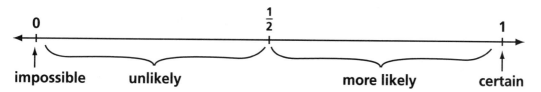

0 $\frac{1}{2}$ **1**

impossible   **unlikely**   **more likely**   **certain**

What is the probability of tossing a **3** on a **1–6** number cube?

Theoretical probability
is a mathematical calculation.

$P(3) = \dfrac{\text{number of ways to toss a 3}}{\text{number of possible outcomes}}$

$P(3) = \dfrac{\text{only one 3 on the number cube}}{\text{six numbers on the cube}}$

$P(3) = \dfrac{1}{6}$

Experimental probability
is what happens in real life.

Toss the number cube **100** times. Suppose
you toss a **3** exactly **18** times.

$P(3) \approx \dfrac{\text{number of times you tossed a 3}}{\text{number of times you tossed the cube}}$

$P(3) \approx \dfrac{18}{100}$ or **0.18**

The probability of tossing a number that is **not 3** means any
number except **3**. The numbers **1, 2, 4, 5,** and **6** on the number
cube are numbers that are not **3**.

$P(\text{not 3}) = \dfrac{\text{numbers 1, 2, 4, 5, 6}}{\text{6 possible numbers}} = \dfrac{5}{6}$

P(3) and *P*(not 3) are **complements**
because their sum is **1**.

Complete. Find the theoretical probability.

1. Spin blue on this spinner.

    a. number of ways to spin blue _____

    b. total number of
       possible outcomes _____

    c. *P*(blue) = _____

2. Select a card that is not a vowel.

   P(not a vowel) = _____

3. Toss an even number on a number cube.

   P(even number) = _____

4. You tossed a number cube **500** times. The
cube landed with the **2** up **85** times. What is
the experimental probability of tossing a **2?** _____

   What is the theoretical probability of tossing a **2?** _____

You can use a tree diagram to find the number of possible outcomes of two events.

| Start with the possible outcomes of the first event. | Extend the tree by listing the possible outcomes of the second event. | List the final outcomes and count them. |

| **Event** | **Tree Diagram** | **Outcomes** |

1. Toss a coin.

Ⓗ Ⓣ

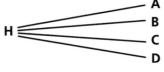

H A   H B   There are

H C   H D   **8**

T A   T B   possible

2. Pick a card.

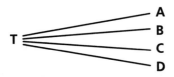

T C   T D   outcomes.

You can also multiply to find the number of possible outcomes. This method is named the **Counting Principle**.

| Find the number of outcomes of the first event. | Multiply by the number of outcomes of the second event. | The product equals the total number of possible outcomes. |

Ⓗ Ⓣ   A B C D

2   ×   4   =   8

Complete. Make a tree diagram to find all the possible outcomes. List the outcomes.

3. Spin this spinner   Then toss this coin.   Tree Diagram   List of Outcomes   Total Number

---

Use the Counting Principle to find the number of possible outcomes.

4. Choose from **3** shoes and **5** socks.

_____ × _____ = _____

_____

5. Choose from **2** cones and **8** flavors.

_____ × _____ = _____

_____

    Teacher Note: Use after Quick Check, page 262 to reteach Unit 9, Lesson p. **(6)**

Name _____

Two events are **independent events** if the outcome of the first event does not affect the outcome of the second event. Tossing a coin and then picking a card are examples of independent events.

What is the probability of tossing a head on a nickel and then drawing a Q from the cards at the right?

| List all outcomes of both events. You may want to use a tree diagram. | > | Count the number of desired outcomes and total outcomes. | > | Write the probability as a ratio. |

$P(\text{a head and a Q}) = \dfrac{1}{12}$

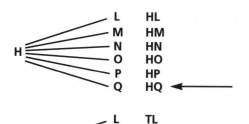

HL
HM
HN
HO
HP
HQ ← **1** way to get a head and a Q

12 possible outcomes

TL
TM
TN
TO
TP
TQ

You can also multiply the probability of the first event by the probability of the second event. The probability of two independent events is a product.

$P(\text{heads, letter Q}) = P(\text{heads}) \times P(\text{letter Q})$

$= \dfrac{1}{2} \times \dfrac{1}{6} \text{ or } \dfrac{1}{12}$

Complete.

1. List all the outcomes for tossing a number cube, then spinning this spinner.

_____

2. How many outcomes have an odd number and a red spin? _____

3. $P(\text{odd, red}) = $ _____

Use multiplication to find the probability of the independent events.

4. Tossing heads on a coin and then spinning a Z on the spinner.

$P(\text{heads}) = \dfrac{1}{2}$ $P(Z) = $ _____

$P(\text{heads and Z}) = $ _____ × _____ or _____

5. Picking a card with a star and then tossing an even number on a number cube

$P(\text{star and even number}) = $ _____ × _____

$P(\text{star and even number}) = $ _____

Teacher Note: Use after Quick Check, page 262, to reteach Unit 9, Lesson 10. **(6)**

Reteach Worksheets

Events are **dependent events** when the outcome of the first event affects the number of outcomes for the second event.

A bag contains **3** white marbles and **3** black marbles. What is the probability of picking a white marble and then a black one?

Independent Events

Find the probability of the first event.

$P(\text{white}) = \frac{3}{6} = \frac{1}{2}$

Put the marble back in the bag.

Dependent Events

Find the probability of the first event.

$P(\text{white}) = \frac{3}{6} = \frac{1}{2}$

Do not put the marble back in the bag.

There are still 6 marbles in the bag.

Find the probability of the second event.

$P(\text{black}) = \frac{3}{6} = \frac{1}{2}$

Now there are only 5 marbles in the bag, 3 black and 2 white.

Find the probability of the second event.

$P(\text{black}) = \frac{3}{5}$

Multiply to find the probability of both.

$P(\text{white and black}) = \frac{1}{2} \cdot \frac{1}{2} = \frac{1}{4}$

Multiply to find the probability of both.

$P(\text{white, then black}) = \frac{1}{2} \cdot \frac{3}{5} = \frac{3}{10}$

Remember that the total number of outcomes changes when the two events are dependent.

Complete. Write _D_ if the events are dependent. Write _I_ if the events are independent.

1. Roll a number cube, then roll it again. _____

2. Pick a card. Do not put it back. Then pick another card. _____

3. Pick a sock from a drawer, put it back. Then pick another sock. _____

4. Toss a coin, then toss a different coin. _____

Find the probability of each pair of dependent events.

5. What is the probability of picking a star, then picking a circle?

$P(\text{star}) = $ _____

$P(\text{circle}) = $ _____

$P(\text{star and circle}) = $ _____ $\cdot$ _____ or _____

6. The cleanup committee is made up of Kordell, Deron, Ashley, Ben, and Megan. What is the probability of picking Kordell and Ashley to do a job?

$P(\text{Kordell}) = $ _____

$P(\text{Ashley}) = $ _____

$P(\text{Kordell and Ashley}) = $ _____ $\cdot$ _____ or _____

126

Teacher Note: Use after Quick Check, page 262, to reteach Unit 9, Lesson 11. **(6)**

When a numerical expression contains more than one operation, the order in which the operations are done must be consistent. You can simplify any expression by following this procedure.

Simplify: $6 - 2(8 - 6) + 4^2 \div 2$

1. Complete operations within parentheses. $= 6 - 2 \ (2) \ + 4^2 \div 2$

2. Evaluate powers. $= 6 - 2 \ (2) \ + 16 \div 2$

3. Multiply and divide from left to right. $= 6 - \ 4 \ + 16 \div 2$

$= 6 - \ 4 \ + \ 8$

4. Add and subtract from left to right. $= \ 2 \ + \ 8$

$= \ 10$

Simplify each expression.

1. $5(8 - 4) + 3^2$

_____ (Parentheses)

_____ (Exponents)

_____ (Multiply and divide.)

_____ (Add and subtract.)

2. $12 \div (9 - 5) + 6$

_____

_____

_____

_____

3. $4^2 - (2 + 8)$

_____

4. $3 \times 6 - 4 \div 2$

_____

5. $5 + 3 \times 4 - 7$

_____

6. $6(3 + 1) - 4^2$

_____

7. $7 + (4 \times 5) \div 2$

_____

8. $15 \div 3 + 6 \times 2 - 4$

_____

Teacher Note: Use before Unit 10, Lesson 1. (6)

Integers include the numbers **1, 2, 3, 4, 5, . . .**, their opposites, and **0**.
Integers can be shown on a number line.

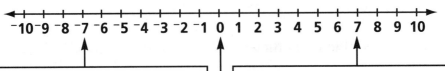

Negative numbers are numbers
less than zero. They are always
written with a negative sign: ⁻**7**.

Positive numbers are numbers
greater than zero. They are
written with or without a positive
sign: ⁺**7** or **7**.

Zero is an integer
that is neither positive
nor negative.

Opposites are integers that are equal distances from zero on the
number line.

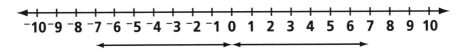

⁻**7** and **7** are both **7** units from zero.
⁻**7** and **7** are opposites.

Zero is its own opposite.

Use the number line to find the opposite of each integer.

1. 3 _____

-10 -9 -8 -7 -6 -5 -4 -3 -2 -1 0 1 2 3 4 5 6 7 8 9 10

2. ⁻6 _____

-10 -9 -8 -7 -6 -5 -4 -3 -2 -1 0 1 2 3 4 5 6 7 8 9 10

3. 7 _____

-10 -9 -8 -7 -6 -5 -4 -3 -2 -1 0 1 2 3 4 5 6 7 8 9 10

4. ⁻2 _____

-10 -9 -8 -7 -6 -5 -4 -3 -2 -1 0 1 2 3 4 5 6 7 8 9 10

5. 6 _____   **6.** 9 _____   **7.** ⁻4 _____

8. ⁻8 _____   **9.** 5 _____   **10.** ⁻7 _____

Teacher Note: Use after Quick Check, page 273, to reteach Unit 10, Lesson 1. **(6)**

To compare two integers, plot them on a number line. The greater number is always to the right of the lesser number.

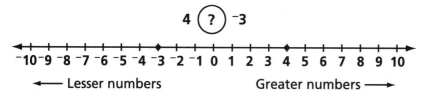

4 (?) ⁻3

⟵ Lesser numbers   Greater numbers ⟶

On the number line, **4** is to the right of ⁻**3**, so **4** is greater than ⁻**3**.

4 > ⁻3

You can compare two negative integers on the number line, too.

⁻7 (?) ⁻2

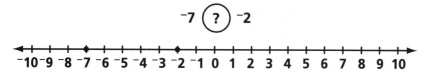

On the number line, ⁻**7** is to the left of ⁻**2**, so ⁻**7** is less than ⁻**2**.

⁻7 < ⁻2

Complete. Plot the numbers on the number line. Then write < or >.

1. ⁻2 ◯ 6

2. ⁻6 ◯ ⁻3

3. 1 ◯ ⁻2

4. 3 ◯ 4

5. 0 ◯ ⁻5

6. 2 ◯ ⁻2

7. ⁻1 ◯ 4

Write < or >.

8. ⁻3 ◯ ⁻5   **9.** 0 ◯ 6   **10.** 5 ◯ ⁻5   **11.** 0 ◯ ⁻2

Teacher Note: Use after Quick Check page 273 to reteach Unit 10, Lesson 2. **(6)**   **129**

You can use a number line to help you add integers. To add a positive number, move that number of units to the right.

Add: ⁻6 + 4

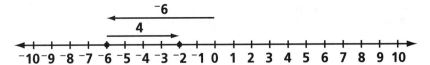

Read the number at the end of the arrow.

So, ⁻6 + 4 = ⁻2.

To add a negative number, move left the given number of units.

Add: ⁻1 + ⁻4

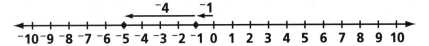

So, ⁻1 + ⁻4 = ⁻5.

Complete. Show the addition on the number line and write the answer.

1. ⁻8 + 5 = _____

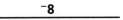

2. 4 + ⁻6 = _____

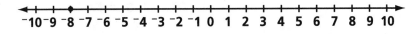

3. ⁻2 + ⁻4 = _____

4. 3 + ⁻9 = _____

5. ⁻1 + 7 = _____

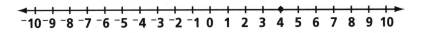

Add.

6. 5 + ⁻7 = _____   **7.** ⁻6 + 8 = _____   **8.** ⁻3 + 5 = _____

Teacher Note: Use after Quick Check, page 273, to reteach Unit 10, Lesson 3. **(6)**

You know how to add **3** to either a positive or negative number on a number line.

Find **4 + 3**.   Find **⁻4 + 3**.

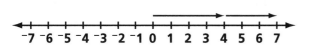   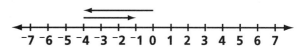

To subtract 3, reverse the direction of the "3" arrow, because subtracting is the opposite of adding.

Find **4 − 3**.   Find **⁻4 − 3**.

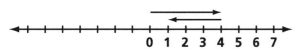   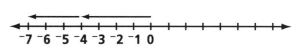

Notice that subtracting an integer is the same as adding its opposite.

You can use this property to subtract negative integers, also. For example, find **4 − ⁻3.**

First rewrite as an addition expression. Use the opposite of the second integer.

$$4 - 3 = 4 + 3$$

Complete as in addition.

$$4 + 3 = 7$$

Subtract by rewriting as an addition expression.

1. $3 - {}^-6 =$ _____ + _____ = _____

2. ${}^-2 - 5 =$ _____ + _____ = _____

3. ${}^-1 - {}^-8 =$ _____ + _____ = _____

4. $9 - {}^-3 =$ _____ + _____ = _____

5. ${}^-7 - {}^-5 =$ _____ + _____ = _____

Subtract by rewriting as an addition expression.

6. ${}^-9 - {}^-4 =$ _____   **7.** $3 - {}^-2 =$ _____   **8.** $0 - {}^-6 =$ _____

9. ${}^-8 - 1 =$ _____   **10.** $5 - {}^-2 =$ _____   **11.** ${}^-1 - {}^-5 =$ _____

12. $4 - 7 =$ _____   **13.** ${}^-1 - {}^-8 =$ _____   **14.** ${}^-3 - {}^-3 =$ _____

Reteach Worksheets

Teacher Note: Use after Quick Check, page 282, to reteach Unit 10, Lesson 4. **(6)**

Multiplying integers is similar to multiplying whole numbers.
But you must remember to put the correct sign in the product.

When you multiply two positive integers, the product is always
positive.

A positive times a positive equals a positive.

$$5 \quad \times \quad 8 \quad = \quad 40$$

When you multiply two negative integers, the product is always
positive.

A negative times a negative equals a positive.

$$^-5 \quad \times \quad ^-8 \quad = \quad 40$$

When you multiply a positive integer and a negative integer, the
product is always **negative**.

A negative times a positive equals a negative.

$$^-5 \quad \times \quad 8 \quad = \quad ^-40$$

A positive times a negative equals a negative.

$$5 \quad \times \quad ^-8 \quad = \quad ^-40$$

Circle whether the product is positive or negative. Then multiply.

1. $^-4 \times ^-8$ Negative   or   Positive   The product is _____.

2. $3 \times ^-4$ Negative   or   Positive   The product is _____.

3. $^-8 \times 2$ Negative   or   Positive   The product is _____.

4. $^-1 \times ^-6$ Negative   or   Positive   The product is _____.

5. 6×5 Negative   or   Positive   The product is _____.

6. $^-4 \times 2$ Negative   or   Positive   The product is _____.

7. $^-5 \times 3$ Negative   or   Positive   The product is _____.

Multiply.

8. $2 \times 5 =$ _____

9. $9 \times ^-4 =$ _____

10. $^-6 \times ^-7 =$ _____

11. $7 \times 2 =$ _____

12. $^-5 \times 4 =$ _____

13. $3 \times ^-9 =$ _____

14. $^-8 \times ^-3 =$ _____

15. $^-7 \times 9 =$ _____

16. $^-9 \times ^-8 =$ _____

Teacher Note: Use after Quick Check, page 282, to reteach Unit 10, Lesson 6. **(6)**

Dividing integers is similar to dividing whole numbers. But you must remember to use the correct sign in the quotient.

When you divide two positive integers, the quotient is always **positive**.

A positive divided by a positive equals a positive.

36   ÷   9   =   4

When you divide two negative integers, the quotient is always **positive**.

A negative divided by a negative equals a positive.

⁻36   ÷   ⁻9   =   4

When you divide a positive integer by a negative integer or a negative integer by a positive integer, the quotient is always **negative**.

A positive divided by a negative equals a negative.

36   ÷   ⁻9   =   ⁻4

A negative divided by a positive equals a negative.

⁻36   ÷   9   =   ⁻4

Circle whether the quotient will be positive or negative. Then divide.

1. 48 ÷ ⁻6   Positive   or   Negative   The quotient is _____.

2. 25 ÷ 5   Positive   or   Negative   The quotient is _____.

3. ⁻16 ÷ ⁻2   Positive   or   Negative   The quotient is _____.

4. 72 ÷ ⁻9   Positive   or   Negative   The quotient is _____.

5. 32 ÷ 4   Positive   or   Negative   The quotient is _____.

6. ⁻49 ÷ 7   Positive   or   Negative   The quotient is _____.

7. 24 ÷ ⁻8   Positive   or   Negative   The quotient is _____.

Divide.

8. 54 ÷ 9 = _____   **9.** 30 ÷ ⁻6 = _____   **10.** 15 ÷ 3 = _____

11. 40 ÷ ⁻8 = _____   **12.** 5 ÷ ⁻5 = _____   **13.** 24 ÷ ⁻4 = _____

14. 64 ÷ 8 = _____   **15.** 81 ÷ ⁻9 = _____   **16.** 18 ÷ 6 = _____

Teacher Note: Use after Quick Check, page 282, to reteach Unit 10, Lesson 7. **(6)**   **133**

To **evaluate** an expression, substitute values
for variables in the expression. Then simplify,
using the order of operations.

As you simplify, work carefully with all
negative signs.

<table>
<tr><td>

Order of Operations

1. Do operations inside parentheses.
2. Evaluate powers.
3. Multiply and divide, left to right.
4. Add and subtract, left to right.

</td></tr>
</table>

Evaluate the expression $(4 - x) - x^2$ for $x = {}^-5$.

$(4 - x) - x^2 = (4 - ({}^-5)) - ({}^-5)^2$　　Substitute for x.

$\qquad = (4 + 5) - ({}^-5)^2$　　Work inside parentheses: subtract $^-5$ by
$\qquad = \quad (9) \quad - ({}^-5)^2$　　adding its inverse, **5**.

$\qquad = \quad 9 - (25)$　　Simplify exponents: multiply $^-5$ by $^-5$.

$\qquad = \quad 9 + ({}^-25)$　　Subtract **25** by adding its inverse, $^-25$.

$\qquad = {}^-16$

Evaluate each expression.

1. $3(8 - x) + 22$ for $x = 12$　　Substitute　　　　$3(8 - \underline{\qquad}) + 22$

　　　　　　　　　　　　　　　Parentheses　　　　_____

　　　　　　　　　　　　　　　Exponents　　　　　_____

　　　　　　　　　　　　　　　Multiply and divide _____

　　　　　　　　　　　　　　　Add and subtract　　_____

2. $x(16 \div 4) - 7$ for $x = {}^-5$　　_____

　　　　　　　　　　　　　　　_____

　　　　　　　　　　　　　　　_____

　　　　　　　　　　　　　　　_____

　　　　　　　　　　　　　　　_____

3. $^-9 + (x^2) \div {}^-3$ for $x = 6$　　　　　　**4.** $45 \div (3 + x)$ for $x = {}^-12$

5. $50 \div (x - 6)^2 - 3$ for $x = 11$　　　　**6.** $2(5 + 3) - x^3$ for $x = {}^-2$

7. $(x - 1)^2 - 30 \div ({}^-6)$ for $x = 7$　　　**8.** $3(x - 2)^2 - 3(x - 10)$ for $x = 3$

　　　　Teacher Note: Use after Quick Check, page 288, to reteach Unit 10, Lesson 8. (6)

Name _____

You can evaluate expressions that have more than one
variable by making as many substitutions as necessary.

When you evaluate an expression, include the sign of the number
you substitute. Then follow the order of operations to simplify.

Evaluate $x - (y - z)$ for $x = 8$, $y = 2$, and $z = {}^-3$.

1. Substitute.	$x - (y - z)$
	$8 - (2 - {}^-3)$
2. Work inside parentheses.	$8 - (2 + 3)$
	$8 - 5$
3. Add and subtract from left to right.	3

Evaluate each expression. You may not need every step in the order of operations.

1. $xy - z^2$ Substitute   _____

     for $x = 7$, $y = {}^-4$, $z = 2$ Exponents   _____

                                  Multiply and divide _____

                                  Add and subtract   _____

2. $z + x - y$ _____

     for $x = 5$, $y = {}^-2$, $z = {}^-3$ _____

                                  _____

3. $y + z - x$ for $x = 8$, $y = {}^-6$, $z = {}^-4$

4. $2xyz$ for $x = {}^-2$, $y = 5$, $z = {}^-3$

_____   _____

5. $x \div (z + y)$ for $x = 8$, $y = 2$, $z = {}^-6$

6. $zx - y$ for $x = {}^-4$, $y = {}^-5$, $z = 3$

_____   _____

7. $y + xz$ for $x = 4$, $y = 3$, $z = {}^-3$

8. $z \div x + y$ for $x = {}^-5$, $y = {}^-3$, $z = 10$

_____   _____

9. $(a + b + c)^2$ for $a = 1$, $b = 2$, $c = {}^-5$

10. $a^2 + b^2 + c^2$ for $a = 1$, $b = 2$, $c = {}^-5$

_____   _____

Teacher Note: Use after Quick Check, page 288, to reteach Unit 10, Lesson 9. **(6)**

To solve addition equations with integers,
you add opposites. To solve subtraction
equations, first rewrite them as addition
equations. Then add opposites to get the
variable alone on one side of the equation.

Addition Property of Equality
If the same number is added to each side of an equation, the two sides are still equal.

Remember to use the properties of equality.

Solve: $x + (^-4) = ^-7$

Add the opposite of −4 to each side of the equation. Then simplify.	$x + (^-4) = ^-7$	Original equation
	$[x + (^-4)] + 4 = ^-7 + 4$	Add **4** to each side.
	$x + [(^-4) + 4] = ^-7 + 4$	Associative property of addition
	$x + 0 = ^-3$	Simplify.
Does your answer check?	$x = ^-3$	Identity property of addition

Solve: $x - 3 = ^-10$

First rewrite this as addition equation. Then add the opposite of −3 to each side and simplify.	$x - 3 = ^-10$	Original equation
	$x + (^-3) = ^-10$	Rewrite as an addition equation.
	$x + (^-3) + 3 = ^-10 + 3$	Add **3** to each side.
	$x + 0 = ^-7$	Simplify.
	$x = ^-7$	Identity property of addition

Does your answer check?

Complete the steps to solve.

1. $y + (^-3) = 9$

$y + (^-3) +$ ____ $= 9 +$ ____   Add ____ to each side.

$y + 0 =$ ____   Simplify.

$y =$ ____   _____ property of addition

2. $z - (^-7) = 4$

$z +$ ____ $= 4$ Rewrite as an addition equation.

$z +$ ____ $+$ ____ $= 4 +$ ____   Add ____ to each side.

$z +$ ____ $=$ ____   Simplify.

$z =$ ____   _____ property of addition

Solve.

3. $k + 5 = -17$

_____

4. $x + (-2) = -8$

_____

5. $(-3) + n = 15$

_____

6. $m - 9 = -22$

_____

7. $h - (-4) = 12$

_____

8. $-25 = p - (-8)$

_____

Teacher Note: Use after Quick Check, page 288, to reteach Unit 10, Lesson 10. **(6)**

The location of a point on a plane can be described using two axes and two numbers called **coordinates**. These two numbers form an **ordered pair.**

The first number of the ordered pair is the *x*-coordinate. It is the distance from the *y*-axis to the point. The second coordinate, the *y*-coordinate, is the distance from the *x*-axis to the point.

To graph the point (2, 1), start at **0**. Move **2** units to the right and **1** unit up.

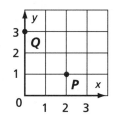

Point *P* is at **(2, 1)**.
Point *Q* is at **(0, 3)**.

To find the coordinates of a point, look beneath it to the *x*-axis. Then look to the left of the point to the *y*-axis.

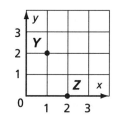

Point *Y* is at **(1, 2)**.
Point *Z* is at **(2, 0)**.

Write the coordinates of each point.

1. Point *H* (4, _____)

2. Point *M* (5, _____)

3. Point *C* (_____, 9)

4. Point *A* (_____, 3)

5. Point *L* _____

6. Point *E* _____

7. Point *D* _____

8. Point *F* _____

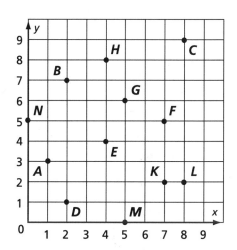

Name the point at each location.

9. (5, 6) _____

10. (2, 7) _____

11. (0, 5) _____

12. (7, 2) _____

Graph each point on the grid at the right.

13. Point *A* (1, 3)

14. Point *B* (0, 7)

15. Point *C* (8, 8)

16. Point *D* (2, 1)

17. Point *E* (5, 3)

18. Point *F* (9, 7)

19. Point *G* (6, 7)

20. Point *H* (3, 8)

21. Point *K* (5, 0)

22. Point *L* (8, 3)

23. Point *P* with the same *x*-coordinate as point *C* and the same *y*-coordinate as point *D*.

24. Do *H* (3, 8) and *L* (8, 3) represent the same point? Explain.

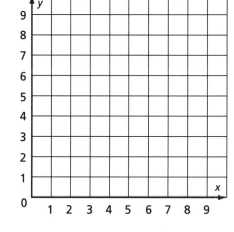

_____

Teacher Note: Use before Unit 11, Lesson 1. (6)

The location of a point on a plane can be described using two axes and two coordinates. The coordinates can be either positive or negative numbers.

Point **A** at (2, 2) is in the first quadrant. Points in this quadrant have two positive coordinates.

Point **B** at (−3, −1) is in the third quadrant. Points in this quadrant have two negative coordinates.

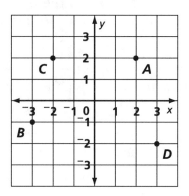

Point **C** at (−2, 2) is in the second quadrant. Point **D** at (3, −2) is in the fourth quadrant.

The first coordinate is the distance left or right of the *y*-axis. The second coordinate is the distance up or down from the *x*-axis.

Write the coordinates of each point.

1. Point *H* (3, _____)

2. Point *D* (−4, _____)

3. Point *C* (_____, 0)

4. Point *F* (_____, −4)

5. Point *L* _____

6. Point *E* _____

7. Point *M* _____

8. Point *A* _____

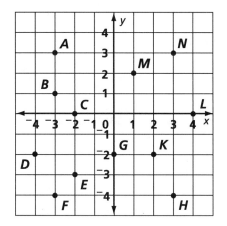

Name the point at each location.

9. (3, 3) _____

10. (0, −2) _____

11. (−3, 1) _____

12. (2, −2) _____

Graph each point on the grid at the right.

13. Point *A* (−4, −2)

14. Point *B* (−3, 1)

15. Point *C* (3, 3)

16. Point *D* (−3, −4)

17. Point *E* (0, −2)

18. Point *F* (4, 0)

19. Point *G* (1, 2)

20. Point *H* (−2, 0)

21. Point *K* (3, −4)

22. Point *L* (3, −3)

23. Point *Q* with the same *x*-coordinate as point *H* and the same *y*-coordinate as point *G*.

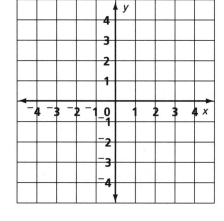

Teacher Note: Use after Quick Check, page 302, to reteach Unit 11, Lesson 1. **(6)**

To make a table for an equation such as
$y = -3x + 2$, follow the steps.

Step 1 Choose any numbers you like for x.

Step 2 Substitute and evaluate.

Step 3 Write the answer as the value for y.

	Step 1	Step 2	Step 3
	↓	↓	↓
	x	$-3x + 2$	y
	0	$-3(0) + 2$	2
	⁻1	$-3(⁻1) + 2$	5
	1	$-3(1) + 2$	−1

Complete the tables to find the value of y for each value of x.

1. $y = ⁻x + 4$

x	$-x + 4$	y
1	$-1 + 4$	3
2	$-2 + 4$	
⁻1	$1 + 4$	

2. $y = ⁻x - 1$

x	$⁻x - 1$	y
1	$⁻1 - 1$	
2	$⁻2 - 1$	
3		

3. $y = 2x - 5$

x	$2x - 5$	y
1	$2 \cdot 1 - 5$	
2		
⁻2	$2(-2) - 5$	

4. $y = -2x + 3$

x	$-2x + 3$	y
0		
⁻1		
1		

Complete the table for each equation.

5. $y = x + 3$

x	y
0	3
⁻1	2
1	

6. $y = ⁻x + 3$

x	y
0	3
1	
3	

7. $y = x - 1$

x	y
2	1
0	
⁻2	

8. $y = x + 4$

x	y
0	4
⁻1	
⁻2	

9. $y = 2x - 1$

x	y
1	
0	
⁻1	

10. $y = ⁻2x + 1$

x	y
2	
⁻1	
0	

11. $y = 3x - 4$

x	y
1	
2	
3	

12. $y = ⁻3x - 7$

x	y
⁻1	
⁻2	
⁻3	

Teacher Note: Use after Quick Check, page 302, to reteach Unit 11, Lesson 2. **(6)**

Any two-variable equation can be graphed from a table of ordered pairs. Here is how to graph the equation $y = -x + 1$.

Step 1 Choose any values for x and find the y-values. Write the ordered pairs.

x	y	
0	1	→ (0, 1)
2	−1	→ (2, −1)
3	−2	→ (3, −2)

Step 2 Graph the ordered pairs. Connect them with a line.

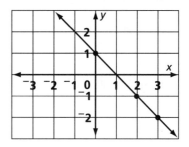

Graph these equations on the grid at the right.

1. $y = {}^-3x - 7$

x	y
−1	−4
−2	−1
−3	

2. $y = x + 3$

x	y
0	3
−1	2
1	

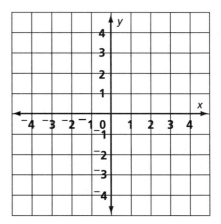

3. $y = 2x - 1$

x	y
1	1
0	
−1	

4. $y = {}^-x + 3$

x	y
0	3
1	
3	

Graph these equations on the grid at the right.

5. $y = 3x - 4$

x	y
1	

6. $y = x + 4$

x	y
0	

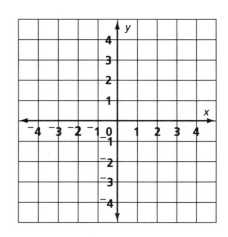

7. $y = {}^-2x + 1$

8. $y = x - 1$

Teacher Note: Use after Quick Check page 302 to reteach Unit 11, Lesson 3. **(6)**

The set of rational numbers includes all numbers that can be written as ratios. To show that a whole number, fraction, decimal, percent, or integer is also a rational number, write it as a ratio.

Show that $2\frac{1}{3}$ is a rational number.

Think:

$2\frac{1}{3}$ equals the fraction $\frac{7}{3}$.

Write:

$2\frac{1}{3} = \frac{7}{3}$

Show that $^-12.42$ is a rational number.

Think:

$^-12.42$ equals the fraction $\frac{^-1242}{100}$.

Write:

$^-12.42 = \frac{^-1242}{100}$

$= \frac{^-621}{50}$

Show that each number is a member of the set of rational numbers. Do this by writing each number as a ratio.

1. $^-17 = \frac{\square}{1}$

2. $^-2 = \frac{^-2}{\square}$

3. $-6 = \frac{\square}{\square}$

4. $3\frac{2}{5} = \frac{\square}{5}$

5. $1\frac{4}{7} = \frac{11}{\square}$

6. $5\frac{1}{12} = \frac{\square}{\square}$

7. $^-9\frac{3}{4} = \frac{\square}{4}$

8. $^-2\frac{3}{8} = \frac{^-19}{\square}$

9. $^-1\frac{5}{6} = \frac{\square}{\square}$

10. $0.6 = \frac{\square}{10}$ or $\frac{\square}{5}$

11. $0.15 = \frac{15}{\square}$ or $\frac{\square}{\square}$

12. $0.08 = \frac{\square}{\square}$ or $\frac{\square}{\square}$

13. $3.47 = \frac{347}{\square}$

14. $^-0.4 = \frac{\square}{10}$ or $\frac{\square}{5}$

15. $^-1.73 = \frac{\square}{\square}$

16. $3\% = \frac{\square}{100}$

17. $14\% = \frac{14}{\square}$ or $\frac{\square}{50}$

18. $65\% = \frac{\square}{\square}$ or $\frac{\square}{\square}$

19. $135\% = \frac{\square}{100}$ or $\frac{\square}{20}$

20. $260\% = \frac{260}{\square}$ or $\frac{\square}{5}$

21. $350\% = \frac{\square}{\square}$ or $\frac{\square}{\square}$

Compare the rational numbers. Write >, <, or =.

22. $1\frac{3}{5}$ ◯ 1.666

23. $^-0.65$ ◯ $\frac{^-5}{8}$

24. $^-5.505$ ◯ $^-5\frac{5}{9}$

25. $^-3.505$ ◯ $^-3.55$

26. $^-1.76$ ◯ 1.06

27. $^-11.21$ ◯ $^-11.212$

Teacher Note: Use after Quick Check, page 310, to reteach Unit 11, Lesson 5. **(6)**

In mathematics, an **inverse** is a number that brings you back to the number that you started with.

The **additive inverse** of a rational number is its opposite. For example, the additive inverse of $-\frac{1}{2}$ is $\frac{1}{2}$, because

$$1 + -\frac{1}{2} + \frac{1}{2} = 1 \text{ and}$$

$$n + -\frac{1}{2} + \frac{1}{2} = n$$

The **multiplicative inverse** of rational number is its reciprocal. For example, the multiplicative inverse of $-\frac{1}{2}$ is -2, because

$$4 \cdot \left(\frac{-1}{2}\right)(-2) = 4 \text{ and}$$

$$n \cdot \left(\frac{-1}{2}\right)(-2) = n$$

Write the additive inverse for each number.

1. 5 _____

2. $^-12$ _____

3. $\frac{2}{3}$ _____

4. $-\frac{4}{5}$ _____

5. $\frac{7}{4}$ _____

6. 0.25 _____

7. $^-1.8$ _____

8. $^-1\frac{1}{6}$ _____

**Write the multiplicative inverse for each number.
If necessary, first write it as a fraction.**

9. $\frac{4}{9}$ _____

10. $-\frac{1}{5}$ _____

11. 6 _____

12. $1\frac{1}{5}$ _____

13. $^-2$ _____

14. 0.75 _____

15. $^-2.5$ _____

16. $^-3\frac{1}{2}$ _____

Circle the one correct number sentence for each question.

17. Which shows that subtraction of whole numbers is NOT commutative?

   a. $4 - 3 \neq 4 + 3$

   b. $4 - 3 \neq 3 - 4$

   c. $4 \times 3 \neq 4 + 3$

18. Which shows that division of whole numbers is NOT commutative?

   a. $8 \div 2 \neq 8 \times 2$

   b. $8 \div 2 \neq 2 \div 8$

   c. $8 - 2 \neq 2 - 8$

19. Which shows that the additive inverse of a whole number is NOT a whole number?

   a. $5 \times \frac{1}{5} = 1$

   b. $5 + (^-5) = 0$

   c. $5 + 0 = 5$

20. Which shows that the multiplicative inverse of a whole number is NOT a whole number?

   a. $3 \times 1 = 3$

   b. $^-3 + 3 = 0$

   c. $3 \times \frac{1}{3} = 1$

21. Complete the number sentence to show that subtraction of rational numbers is not associative.

$$\left(\frac{1}{2} - \frac{3}{4}\right) - 1 \neq \underline{\hspace{3cm}}$$

Teacher Note: Use after Quick Check, page 310, to reteach Unit 11, Lesson 6. **(6)**

An expression such as **2a + b** can be evaluated by substituting a
value for each variable. Sometimes inserting new parentheses can
help you keep track of negative signs.

Complete the steps to evaluate each expression.

1. Evaluate $2a - b - 2c$ for $a = \frac{1}{2}$ $b = \frac{-1}{3}$ $c = \frac{2}{3}$

Substitute. $2\left(\frac{1}{2}\right) - \left(\frac{-1}{3}\right) - 2\left(\frac{2}{3}\right)$

Multiply. Work from left to right. $1 + \frac{1}{3} - \underline{\hspace{1cm}}$

Add and subtract from left to right. $\frac{3}{3} + \frac{1}{3} - \underline{\hspace{1cm}} = \underline{\hspace{1cm}}$

2. Evaluate $a^2 + b - c^2$ for $a = \frac{-1}{3}$ $b = \frac{-4}{9}$ $c = 2\frac{2}{3}$

Substitute. $\left(\frac{-1}{3}\right)^2 + \left(\frac{-4}{9}\right) - \left(\underline{\hspace{1cm}}\right)^2$

Evaluate the squared numbers. $\frac{1}{9} - \frac{4}{9} - \underline{\hspace{1cm}}$

Add and subtract from left to right. $\frac{1}{9} - \frac{4}{9} - \underline{\hspace{1cm}} = \underline{\hspace{1cm}}$

Evaluate each expression.

3. Evaluate $a + b + c$ for

$a = \frac{-1}{2}$ $b = \frac{2}{3}$ $c = \frac{-1}{3}$

$a + b + c = \underline{\hspace{1cm}}$

4. Evaluate $2a + b - c$ for

$a = \frac{-1}{4}$ $b = \frac{1}{2}$ $c = \frac{1}{4}$

$2a + b - c = \underline{\hspace{1cm}}$

5. Evaluate $2a^2 - 3b - c$ for

$a = \frac{1}{2}$ $b = \frac{-1}{4}$ $c = \frac{3}{4}$

$2a^2 - 3b - c = \underline{\hspace{1cm}}$

6. Evaluate $a^2 + b^2 + 2c$ for

$a = \frac{-2}{3}$ $b = \frac{1}{3}$ $c = \frac{-1}{3}$

$a^2 + b^2 + 2c = \underline{\hspace{1cm}}$

7. Evaluate $2a + 3b - 2a$ for $a = \frac{-1}{10}$ and $b = \frac{3}{10}$. _____

Extension
Worksheets

Extension Worksheets

NOTES

You can estimate a product or quotient using mental math.
Replace each factor, dividend, or divisor with a number that
is easy to use mentally.

Using Rounding

To estimate **63 × 48**:

63 rounds to **60**.

Round both numbers
to the nearest **10**.

48 rounds to **50**.

| Round down when the ones digit is less than **5**. |
| Round up when the ones digit is **5** or greater. |

So **63 × 48** is about **60 × 50**, or **3,000**.

Using Front-End Estimation

To estimate **79 × 278**:

Use only the first digit of each factor.

79 → 70   **278 → 200**

So **79 × 278** is about **70 × 200**, or **14,000**.

Using Compatible Numbers

To estimate **178 ÷ 4**:

Replace **178** by a number that is divisible by **4**
and that you can divide mentally.

Use **200 ÷ 4 = 50** or, use **160 ÷ 4 = 40**.

So **178 ÷ 4** is between **40** and **50**.

Use rounding to estimate each product.

1. 25 × 47

2. 54 × 93

3. 49 × 33

_____

_____

_____

4. 367 × 768 (nearest 100)

5. 643 × 825

6. 284 × 132

_____

_____

_____

Use front-end estimation.

7. 18 × 36

8. 47 × 138

9. 372 × 997

_____

_____

_____

Use compatible numbers to estimate each quotient.

10. 181 ÷ 8

Between _____ and _____

11. 91 ÷ 27

Between _____ and _____

12. 468 ÷ 18

Between _____ and _____

13. 1,290 ÷ 431

Between _____ and _____

Name _____

Think of a number that is
the area of a square, such as **16**.

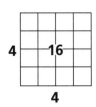

Then a **square root** of that number
is the length of a side.

A square root of **16** is **4**,
which is written $\sqrt{16} = 4$.

Numbers whose square roots are whole
numbers are called **perfect squares**.

Since **3 × 3 = 9**, the square root of **9** is **3**,
which is written $\sqrt{9} = 3$.

Numbers that are not perfect squares, such
as **12**, can be fitted between two perfect
squares to estimate square roots.

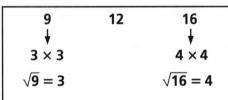

Write the area of each square and the length of its side.

1.

Area = _____

Side = _____

2.

Area = _____

Side = _____

3.

Area = _____

Side = _____

4.

Area = _____

Side = _____

5.

Area = _____

Side = _____

Write the square root of each perfect square.

6. $\sqrt{36} =$ _____ **7.** $\sqrt{81} =$ _____ **8.** $\sqrt{121} =$ _____ **9.** $\sqrt{144} =$ _____

**Fit the given number between the two closest perfect
squares. Estimate the square root.**

10. 5 is between _____ and _____.

So $\sqrt{5}$ is between _____ and _____.

11. 11 is between _____ and _____.

So $\sqrt{11}$ is between _____ and _____.

12. 40 is between _____ and _____.

So $\sqrt{40}$ is between _____ and _____.

13. 95 is between _____ and _____.

So $\sqrt{95}$ is between _____ and _____.

Estimate the square root.

14. $\sqrt{55} =$ _____ **15.** $\sqrt{53} =$ _____ **16.** $\sqrt{130} =$ _____

Teacher Note: Use after Unit 1, Lesson 6. (6)

A number in **scientific notation** is a product of two factors.
The first factor is greater than or equal to **1** and less than **10**.
The second factor is a power of **10**.

To write **14,000,000** in scientific notation:

Step **1**	Note the location of the decimal point in the given number.	**1 4 0 0 0 0 0.**
Step **2**	Position a new decimal point to get a number between **1** and **10**.	**1.4 0 0 0 0 0 0**
Step **3**	Count the number of places from the new decimal point to the original.	**1.4 0 0 0 0 0 0.** ← **7** places from the new point to the original.
Step **4**	Use that number as the power of **10**.	1.4×10^7 ← Use the **7th** power of **10**.

Complete.

1. In **730,000,** the decimal point is located at the end of the number. In scientific notation, the decimal point will be

between the digits _____ and _____.

2. In scientific notation, the first factor of **8,700,000** will be _____.

3. In scientific notation, **548,000** = **5.48 × 10⎯**.

Write the number in scientific notation.

4. 19,000

_____

5. 260,000

_____

6. 3,700,000

_____

7. 145,000

_____

8. 4,370,000

_____

9. 328,900

_____

Complete.

10. Multiplying **1.6** by 10^4 moves the decimal point _____ places

to the right. So in standard form, 1.6×10^4 is _____.

Write the number in standard form.

11. 3.2×10^6

_____

12. 4.9×10^5

_____

13. 7.14×10^5

_____

Extension Worksheets

Here's how to use the **divide-and-average method** to find the square root of any whole number or decimal. Use this method when the number is not a perfect square.

To find $\sqrt{32}$ to the nearest tenth:

Step 1 *Estimate* $\sqrt{32}$.

32 fits between the perfect squares **25** and **36**.

$\sqrt{32}$ is about **5.5**.

Step 2 *Divide* **32** by the estimate.
Divide to two decimal places and round.

$$\begin{array}{r} 5.81 \leftarrow \text{Rounds to } 5.8. \\ 5.5\overline{)32.0.00} \end{array}$$

Step 3 *Average* the divisor and the quotient.

$$\frac{5.5 + 5.81}{2} = 5.65 \leftarrow \text{Rounds to } 5.7.$$

So to the nearest tenth, $\sqrt{32} = 5.7$.

Check the accuracy. **5.7 × 5.7 = 32.49**, which rounds to **32**.

Estimate the square root of the number to the nearest whole number by fitting the given number between two perfect squares.

1. $\sqrt{19}$
Between _____ and _____

2. $\sqrt{54}$
Between _____ and _____

3. $\sqrt{78}$
Between _____ and _____

4. $\sqrt{136}$
Between _____ and _____

Find the square root to the nearest tenth by using the divide-and-average method. Check your result by multiplying.

5. $\sqrt{46}$

6. $\sqrt{63}$

7. $\sqrt{93}$

8. $\sqrt{112}$

$\sqrt{46} =$ _____

$\sqrt{63} =$ _____

$\sqrt{93} =$ _____

$\sqrt{112} =$ _____

Check:

_____

_____

_____

_____

Teacher Note: Use after Unit 2, Lesson 9. **(6)**

When the **GCF** of two numbers is **1**, the numbers are **relatively prime**.

Two prime numbers are always relatively prime.

$$\left.\begin{array}{l}5 = 1 \cdot 5 \\ 7 = 1 \cdot 7\end{array}\right\} \text{ The GCF is } \mathbf{1.}$$

One prime number and one composite number may be relatively prime.

$$\left.\begin{array}{l}11 = 1 \cdot 11 \\ 35 = 1 \cdot 5 \cdot 7\end{array}\right\} \text{ The GCF is } \mathbf{1.}$$

Two composite numbers may be relatively prime.

$$\left.\begin{array}{l}10 = 1 \cdot 2 \cdot 5 \\ 27 = 1 \cdot 3 \cdot 3 \cdot 3\end{array}\right\} \text{ The GCF is } \mathbf{1.}$$

A number that equals the sum of all its factors that are less than itself is a **perfect number**.

The smallest perfect number is **6**. The factors of **6** are **1, 2, 3, 6** and **1 + 2 + 3 = 6**.

Some numbers, such as **8**, are "less than perfect."

The factors of **8** are **1, 2, 4, 8** and **1 + 2 + 4 < 8**.

Some numbers, such as **12**, are "more than perfect."

The factors of **12** are **1, 2, 3, 4, 6, 12** and **1 + 2 + 3 + 4 + 6 > 12**.

Are the numbers relatively prime? Write *yes* or *no*.

1. 13 and 26 _____

2. 4 and 15 _____

3. 14 and 49 _____

4. 17 and 32 _____

5. 24 and 35 _____

6. 23 and 37 _____

7. 27 and 42 _____

8. 25 and 36 _____

9. 9 and 75 _____

Complete.

10. Write all the factors of **28**. _____

11. Show that **28** is a perfect number. _____

_____

12. Write all the factors of **496** and show that **496** is a perfect

number. _____

_____

13. Is **64** more or less than perfect? Explain. _____

_____

_____

Extension Worksheets

Name _____

Special circle diagrams, called **Venn diagrams**, can be used to display factors.

This Venn diagram shows all prime factors of **36** and of **48**.

36 = 2 · 2 · 3 · 3 and **48 = 2 · 2 · 2 · 2 · 3**

The common prime factors **2, 2, 3** are shown once in the overlap of the circles.

Factors of 36 and 48

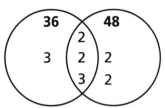

To write the GCF, multiply all the factors in the overlap.

GCF = **2 · 2 · 3**, or **12**

To write the LCM, multiply all the factors in each circle, using those in the overlap only once.

LCM = **3 · 2 · 2 · 3 · 2 · 2**, or **144**

Use the Venn diagrams to answer the questions.

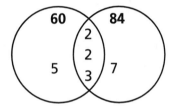

1. Write the prime factorization.

60 = _____

84 = _____

2. Write the GCF of **60** and **84**. _____

3. Write the LCM of **60** and **84**. _____

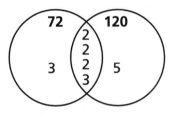

4. Write the prime factorization.

72 = _____

120 = _____

5. Write the GCF of **72** and **120**. _____

6. Write the LCM of **72** and **120**. _____

The Venn diagram below shows all the prime factors of two numbers.

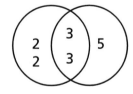

7. Write the GCF and the LCM of the two numbers. _____

8. Write the two numbers. _____

9. Complete the Venn diagram below to show all the prime factors of **30** and **36**.

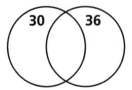

10. Write the GCF of **30** and **36**. _____

11. Write the LCM of **30** and **36**. _____

Teacher Note: Use after Unit 3, Lesson 6. **(6)**

Unit fractions are fractions that have a numerator of **1**, such as $\frac{1}{2}, \frac{1}{3}, \frac{1}{4}$ and $\frac{1}{5}$.

Ancient Egyptians used the sign $\bigcirc$ over a whole number to represent a unit fraction. They represented other fractions as a sum of unit fractions.

Egyptian Numerals

| meant **1** $\cap$ meant **10**

$\bigcirc$
|||| meant $\frac{1}{6}$
||

$\bigcirc$
$\cap$ meant $\frac{1}{12}$
||

To show $\frac{99}{100}$ in the Egyptian way, use these steps.

Step 1 Find the greatest unit fraction less than $\frac{99}{100}$, and subtract.

$$\frac{99}{100} - \frac{1}{2} = \frac{49}{100}$$

Step 2 Find other unit fractions. Continue subtracting until the difference is **0**.

$$\frac{49}{100} - \frac{1}{4} = \frac{24}{100} \qquad \frac{24}{100} - \frac{1}{5} = \frac{4}{100} \qquad \frac{4}{100} - \frac{1}{25} = 0$$

Step 3 Add these unit fractions to represent $\frac{99}{100}$.

$$\frac{99}{100} = \frac{1}{2} + \frac{1}{4} + \frac{1}{5} + \frac{1}{25}$$

Step 4 Write the answer in the Egyptian way.

$$\frac{99}{100} = \bigcirc \quad \bigcirc \quad \bigcirc \quad \bigcirc$$
$$|| \quad |||| \quad ||||| \quad \cap\cap$$
$$|||||$$

Represent the fractions as a sum of unit fractions and then in the Egyptian way.

1. $\frac{7}{8} =$ _____

2. $\frac{19}{24} =$ _____

Complete each equation by filling in the missing denominator.

3. $\frac{1}{2} = \frac{1}{3} + \frac{1}{\underline{}}$ 　　　 **4.** $\frac{1}{3} = \frac{1}{4} + \frac{1}{\underline{}}$ 　　　 **5.** $\frac{1}{4} = \frac{1}{5} + \frac{1}{\underline{}}$ 　　　 **6.** $\frac{1}{5} = \frac{1}{6} + \frac{1}{\underline{}}$

Look for a pattern in Exercises 3–6.

7. Describe the pattern. _____

8. Use the pattern to write $\frac{1}{10}$ as a sum of unit fractions. _____

A **complex fraction** has fractions in the numerator or denominator or both.

Simplify $\dfrac{\frac{1}{2}}{\frac{2}{3}}$.

Step 1 Write a complex fraction that contains the reciprocal of the denominator in both its numerator and denominator.

$$\dfrac{\frac{3}{2}}{\frac{3}{2}} \leftarrow \text{This fraction is a name for for } \mathbf{1}.$$

Step 2 Multiply the original fraction by this new complex fraction. Simplify.

$$\dfrac{\frac{1}{2}}{\frac{2}{3}} \times \dfrac{\frac{3}{2}}{\frac{3}{2}} = \dfrac{\frac{1 \times 3}{2 \times 2}}{1} = \dfrac{\frac{3}{4}}{1} = \dfrac{3}{4}$$

$\uparrow$
The product of reciprocals is **1**.

Simplify each complex fraction.

1. $\dfrac{\frac{1}{4}}{\frac{3}{5}}$

2. $\dfrac{\frac{2}{5}}{\frac{3}{10}}$

3. $\dfrac{\frac{3}{8}}{\frac{5}{16}}$

_____   _____   _____

4. $\dfrac{\frac{2}{7}}{14}$

5. $\dfrac{\frac{3}{8}}{24}$

6. $\dfrac{\frac{4}{5}}{20}$

_____   _____   _____

7. $\dfrac{16}{\frac{8}{3}}$

8. $\dfrac{50}{\frac{2}{5}}$

9. $\dfrac{45}{\frac{5}{9}}$

_____   _____   _____

Copyright © Houghton Mifflin Company. All rights r...

Teacher Note: Use after Unit 4, Lesson 12. **(6)**

Although made carefully, measurements are not perfectly accurate. The **precision** of a measurement will depend on the unit of measure used. The smaller the unit, the more precise the measurement. The level of precision is expressed by the **greatest possible error** (G.P.E.) of the measurement. It is one half the smallest unit used to make the measurement.

$1\frac{7}{8}$ in.

A ●———————————● B

Line segment *AB* at the right measures $1\frac{7}{8}$ in.

But since it is measured to the nearest $\frac{1}{8}$ in., the length may be off by $\frac{1}{16}$ in. in either direction. This is written as

$$\pm\frac{1}{16} \text{ in. (read as "plus or minus } \frac{1}{16} \text{ in.").}$$

So the range is from $1\frac{7}{8} - \frac{1}{16}$ to $1\frac{7}{8} + \frac{1}{16}$ or $1\frac{13}{16}$ in. to $1\frac{15}{16}$ in.

Line segment *RT* measures **12 millimeters**.

12mm

R ●——● T

The measure is in millimeters, so the G.P.E. is ± **0.5 mm**. The range of the length is from **11.5** mm to **12.5** mm.

Write the G.P.E. and the range of the length.

1. $10\frac{3}{4}$ in.

G.P.E.: _____

Range:

_____ to _____

2. $6\frac{3}{8}$ in.

G.P.E.: _____

Range:

_____ to _____

3. $9\frac{7}{10}$ in.

G.P.E.: _____

Range:

_____ to _____

4. 8 mm

G.P.E.: _____

Range:

_____ to _____

5. 9 mm

G.P.E.: _____

Range:

_____ to _____

6. 13 cm

G.P.E.: _____

Range:

_____ to _____

Measure the line segment using the given unit. State the G.P.E and the range of length.

M ●———————————● N

7. To the nearest eighth of an inch,

MN = _____

G.P.E.: _____

Range: _____ to _____

8. To the nearest millimeter,

MN = _____

G.P.E.: _____

Range: _____ to _____

Teacher Note: Use after Unit 5, Lesson 1. **(6)**

Extension Worksheets

You can use a chart to help you to organize facts and draw conclusions.

Jenny, Zoe, and Carrie are sisters who enjoy different sports. One likes diving, another bowling, and the third snorkels. Use these clues to find the favorite sport of each sister.

Make a chart to organize the facts. Then you can reason out the situation and draw a conclusion.

From clue (a), say *no* to *diving* and *snorkeling* for Carrie. So, Carrie must like *bowling* and Jenny and Zoe don't.

From clues (b) and (c), say *no* to *diving* for Zoe. Since Zoe already had a *no* for *bowling*, she must like *snorkeling*.

Since Zoe has the only *yes* for *snorkeling*, then Jenny doesn't like it. Since Jenny has *no* for *bowling* and *snorkeling*, Jenny likes *diving*.

Conclusion:
Jenny likes diving, Zoe likes snorkeling, and Carrie likes bowling.

Clues
a. Carrie doesn't like water sports.
b. Zoe is the youngest.
c. The oldest likes diving.

	Diving	Bowling	Snorkeling
Jenny	yes	no	no
Zoe	no	no	yes
Carrie	no	yes	no

Use a chart to organize the facts in the problem.

1. Art, Bill, and Cliff have the pets Allie, an alligator, Burt, a beaver, and Cindy, a cat, not in that order. Use these clues to find each boy's pet.
a. No boy has the same initials as his pet.
b. Bill is allergic to cats.

	Allie	Burt	Cindy
Art			
Bill			
Cliff			

Conclusion: _____

2. Al Teacher, Jo Doctor, and Rita Tailor are a teacher, a doctor, and a tailor. Use these clues to find each person's occupation.
a. Their occupations do not match their names.
b. Al Teacher is the tailor's cousin.

	Teacher	Doctor	Tailor
Al Teacher			
Jo Doctor			
Rita Tailor			

Conclusion: _____

3. Ann, Dan, and Jan all study math, science, and French, and each has a different favorite. Use these clues to find each student's favorite subject.
a. One of Ann's classmates in the group likes science best.
b. Neither Ann nor Jan likes French best.
c. Once Jan liked math best but doesn't now.

Conclusion: _____

Teacher Note: Use after Unit 5, Lesson 4. **(6)**

To write metric measurements using customary units or vice versa, you can write a proportion using equivalent measures, such as those shown in the table.

Equivalencies
1 in. = 2.54 cm
1 yd ≈ 0.9 m
1 mi ≈ 1.6 km

Find the number of centimeters in **7.5 inches.**

| Let n be the number of cm. | > | Write a proportion. $\dfrac{1 \text{ in.}}{2.54 \text{ cm}} = \dfrac{7.5 \text{ in.}}{n \text{ cm}}$ | > | Cross-multiply. $1 \times n = 2.54 \times 7.5$ $n = 19.05$ | > | There are **19.05** cm in **7.5** in. |

Find the number of miles in **60 kilometers.**

| Let n be the number of mi. | > | Write a proportion. $\dfrac{1 \text{ mi}}{1.6 \text{ km}} = \dfrac{n}{60 \text{ km}}$ | > | Cross-multiply. $1.6 \times n = 1 \times 60$ $n \approx \dfrac{60}{1.6} \approx 37.5$ | > | There are about **37.5** mi in **60** km. |

Complete by writing the measurement in metric units.
Show the proportion you used.

1. 6 in. = _____ cm

2. 4 yd ≈ _____ m

3. 40 mi ≈ _____ km

4. 7.2 yd ≈ _____ m

5. 65.7 mi ≈ _____ km

6. 8.2 in. = _____ cm

Complete by writing the measurement in customary units.
Show the proportion you used. Round the result to the nearest tenth.

7. 14 cm = _____ in.

8. 9 m ≈ _____ yd

9. 100 km ≈ _____ mi

10. 16.5 m ≈ _____ yd

11. 85.6 km ≈ _____ mi

12. 35.8 cm = _____ in.

13. 10 m ≈ _____ ft

14. 155 mm = _____ in.

15. 0.6 m = _____ in.

Extension Worksheets

Teacher Note: Use after Unit 6, Lesson 4. **(6)**

Each of the ratios $\frac{2}{4}$, $\frac{3}{6}$, $\frac{4}{8}$, and $\frac{5}{10}$ is equivalent to $\frac{1}{2}$.

The table below shows the five ratios, with the numerators of the ratios in the first row and the denominators in the second.

Numerator	1	2	3	4	5
Denominator	2	4	6	8	10

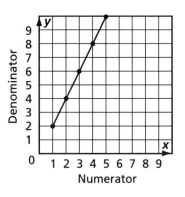

From the table, read each set of values as a coordinate pair: (numerator, denominator).

Plot a point for each coordinate pair.

When the points that represent equivalent ratios or rates are connected on a graph, they form a line.

Complete a table of values for the rates. Plot the points using the values in the table for the coordinates.

1. Trish is making bracelets. She uses **1** foot of cord for every **2** bracelets.

Feet of Cord	1	2	3	4
Number of Bracelets	2	4	6	8

2. Do the points lie on a line?

_____

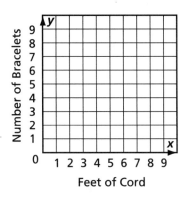

3. Desmond is making model airplanes that use a scale of **2 cm = 5 ft.**

Length in cm	0	2	4	6	8
Length in ft	0	5			

4. A box of waffle mix says that **2** cups of mix will make **3** waffles.

No. of Cups	2	4	6	8	10
No. of Waffles	3				

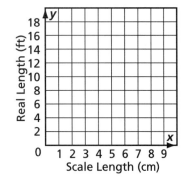

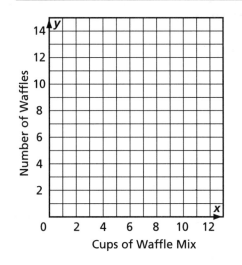

Teacher Note: Use after Unit 6, Lesson 4. **(6)**

A **transversal** is a line that intersects two or more lines in the same plane.

Transversal $\overleftrightarrow{EF}$ intersects $\overleftrightarrow{AB}$ and $\overleftrightarrow{CD}$.

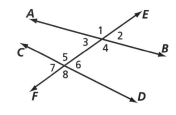

Notice that **8** angles are formed. Pairs of angles that are in the same relative position in the diagram are **corresponding angles**. The pairs of corresponding angles are: ∠1 and ∠5 ∠2 and ∠6 ∠3 and ∠7 ∠4 and ∠8.

When the two lines intersected by the transversal are parallel, the pairs of corresponding angles are congruent. These angle pairs are not congruent when the lines are not parallel.

Corresponding Angles

Below, $\overline{BD} \parallel \overline{AC}$ and ∠DBA = **100°**. Find the measure of ∠BAC.

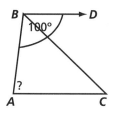

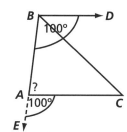

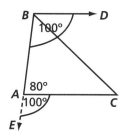

The lines with arrowheads are parallel. Name all congruent corresponding angles that are labeled.

1.

_____

2.

_____

3.

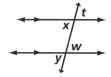

_____

The lines with arrowheads are parallel. Find the value of x.

4.

x = _____

5.

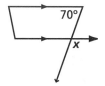

x = _____

6.

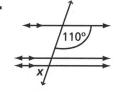

x = _____

Extension Worksheets

A **transformation** moves each point of a plane figure according to some rule. It maps the original figure onto an **image** so that there is a one-to-one correspondence between every point of the original figure and a corresponding point on the image.

Reflection	**Rotation**	**Translation**
a mirror image	*a turning*	*a slide*

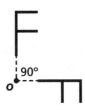

The letter F is reflected across line *l*.

The letter F is rotated **90°** clockwise about point *O*.

The letter F is translated **4** units right and **1** unit up.

Use the diagram at the right. Name the image of each point after reflecting it over $\overleftrightarrow{PQ}$.

1. *A* _____

2. *B* _____

3. *K* _____

4. *L* _____

5. *J* _____

6. *D* _____

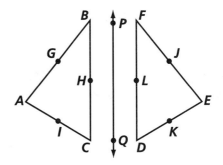

The diagram at the right shows 12 congruent circles. One translation moves *K* to *E*.

7. Describe that translation. _____

8. Under that translation, find the image of

    a. *P* _____   b. *O* _____   b. *L* _____

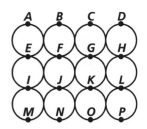

The figure at the right shows polygon *KLMNOP* and its image after rotating it 180° about point *X*. Name the image of each point.

9. *K* _____   **10.** *N* _____   **11.** *R* _____

12. *L* _____   **13.** *P* _____   **14.** *X* _____

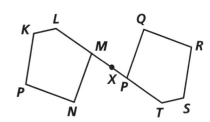

Teacher Note: Use after Unit 7, Lesson 5. **(6)**

The word **bisect** means to cut into halves. You can use a compass to bisect segments or angles.

These steps show how to bisect segment **AB.**

Step **1**	Step **2**	Step **3**
From **A,** mark an arc.	Use the same setting. Draw an arc from **B.**	Draw the bisecting line.

These steps show how to bisect angle **C.**

Step **1**	Step **2**	Step **3**	Step **4**
Mark off arcs the same distance from **C.**	From **B** mark a third arc.	From **A,** mark a fourth arc.	Draw the bisecting ray.

Use a compass and straightedge.

1. Bisect the segment.

2. Bisect the angle.

3. Divide $\overline{PQ}$ into four congruent parts.

4. Construct a line segment that is $2\frac{1}{2}$ (*RS*).

5. Construct an angle one-fourth the size of ∠*ABC.*

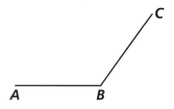

6. Construct an angle of **45°** with vertex at **V.**

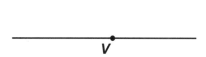

Teacher Note: Use after Unit 7, Lesson 5. **(6)**

Name _____

You can use an area or a perimeter formula to find a missing dimension of a figure.

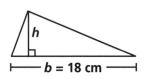

The area and base of a triangle are known, as shown in the diagram. To find the height h, use these steps.

Area of triangle: **72** cm²

Step 1 Write the area formula for a triangle.

$$A = \frac{1}{2}bh$$

Step 2 Substitute **72** for A and **18** for b.

$$72 = \frac{1}{2} \cdot 18 \cdot h$$

Step 3 Solve the equation.

$$72 = 9h$$

$$\frac{72}{9} = \frac{9h}{9}$$

$$8 = h$$

So the height is **8** cm.

Find the missing dimension.

1. Area = **112.5** m²

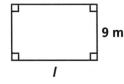

9 m

l

$l =$ _____

2. Area = **94.5** cm²

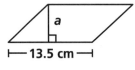

a

$\vdash$ 13.5 cm $\dashv$

$a =$ _____

3. Area = **85.86** mm²

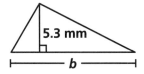

5.3 mm

$\vdash$ b $\dashv$

$b =$ _____

4. Area = **628** m²

r

$r \approx$ _____

---

5. The perimeter of an equilateral triangle is **42** cm. Find the length of a side.

_____

6. The perimeter of a square is **44** m. Find its area.

_____

7. The area of a rhombus is **136** cm². Its height is **8** cm. What is the length of each side?

_____

8. An isosceles triangle has a perimeter of **50** m and an area of **120** m². Its base is **16** cm long.

  a. What is the length of each congruent side?

_____

  b. What is the height of the triangle?

_____

The circumference of a circle is 50π cm.

9. Find the diameter.

10. Find the radius.

11. Find the area.

_____ _____ _____

Teacher Note: Use after Unit 8, Lesson 3. **(6)**

Geometric measures of similar figures are related to the scale factor. Use the similar rectangles R, I, II, and III below to look for these patterns.

R

3

Perimeter = 8
Area = 3

I

6

Perimeter = 16
Area = 12

II

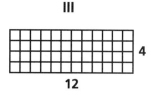

Perimeter = 24
Area = 27

III

Perimeter = 32
Area = 48

Rectangles	Scale Factor	Ratio of Perimeters	Ratio of Areas
I : R	2 : 1	16 : 8 or 2 : 1	12 : 3 or 4 : 1 or $2^2 : 1^2$
II : R	3 : 1	24 : 8 or 3 : 1	27 : 3 or 9 : 1 or $3^2 : 1^2$
III : R	4 : 1	32 : 8 or 4 : 1	48 : 3 or 16 : 1 or $4^2 : 1^2$

The ratio of the perimeters equals the scale factor ratio.

The ratio of the areas equals the ratio of the squares of the scale factor terms.

Use the similar figures to find: a. the ratio of the perimeters, and b. the ratio of the areas.

1.

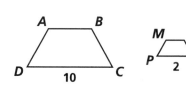

ABCD ~ MNOP

a. _____ b. _____

2.

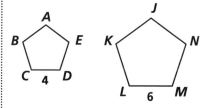

ABCDE ~ JKLMN

a. _____ b. _____

3.

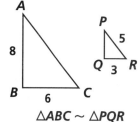

△*ABC ~* △*PQR*

a. _____ b. _____

Calculate the volume of the similar rectangular prisms.

4. $P : 2 \times 3 \times 5$ V = _____

5. $I : 4 \times 6 \times 10$ V = _____

6. $II : 6 \times 9 \times 15$ V = _____

7. $III : 8 \times 12 \times 20$ V = _____

8. Complete the table using the prisms in Exercises **4–7.** Express ratios in simplest terms.

9. How are the ratio of the volumes of similar solids related?

Prism	Scale Factor	Ratio of Volumes
I : P		
II : P		
III : P		

Teacher Note: Use after Unit 8, Lesson 8. (6)

Units of measure for area and volume correspond to
the units used for length.

Length	Area	Volume
in.	in.^{2}	in.^{3}

Equivalent Lengths

1 ft = 12 in.
1 yd = 3 ft = 36 in.

To find the area of the rectangle shown, first express
both dimensions using the same unit.

l = 3 ft or 36 in. l = 3 ft
w = 18 in. w = 18 in. or 1.5 ft
$A = l\,w$ $A = l\,w$
  = 36 · 18 = 648 in.^{2} = 3 · 1.5 = 4.5 ft^2

w = 18 in.
l = 3 ft

So, the area is **648** in.^{2} or **4.5** ft^2.

**Find the area or the surface area and volume. Write the
answer in two ways.**

1.
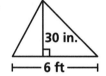
30 in.
6 ft

$A =$ _____

$A =$ _____

2.

$1\frac{1}{2}$ yd
2 ft

$A =$ _____

$A =$ _____

3.
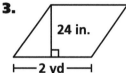
24 in.
2 yd

$A =$ _____

$A =$ _____

4.
3 ft

$A =$ _____

$A =$ _____

5.
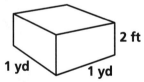
2 ft
1 yd   1 yd

$V =$ _____ $V =$ _____

$SA =$ _____ $SA =$ _____

6.
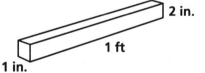
2 in.
1 ft
1 in.

$V =$ _____ $V =$ _____

$SA =$ _____ $SA =$ _____

Complete.

7. Since 1 ft = 12 in., then

  a. 1 ft^2 = 12 in. × 12 in. or _____ in.^{2}

  b. 1 ft^3 = _____ in.^{3}

9. 1 in.^{2} = _____ ft^2

11. 36 in.^{2} = _____ ft^2

13. 1 in.^{3} = _____ ft^3

8. Since 1 yd = 3 ft, then

  a. 1 yd^2 = _____ ft^2

  b. 1 yd^3 = _____ ft^3

10. 8 ft^2 = _____ yd^2

12. $\frac{1}{3}$ yd^2 = _____ ft^2

14. 1 ft^3 = _____ yd^3

Teacher Note: Use after Unit 8, Lesson 8. **(6)**

You can use a **double stem-and-leaf plot** to compare two sets of similar data. Use the same stem for each set. Write the second set of leaves to the left of the stem. Arrange the numbers at the left from greatest to least.

Winning Scores leaf	stem	Losing Scores leaf
	0	3 6 7 7 7 7 7 9
6 6 6 4	1	0 0 0 0 3 4 4 6 7 7 9
7 7 7 6 4 4 3 1	2	1
8 8 5 5 3 2 2 1	3	1
6	4	

Superbowl Scores (Superbowls I–XXI)

Key

The scores $5\,|\,2\,|\,1$ are read "winning score: **25**, losing score **21**."

Write the range, mean, median, and mode of the series.

Winning Scores

1. Range: _____

3. Mean: _____

5. Median: _____

7. Mode: _____

Losing Scores

2. Range: _____

4. Mean: _____

6. Median: _____

8. Mode: _____

9. In one game, the losing team scored **31** points. What are the possible scores of the winning team? _____

10. In one game, the winning team scored **16** points. What are the possible scores of the losing team? _____

---

11. Use the data below to make a double stem-and-leaf plot.

Winning Scores							
46	60	39	53	46	42	49	43
58	58	46	71	68	80	69	92

Losing Scores							
33	42	34	38	34	40	45	40
47	42	36	68	58	63	68	76

Write the range, mean, median, and mode of the scores.

Winning Scores

12. Range: _____

14. Mean: _____

16. Median: _____

18. Mode: _____

Losing Scores

13. Range: _____

15. Mean: _____

17. Median: _____

19. Mode: _____

Teacher Note: Use after Unit 9, Lesson 1. **(6)**

To find the quartiles of a set of data, find the median of the upper half of the data and of the lower half of the data.

Age of Vice Presidents at Inauguration							
54	45	69	43	57	53	67	52
54	66	43	51	51	49	36	57

1 Make a stem-and-leaf plot to order the data.

Stem	Leaf
3	6
4	3 3 5 9
5	1 1 2 3 4 4 7 7
6	6 7 9

2 Find the median of the data and draw a line. The median is **52.5.**

Stem	Leaf
3	6
4	3 3 5 9
5	1 1 2/3 4 4 7 7
6	6 7 9	⎯ Median

3 Look at the **8** items of data greater than the median. Find the median of these items. This is the upper quartile, **57.**

Stem	Leaf
3	6
4	3 3 5 9
5	1 1 2/3 4 4 7/7	⎯ Upper quartile
6	6 7 9

4 Look at the data less than the median. Find the median of these data. This is the lower quartile, **47.**

Stem	Leaf
3	6	⎯ Lower quartile
4	3 3 5/9
5	1 1 2/3 4 4 7/7
6	6 7 9

Complete.

1. Find the median and the upper and lower quartiles in this stem-and-leaf plot.

Monthly Normal Temperatures: Albany, NY

Stem	Leaf
2	1 4 7
3	4
4	0 6
5	0 8
6	1 7
7	0 2

2. Find the median and the upper and lower quartiles in this stem-and-leaf plot.

Zoo Budgets (to nearest million)

Stem	Leaf
0	4 6 7 7 7 8 9 9 9 7
1	0 0 2 3 3 4 5 5 5
2	1 3 4
3	5 8

3. Use this set of data to draw a stem-and-leaf plot. Find the median and the upper and lower quartiles.

Age of Presidents (at their deaths)					
67	90	83	85	56	66
73	80	78	79	71	63
68	71	53	65	67	70
74	64	77	56	71	49

You can show all the solutions to an
inequality such as *x* > ⁻**3** on a number line.
The number line at the right shows these
solutions.

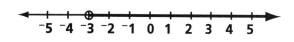

The open circle means that ⁻**3** is **not** included
in the solution set.

This line shows *x* ≤**2**. The solid circle means
that **2** is included in the solution set.

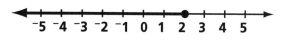

This number line shows ⁻**3** < *x* ≤ **1**. The
solution set is all numbers that are greater
than ⁻**3** and less than or equal to **1**.

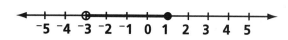

Show all the solutions to the inequality on the number line.

1. *x* < ⁻1

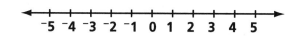

2. *x* ≥ ⁻3

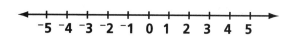

3. *x* ≤ 0

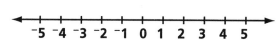

4. *x* > 2

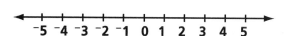

5. *x* ≥ 2

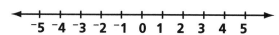

6. *x* > ⁻1

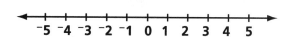

7. *x* < 3

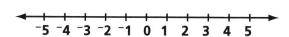

8. *x* ≤ ⁻4

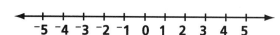

9. ⁻2 ≤ *x* ≤ 3

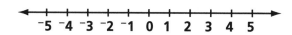

10. ⁻5 < *x* < ⁻1

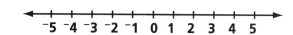

11. ⁻4 ≤ *x* < ⁻1

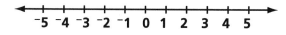

12. ⁻2 < *x* ≤ 5

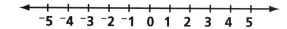

Extension Worksheets

Equations of the form $A(x - B) = C$ $(A \neq 0)$ can be solved in more than one way. Before using the addition property of equality, you can either

(1) divide both sides by A,

or

(2) multiply A times $(x - B)$ to simplify the left side.

$$3(x - 4) = 18$$

$$\frac{3(x - 4)}{3} = \frac{18}{3}$$

$$x - 4 = 6$$
$$x = 10$$

$$3(x - 4) = 18$$
$$3x - 12 = 18$$
$$3x - 12 + 12 = 18 + 12$$
$$3x = 30$$
$$x = 10$$

Follow the steps to solve the equation in two ways.

1. $6(x - 1) = 18$
Divide each side by **6** to get

(_____ − _____) = _____.
Add **1** to each side to get

$x =$ _____.

2. $6(x - 1) = 18$
Multiply **6** times $(x - 1)$ to get

_____ − _____ = _____.
Add **6** to each side to get

_____ = _____.
Divide each side by **6** to get $x =$ _____.

---

3. $2(x + 3) = -10$
Divide each side by **2** to get

(_____ + _____) = _____.
Subtract **3** from each side to get

$x =$ _____.

4. $2(x + 3) = -10$
Multiply **2** times $(x + 3)$ to get

_____ + _____ = _____.
Subtract **6** from each side to get

_____ = _____.
Divide each side by **2** to get $x =$ _____.

Solve the equation in two ways. Show your work on another sheet of paper.

5. $-4(x - 1) = 20$

Begin by dividing each side by **−4**.

6. $-4(x - 1) = 20$

Begin by simplifying the left side.

7. $-2(x + 5) = -22$

Begin by dividing each side by **−2**.

8. $-2(x + 5) = -22$

Begin by simplifying the left side.

9. $15 = -3(x + 4)$

Begin by dividing each side by **−3**.

10. $15 = -3(x + 4)$

Begin by simplifying the right side.

Teacher Note: Use after Unit 10, Lesson 10. **(6)**

An equation with two variables, such as $y = x^2$, can be graphed from a table of values. Use the values to form ordered pairs, as shown at the right.

If the graph is a curved line, you may need more than two or three points to see the shape of the graph.

x	y
3	9

→ (3, 9)

Complete the table of values. Then graph the ordered pairs on the grid at the right. Use different colors to show the two graphs.

1. $y = x^2$

x	y
3	
2	
1	
0	
−1	
−2	
−3	

2. $y = -x^2$

x	y
3	
2	
1	
0	
−1	
−2	
−3	

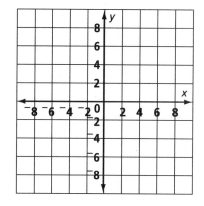

3. $y = x^2 + 1$

x	y
3	
2	
1	
0	
−1	
−2	
−3	

4. $y = \frac{1}{2} x^2$

x	y
6	
4	
2	
0	
−2	
−4	
−6	

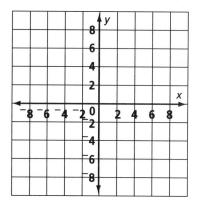

Teacher Note: Use after Unit 11, Lesson 2. **(6)**

Two temperature scales are shown on the
circular thermometer. The outer scale is in
degrees Fahrenheit; the inner scale is in
degrees Celsius.

To estimate temperature readings between
Fahrenheit and Celsius, you can use a
thermometer.

To find more precise temperatures, use
either one of these formulas:

$$F = \frac{9}{5}C + 32 \qquad\qquad C = \frac{5}{9}(F - 32)$$

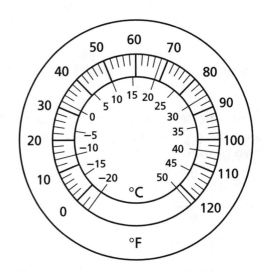

**Use the diagram of the thermometer to estimate the
temperature.**

1. 15°C is about _____ °F

2. 40°C is about _____ °F

3. −5°C is about _____ °F

4. 30°C is about _____ °F

5. 68°F is about _____ °C

6. 5°F is about _____ °C

7. 41°F is about _____ °C

8. 14°F is about _____ °C

**Use a formula. Write the temperature to the nearest tenth
of a degree. Write the formula you used.**

9. 17°C = _____ °F

10. 53°C = _____ °F

11. 43°C = _____ °F

12. −30°C = _____ °F

13. −13°C = _____ °F

14. −36°C = _____ °F

15. 24°F = _____ °C

16. 72°F = _____ °C

17. 16°F = _____ °C

18. −10°F = _____ °C

19. −25°F = _____ °C

20. −8°F = _____ °C

Teacher Note: Use after Unit 11, Lesson 7. **(6)**

Teaching Resources

Teaching Resources

Unit ____ Cumulative Review

Mark the space for the answer you have chosen.

1. Ⓐ Ⓑ Ⓒ Ⓓ Ⓔ
2. Ⓕ Ⓖ Ⓗ Ⓙ Ⓚ
3. Ⓐ Ⓑ Ⓒ Ⓓ Ⓔ
4. Ⓕ Ⓖ Ⓗ Ⓙ Ⓚ
5. Ⓐ Ⓑ Ⓒ Ⓓ Ⓔ
6. Ⓕ Ⓖ Ⓗ Ⓙ Ⓚ
7. Ⓐ Ⓑ Ⓒ Ⓓ Ⓔ
8. Ⓕ Ⓖ Ⓗ Ⓙ Ⓚ
9. Ⓐ Ⓑ Ⓒ Ⓓ Ⓔ
10. Ⓕ Ⓖ Ⓗ Ⓙ Ⓚ
11. Ⓐ Ⓑ Ⓒ Ⓓ Ⓔ
12. Ⓕ Ⓖ Ⓗ Ⓙ Ⓚ
13. Ⓐ Ⓑ Ⓒ Ⓓ Ⓔ
14. Ⓕ Ⓖ Ⓗ Ⓙ Ⓚ
15. Ⓐ Ⓑ Ⓒ Ⓓ Ⓔ
16. Ⓕ Ⓖ Ⓗ Ⓙ Ⓚ

Mark the space for the answer you have chosen.

1. Ⓐ Ⓑ Ⓒ Ⓓ Ⓔ	**31.** Ⓐ Ⓑ Ⓒ Ⓓ Ⓔ	
2. Ⓕ Ⓖ Ⓗ Ⓙ Ⓚ	**32.** Ⓕ Ⓖ Ⓗ Ⓙ Ⓚ	
3. Ⓐ Ⓑ Ⓒ Ⓓ Ⓔ	**33.** Ⓐ Ⓑ Ⓒ Ⓓ Ⓔ	
4. Ⓕ Ⓖ Ⓗ Ⓙ Ⓚ	**34.** Ⓕ Ⓖ Ⓗ Ⓙ Ⓚ	
5. Ⓐ Ⓑ Ⓒ Ⓓ Ⓔ	**35.** Ⓐ Ⓑ Ⓒ Ⓓ Ⓔ	
6. Ⓕ Ⓖ Ⓗ Ⓙ Ⓚ	**36.** Ⓕ Ⓖ Ⓗ Ⓙ Ⓚ	
7. Ⓐ Ⓑ Ⓒ Ⓓ Ⓔ	**37.** Ⓐ Ⓑ Ⓒ Ⓓ Ⓔ	
8. Ⓕ Ⓖ Ⓗ Ⓙ Ⓚ	**38.** Ⓕ Ⓖ Ⓗ Ⓙ Ⓚ	
9. Ⓐ Ⓑ Ⓒ Ⓓ Ⓔ	**39.** Ⓐ Ⓑ Ⓒ Ⓓ Ⓔ	
10. Ⓕ Ⓖ Ⓗ Ⓙ Ⓚ	**40.** Ⓕ Ⓖ Ⓗ Ⓙ Ⓚ	
11. Ⓐ Ⓑ Ⓒ Ⓓ Ⓔ	**41.** Ⓐ Ⓑ Ⓒ Ⓓ Ⓔ	
12. Ⓕ Ⓖ Ⓗ Ⓙ Ⓚ	**42.** Ⓕ Ⓖ Ⓗ Ⓙ Ⓚ	
13. Ⓐ Ⓑ Ⓒ Ⓓ Ⓔ	**43.** Ⓐ Ⓑ Ⓒ Ⓓ Ⓔ	
14. Ⓕ Ⓖ Ⓗ Ⓙ Ⓚ	**44.** Ⓕ Ⓖ Ⓗ Ⓙ Ⓚ	
15. Ⓐ Ⓑ Ⓒ Ⓓ Ⓔ	**45.** Ⓐ Ⓑ Ⓒ Ⓓ Ⓔ	
16. Ⓕ Ⓖ Ⓗ Ⓙ Ⓚ	**46.** Ⓕ Ⓖ Ⓗ Ⓙ Ⓚ	
17. Ⓐ Ⓑ Ⓒ Ⓓ Ⓔ	**47.** Ⓐ Ⓑ Ⓒ Ⓓ Ⓔ	
18. Ⓕ Ⓖ Ⓗ Ⓙ Ⓚ	**48.** Ⓕ Ⓖ Ⓗ Ⓙ Ⓚ	
19. Ⓐ Ⓑ Ⓒ Ⓓ Ⓔ	**49.** Ⓐ Ⓑ Ⓒ Ⓓ Ⓔ	
20. Ⓕ Ⓖ Ⓗ Ⓙ Ⓚ	**50.** Ⓕ Ⓖ Ⓗ Ⓙ Ⓚ	
21. Ⓐ Ⓑ Ⓒ Ⓓ Ⓔ	**51.** Ⓐ Ⓑ Ⓒ Ⓓ Ⓔ	
22. Ⓕ Ⓖ Ⓗ Ⓙ Ⓚ	**52.** Ⓕ Ⓖ Ⓗ Ⓙ Ⓚ	
23. Ⓐ Ⓑ Ⓒ Ⓓ Ⓔ	**53.** Ⓐ Ⓑ Ⓒ Ⓓ Ⓔ	
24. Ⓕ Ⓖ Ⓗ Ⓙ Ⓚ	**54.** Ⓕ Ⓖ Ⓗ Ⓙ Ⓚ	
25. Ⓐ Ⓑ Ⓒ Ⓓ Ⓔ	**55.** Ⓐ Ⓑ Ⓒ Ⓓ Ⓔ	
26. Ⓕ Ⓖ Ⓗ Ⓙ Ⓚ	**56.** Ⓕ Ⓖ Ⓗ Ⓙ Ⓚ	
27. Ⓐ Ⓑ Ⓒ Ⓓ Ⓔ	**57.** Ⓐ Ⓑ Ⓒ Ⓓ Ⓔ	
28. Ⓕ Ⓖ Ⓗ Ⓙ Ⓚ	**58.** Ⓕ Ⓖ Ⓗ Ⓙ Ⓚ	
29. Ⓐ Ⓑ Ⓒ Ⓓ Ⓔ	**59.** Ⓐ Ⓑ Ⓒ Ⓓ Ⓔ	
30. Ⓕ Ⓖ Ⓗ Ⓙ Ⓚ	**60.** Ⓕ Ⓖ Ⓗ Ⓙ Ⓚ	

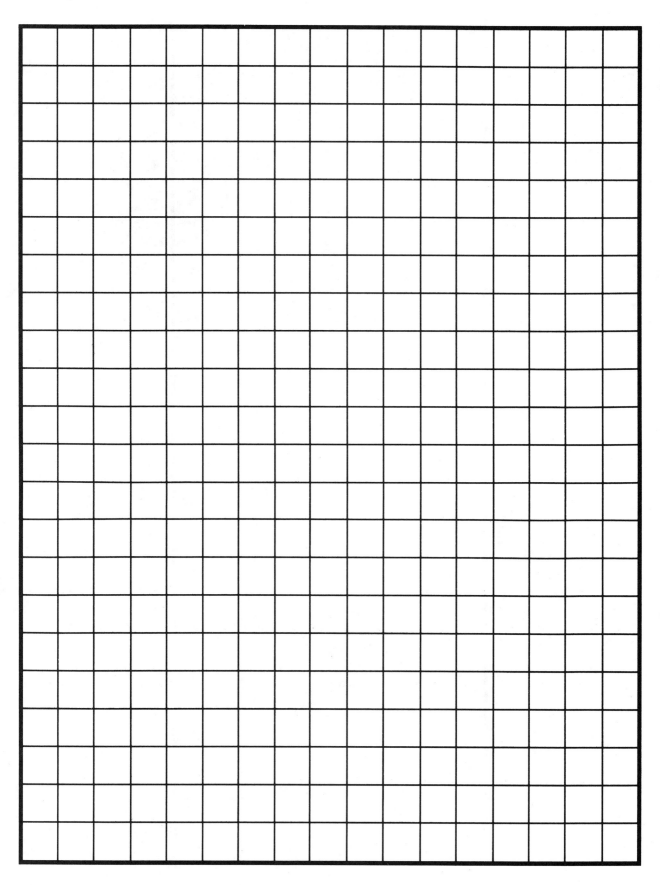

Teaching Resources

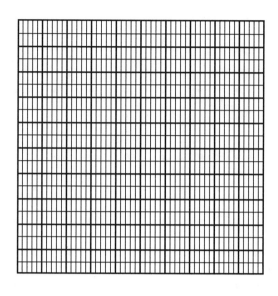

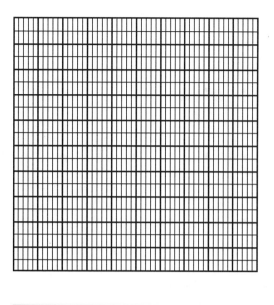

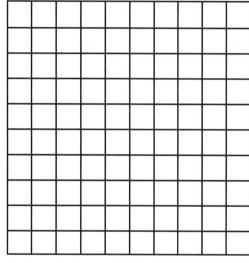

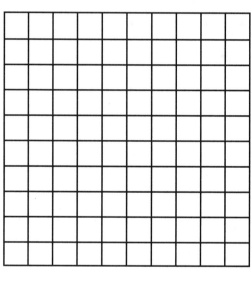

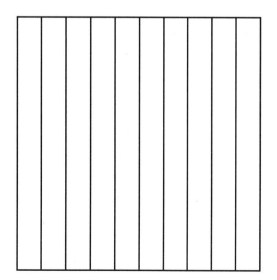

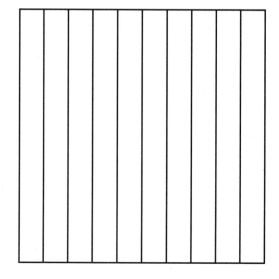

Teaching Resources

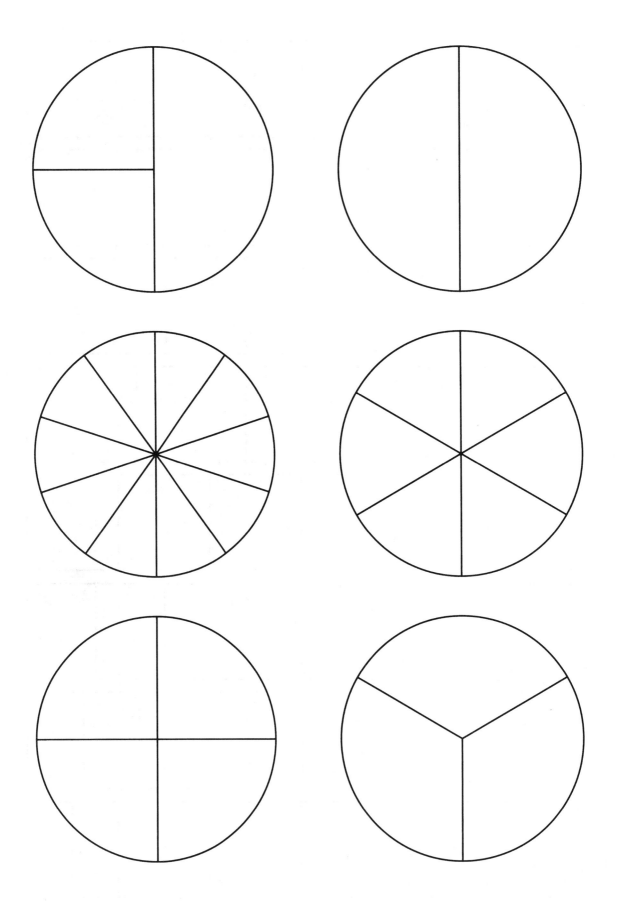

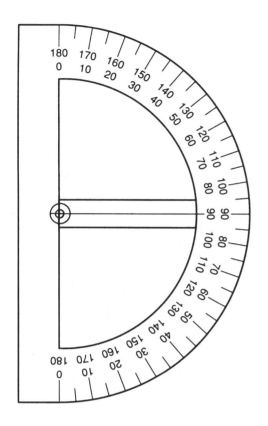

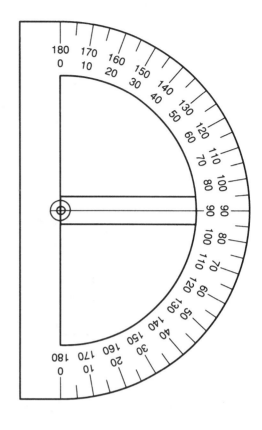

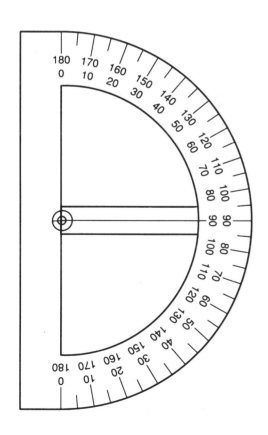

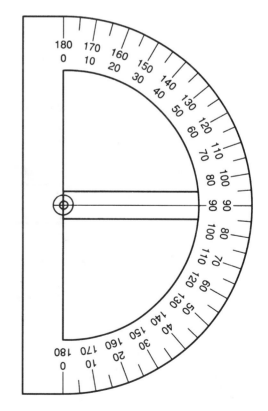

Teaching Resources

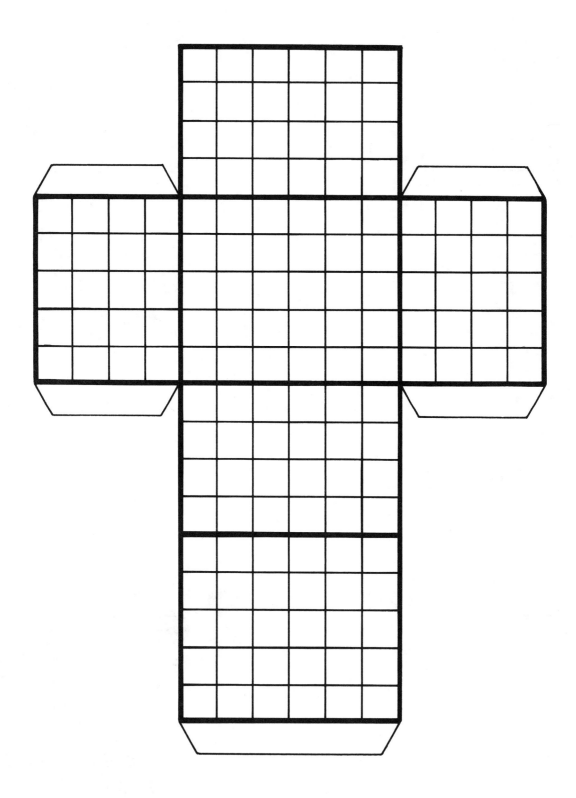

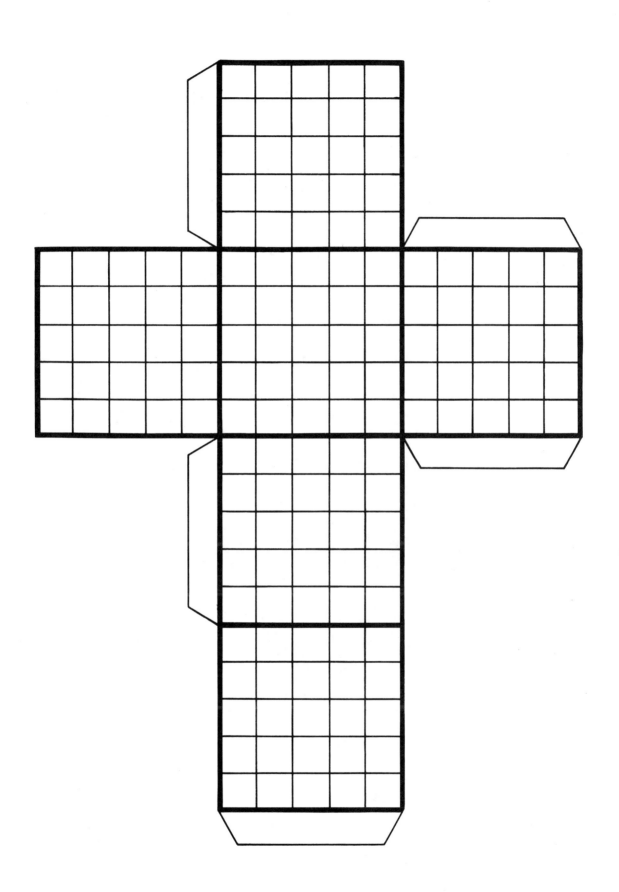

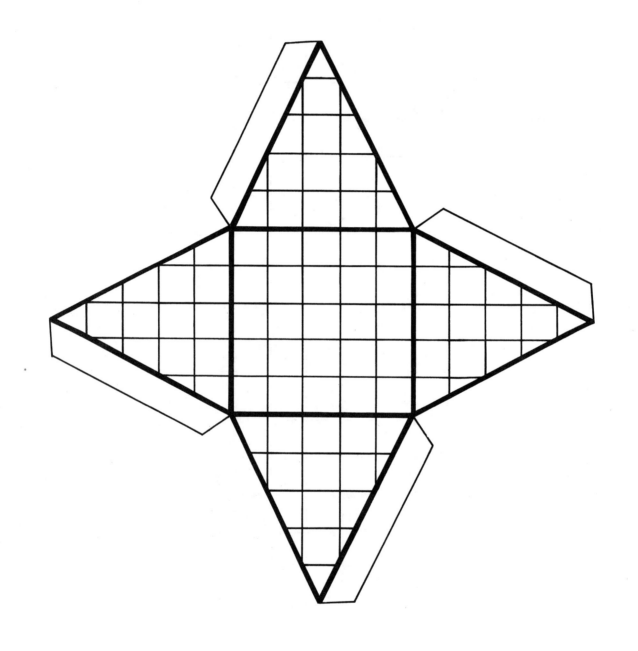

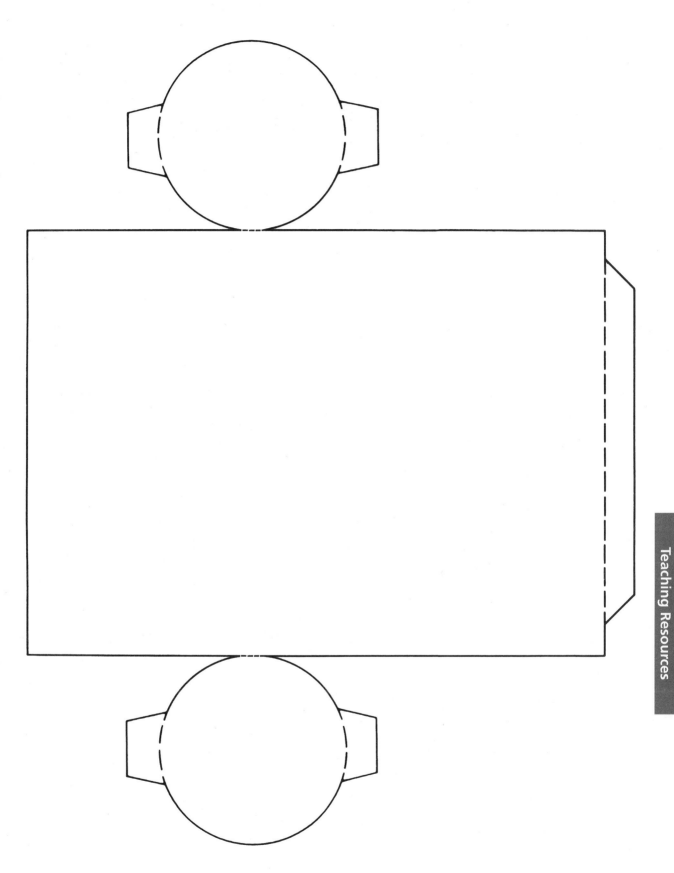

Teaching Resources

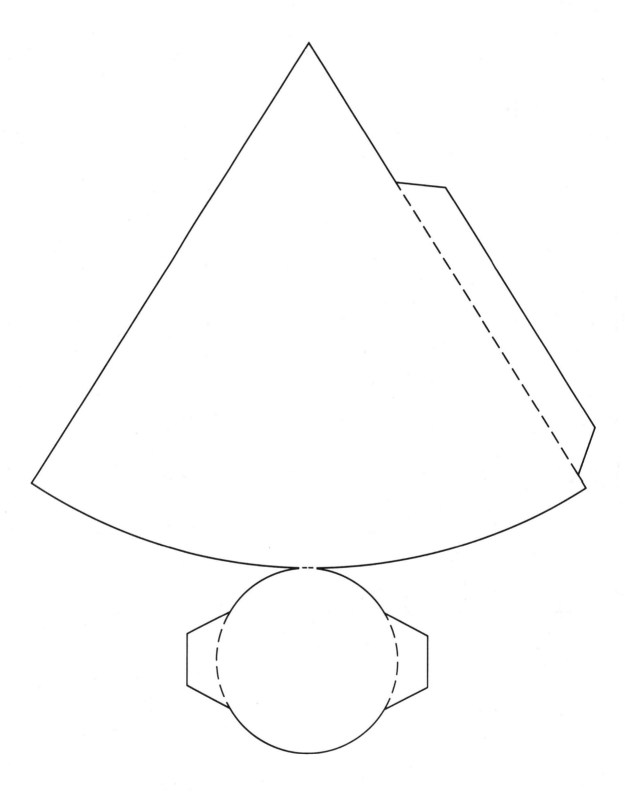

Name _____

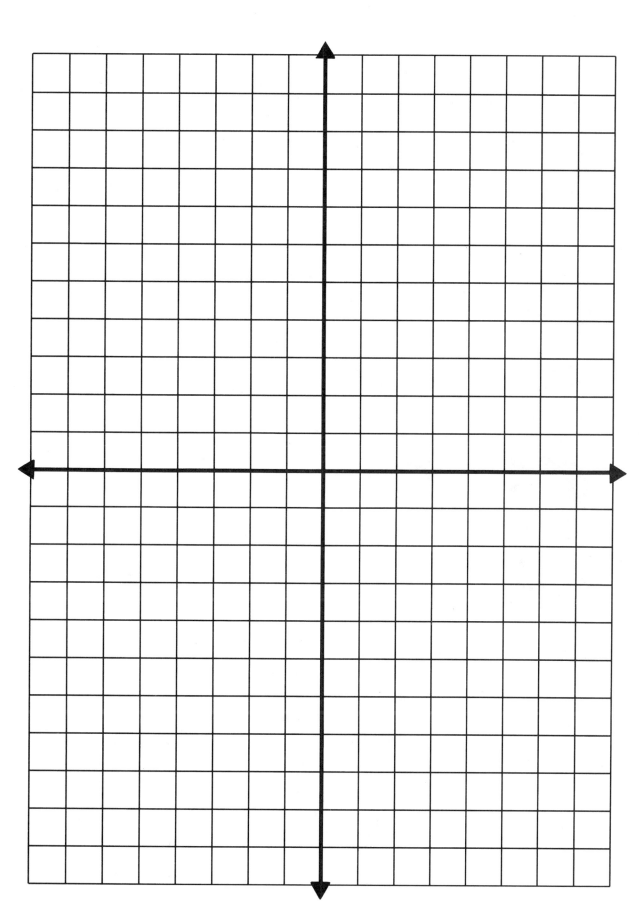

0 1 2 3

4 5 6 7

8 9 + −

× ÷ = >

10	11	12	13
14	15	16	17
18	19	20	(
)	n	$\neq$	$<$

Teaching Resources

thousands	hundreds	tens	ones	.	tenths	hundredths	thousandths
				.			
				.			
				.			

thousands	hundreds	tens	ones	.	tenths	hundredths	thousandths
				.			
				.			
				.			

thousands	hundreds	tens	ones	.	tenths	hundredths	thousandths
				.			
				.			
				.			

thousands	hundreds	tens	ones	.	tenths	hundredths	thousandths
				.			
				.			
				.			

thousands	hundreds	tens	ones	.	tenths	hundredths	thousandths
				.			
				.			
				.			

thousands	hundreds	tens	ones	.	tenths	hundredths	thousandths
				.			
				.			
				.			

Work with a family member to collect the data for this activity.

Remember:

The **mean** (or **average**) of a set of data is the sum of the items divided by the number of items.

This is a list of the number of students in each seventh grade class who attended the school play:

Mr. Farley's class	Ms. Ruiz's class	Mr. DeCarlo's class	Ms. Liu's class	Mrs. Morgan's class
18	16	14	10	17

The average number of students who attended is:

$$\frac{18 + 16 + 14 + 10 + 17}{5} = \frac{75}{5} \text{ or } \textbf{15} \text{ students}$$

Collect the data for each item below. Find each average.

The average number of hours members of your family watch TV in one day	The average height of the members of your family in inches or centimeters	The average number of sandwiches eaten by members of your family in the past week
_____ _____ Average_____	_____ _____ Average_____	_____ _____ Average_____
The average number of pages in 4 of your text-books	The average outdoor temperature for the past week	The average number of phone calls you made each day last week
_____ _____ Average_____	_____ _____ Average_____	_____ _____ Average_____

✂ -

Family Note:

- Have your child complete one item above each day. Help him or her collect the data.
- Ask questions that help your child understand the reasonableness or unreasonableness of using an "average" to describe a set of data.

   EXAMPLE: Suppose the ages of people in your family are 38, 36, 14, 10, and 7. The average age is 21. However, this average is not a good description of the data, because the ages do not cluster around a "typical" age. You could find the average of the children's ages and the average of the adult's ages to give a reasonable description of the data.

Family Projects

Work with a family member.
Find the total cost of each item. Round the total cost to the nearest cent.

A	B	C
Bananas **$0.59** per pound Bought **1.28** pounds _____	Peaches **$2.98** per pound Bought **1.06** pounds _____	Lemons **$0.99** per pound Bought **1.78** pounds _____
D	E	F
Oranges **$0.79** per pound Bought **1.52** pounds _____	Grapes **$1.98** per pound Bought **2.04** pounds _____	Apples **$1.39** per pound Bought **2.71** pounds _____
G	H	I
Broccoli **$0.79** per pound Bought **1.36** pounds _____	Potatoes **$0.59** per pound Bought **2.54** pounds _____	Cherries **$2.39** per pound Bought **0.75** pounds _____

For each item above, how does the unit cost compare to the unit cost of the same items in your local supermarket?

• **Find out the unit cost of each item in your supermarket. Use < or > to compare them.**

• **The costs above are typical for one store in California. Do you think these costs may be different from the costs in your area? Why or why not?**

✂ ━ ✂ ━ ━ ━ ━

Family Note:
• Work with your child to multiply and round the decimals above. You may wish to do only one or two exercises each day.
• On your next trip to the supermarket, ask your child to record the unit costs of each item. Unit costs can be found on the tags where the items are displayed.
• When your child compares the unit costs for your location to the costs for the location above, talk about what might influence how a store establishes its prices. Talk about proximity to where food is grown, seasonal abundance, or ability of a store to buy items in large quantities.

Answers: A. $.76   **B.** $3.16   **C.** $1.76   **D.** $1.20   **E.** $4.04   **F.** $3.77   **G.** $1.07   **H.** $1.50   **I.** $1.79

Name _____

Family Project Unit 3

Factors, Multiples, and
Simplest Form

Play this game with an adult in your family.

• The first player chooses a box and completes it. The second player decides whether the answer is correct. If it is, the first player puts his or her initial in the box. If it is not, the first player loses a turn.

• The player with the most boxes wins.

Find two factors of 19. _____ and _____	Find two multiples of 12. _____ and _____	Write in simplest form. $\frac{6}{9}$ _____
Find a common multiple of 3 and 7. _____	Find a common factor of 12 and 21. _____	Write in simplest form. $\frac{18}{6}$ _____
Write four factors of 20. _____	Find the Greatest Common Factor of 24 and 48. _____	Find the Least Common Multiple of 6 and 8. _____
Write in simplest form. $8\frac{9}{15}$ _____	Find a common multiple of 4 and 10. _____	Write in simplest form. $\frac{15}{27}$ _____
Find the Greatest Common Factor of 8 and 32. _____	Write in simplest form. $\frac{56}{14}$ _____	Find the Least Common Multiple of 7 and 12. _____

✂ -

Family Note: Use these descriptions to refresh the concepts on this page.
• **Factor** A number that divides another number evenly. A **common factor** is a number that divides 2 numbers evenly. The **Greatest Common Factor (GCF)** is the largest number that is a common factor of 2 numbers.
• **Multiple** The product of the number and any other whole number. For example, a multiple of 3 is 6 because $3 \times 2 = 6$. A **common multiple** is any number that is a multiple of two or more numbers. The **Least Common Multiple (LCM)** is the smallest number that is a common multiple of two or more numbers. For example, the LCM of 6 and 4 is 12, although 24 and 36 are also common multiples.
• **Simplest form of a fraction** A fraction less than 1 is in simplest form if there is no whole number that divides evenly into both the numerator and denominator. A fraction greater than 1 must be written as a whole number and a fraction. For example the simplest form of $\frac{8}{7}$ is $1\frac{1}{7}$ and of $\frac{34}{16}$ is $2\frac{1}{8}$.

Answers: A. 1 and 19 **B.** Sample: 24 and 36 **C.** $\frac{2}{3}$ **D.** Sample: 21 **E.** 3 **F.** 3 **G.** Sample : 2, 4, 5, 10

H. 24 **I.** 24 **J.** $8\frac{3}{5}$ **K.** Sample :20 **L.** $\frac{5}{9}$ **M.** 8 **N.** 4 **O.** 84

Family Project Unit 3 (6)

195

Work with a family member. Multiply with fractions to adjust each recipe.

A A recipe for banana bread calls for $\frac{1}{2}$ cup vegetable oil. If you want to make half the recipe, how much oil will you need? Adjusted Amount_____	**B** A carrot cake recipe calls for $\frac{1}{4}$ cup sugar. If you want to make three times the recipe, how much sugar will you need? Adjusted Amount_____
C An oatmeal cookie recipe calls for $\frac{1}{3}$ cup milk. If you want to make two times the recipe, how much milk will you need? Adjusted Amount_____	**D** A recipe for zucchini bread calls for $\frac{1}{2}$ cup butter. If you want to make two times the recipe, how much butter will you need? Adjusted Amount_____
E A recipe for 3 loaves of bread calls for $1\frac{1}{2}$ cup raisins. If you want to make only 1 loaf, how many cups of raisins will you need? Adjusted Amount_____	**F** A cookie recipe calls for $\frac{1}{4}$ cup peanut butter. If you want to make half as much, how much peanut butter will you need? Adjusted Amount_____
G Adjusted Amount_____	**H** Adjusted Amount_____

✂ --

Family Note:
- Have your child show you how to solve each problem. Multiplying with factions gives results unlike multiplying with whole numbers. When you multiply a whole number and a fraction, the product is less than the whole number factor: $3 \times \frac{1}{2} = 1\frac{1}{2}$. When you multiply two fractions that are less than 1, the result is less than either of the factors:
  $\frac{2}{3} \times \frac{3}{8} = \frac{6}{24}$ or $\frac{1}{4}$.
- Work with your child to find recipes to adjust for **G** and **H** above. Together, choose two recipes from a cookbook or magazine. Decide whether to increase or decrease the recipe. Show how to adjust the amounts for two ingredients in each recipe.

Answers: A. $\frac{1}{2} \times \frac{1}{2} = \frac{1}{4}; \frac{1}{4}$ cup   **B.** $\frac{1}{4} \times 3 = \frac{3}{4}; \frac{3}{4}$ cup   **C.** $\frac{1}{3} \times 2 = \frac{2}{3}; \frac{2}{3}$ cup   **D.** $\frac{1}{2} \times 2 = \frac{2}{2}$ or 1; 1 cup
   E. $\frac{3}{2} \times \frac{1}{3} = \frac{3}{6}$ or $\frac{1}{2}; \frac{1}{2}$ cup   **F.** $\frac{1}{4} \times \frac{1}{2} = \frac{1}{8}; \frac{1}{8}$ cup

Name _____

Work with a family member.

Each measurement is in the wrong statement.

• Read all the statements first.

• Decide where each of the given measurements belongs.

• Write the correct measurement in the space at the right.

1. A newspaper advertisement shows the capacity of an oval-shaped, above-ground pool as **5 mL**.

   _____

2. The width of a store front on First Avenue is **200 km**.

   _____

3. Arnold said that his social studies book had a mass of **7 g**.

   _____

4. It was much colder than Lorna expected. Heir light coat did not provide enough warmth on a day when the temperature was only **35°C**.

   _____

5. The instructions said to use a nail that is **20 cm** long to attach the picture frame.

   _____

6. If you want to be comfortable when the temperature is **5°C**, wear a white cotton T-shirt, a straw hat, and sandals.

   _____

7. Don't you agree that **80,000 L** of vanilla is just right for flavoring the sugar cookies?

   _____

8. Everyone knows that the distance between New York City and Hartford, Connecticut, is at least **12 m**.

   _____

9. The jeweler placed the wristwatch in a box that was **7 mm** long.

   _____

10. The naturalist estimated the mass of the earthworm to be **2 kg**.

   _____

✂ —

Family Note: If you are unfamiliar with the metric system, here are some hints for you.
• **Units of length** 1 kilometer (km) is about $\frac{2}{3}$ mile; 1 meter (m) is a little more than 1 yard; 1 centimeter (cm) is a little less than $\frac{1}{2}$ inch; 1 millimeter (mm) is very small: 10 mm = 1 cm.
• **Units of capacity** 1 liter (L) is a little more than 1 quart; a milliliter (mL) is a very small amount of liquid: about 5 mL make a teaspoon.
• **Units of mass** 1 kilogram (kg) is about 2.2 pounds; 1 gram (g) is a very small mass: the mass of a nickel is about 5 grams.

Answers 1. 80,000 L   **2.** 12 m   **3.** 2 kg   **4.** 5°C   **5.** 7 mm   **6.** 35°C   **7.** 5 mL   **8.** 200 km   **9.** 20 cm
        10. 7 g

Work with a family member. Shade the grid to show each value. Write equivalent fractions, decimals, and percents. Write fractions in simplest form.

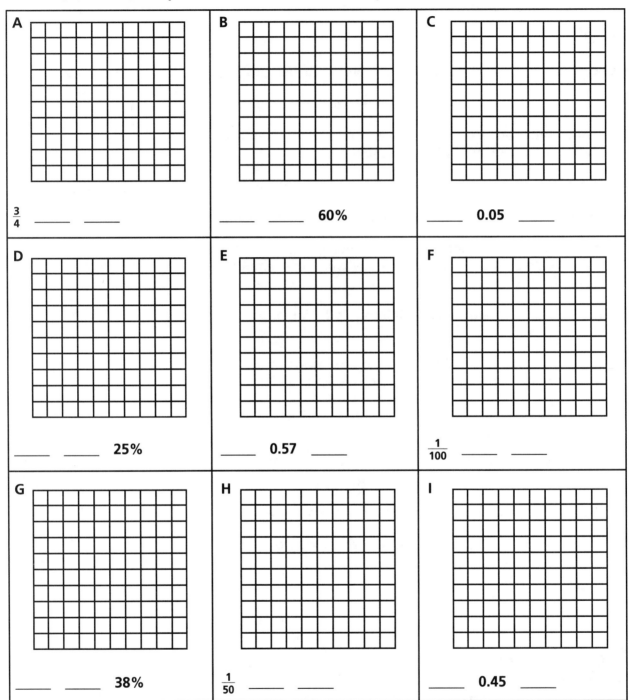

A

$\frac{3}{4}$ _____ _____

B

_____ _____ **60%**

C

_____ **0.05** _____

D

_____ _____ **25%**

E

_____ **0.57** _____

F

$\frac{1}{100}$ _____ _____

G

_____ _____ **38%**

H

$\frac{1}{50}$ _____ _____

I

_____ **0.45** _____

✂ ━ ✂ ━ ━ ━ ━

Family Note:
- The skill of writing equivalent fractions, decimals, and percents is important for later work with equations. Work with your child to make up and solve other similar problems.

Answers: **A.** Shade 75 squares, 0.75, 75%   **B.** Shade 60 squares, $\frac{3}{5}$, 0.60   **C.** Shade 5 squares, $\frac{1}{20}$, 5%

D. Shade 25 squares, $\frac{1}{4}$, 0.25   **E.** Shade 57 squares, $\frac{57}{100}$, 57%   **F.** Shade 1 square, 0.01, 1%

G. Shade 38 squares, $\frac{19}{50}$, 0.38,   **H.** Shade 2 squares, 0.02, 2%   **I.** Shade 45 squares, $\frac{9}{20}$, 45%

Cut out the cards on this sheet. Then play a game of Concentration with a member of your family.

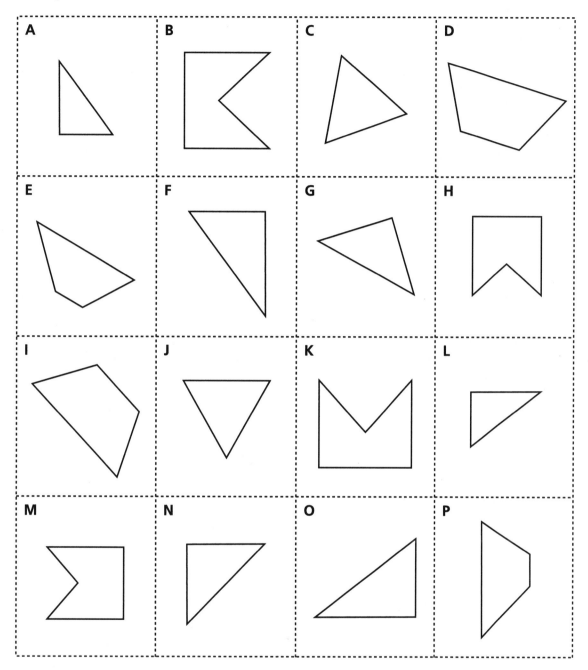

✂ - ✂ - - - - -

Family Note:
- Play a game in which the goal is to get pairs of cards where the figure on one card is congruent to the figure on the other card.
- Put all the cards face down in rows of 4 cards each. Each player takes a turn, turning over two cards. When a match is made the player keeps both cards.
- When all the cards are matched, the player with the most cards wins. Verify matches by tracing the figures, or by measuring sides and angles.

Answers: These cards match: **A** and **L**; **B** and **K**; **C** and **J**; **D** and **I**; **E** and **P**; **F** and **O**; **G** and **N**; **H** and **M**

Work with a family member to find the perimeter and area of this complex figure.

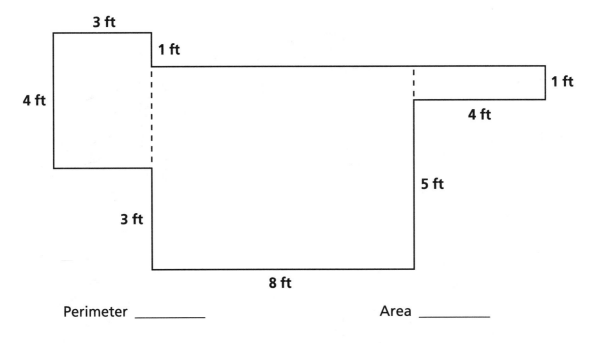

Perimeter _____   Area _____

Measure these items in your home. Find the perimeters and areas.

Rug or Floor	Gameboard or Newspaper	Tabletop
Perimeter_____ Area_____	Perimeter_____ Area_____	Perimeter_____ Area_____
Placemat or Napkin	**Bottom of a Drawer**	**TV screen**
Perimeter_____ Area_____	Perimeter_____ Area_____	Perimeter_____ Area_____

✂ —

Family Note:

- Complex figures are made up of more than one geometric figure. The complex figure above is made up of 3 rectangles. To find the area of the complex figure, you can find the areas of each of the 3 rectangles and find the sum of the 3 areas.
- The measuring activity above provides your child with practice finding perimeter and area. Check that your child expresses all areas in square units.

Answer: **Perimeter:** $8 + 5 + 4 + 1 + 12 + 1 + 3 + 4 + 3 + 3 = 44$ feet

Area: $48\ \text{feet}^2 + 12\ \text{feet}^2 + 4\ \text{feet}^2 = 64\ \text{feet}^2$

Keep a tally of how many glasses of water you and a family member drink each day for 1 week. Make a double bar graph to show the results.

Then, write questions about the graph in the space below.

Tally of Water We Drank							
	Mon	**Tues**	**Wed**	**Thur**	**Fri**	**Sat**	**Sun**
Me							

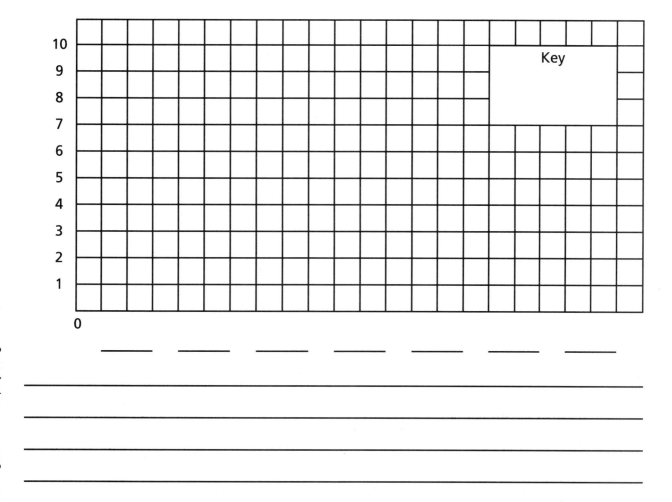

_____

_____

_____

_____

_____

✂ ‑ ✂ ‑ ‑ ‑

Family Note:
• Keep a tally of all the glasses of water you drink every day for 7 days. Work with your child to graph the results.
• Together, choose 2 different colors for the bars and show them in the key. Decide on a title for the graph and the labels for the axes.
• When the graph is done, take turns asking and recording questions about the data.
  EXAMPLES: On what day did we both drink the same number of glasses of water? On Tuesday, who drank fewer glasses of water? How much more did _____ drink than ___?

Do this activity with a family member to show the meaning of adding integers.

• Cut out the positive and negative squares below.

• To represent a negative integer such as –2 , use 2 white squares.

• To represent a positive integer such as 1, use 1 shaded square.

• To represent -2 + 1, place the squares as shown in the first example below.

Match one white square and one shaded square to form a zero pair. Remove the zero pair. The sum is the unmatched square or squares.

‾2 + 1 = ‾1   ‾1 + 1 = 0   -1 + ‾1 = –2   1 +1 = 2   ‾1 + 2 = 1

• Study the examples above. To find the sum of positive and negative integers with the squares, make as many zero pairs as possible. If there are no unmatched squares, the sum is zero.

Use the squares to find the sum.

A. 3 + 2 = _____   B. 3 + ‾2 = _____   C. 3 + 2 = _____

D. ‾3 + 1 = _____   E. 3 + ‾1 = _____   F. 3 + 1 = _____

G. ‾3 + 3 = _____   H. ‾3 + ‾3 = _____   I. 3 + 3 = _____

J. 4 + -5 = _____   K. ‾4 + 5 = _____   L. ‾6 + 6 = _____

M. ‾9 + 8 = _____   N. 7 + ‾3 = _____   O. ‾8 + ‾8 = _____

P. 6 + -1 = _____   Q. ‾3 + 2 + ‾1 = _____   R. 7 + ‾2 + = _____

+	+	+	+	+	+	+	+	+	+	+
–	–	–	–	–	–	–	–	–	–	–

✂ –

Family Note:

• Using integers in equations is a skill used later in algebra. Your child needs many opportunities to work with integers. This activity can provide ongoing practice with addition of integers. Encourage your child to make up and solve exercises similar to those above.

Answers: A. 1 B. 1 C. 5 D. ‾2 E. 2 F. 4 G. 0 H. ‾6 I. 6 J. ‾1 K. 1 L. 0 M. ‾1 N. 4 O. 0
     P. 5 Q. ‾2 R. 7

Work with a family member. Complete each table of values and each statement.

1. $x + y = 9$

When $x = 3$,
the value of y is _____.

When $x = $ _____,
the value of y is 8.

x	y
3	
	8
¯1	
¯3	
	14

2. $x + y = 3$

When $x = 5$,
the value of y is _____.

When $x = 5$,
the value of y is _____.

When $x = $ _____,
the value of y is 2.

x	y
5	
3	
	2
	4
¯2	

3. $y = x - 3$

When $x = $ _____,
the value of y is 2.

When $x = 2$,
the value of y is _____.

x	y
	2
2	
0	
	¯4
¯3	

4. $y = 2x$

When $x = 3$,
the value of y is _____.

When $x = $ _____,
the value of y is 4.

x	y
3	
	4
	¯2
¯3	
	¯8

✂ —

Family Note:
- In each equation above, have your child find possible values for x and y.
- To check the solutions, substitute the values for x and y into the equation.
- If the quantity on the left side of the equal sign is equal to the quantity on the right side of the equal sign, then the equation is true. Then you know that the values you found for x and y are correct.
- Completing tables of value is a skill needed for solving and graphing equations.

Answers: 1. 3, 6; 1, 8; ¯1, 10; 3. ¯3, 12; ¯5, 14   **2.** 5, ¯2; 3, 0; 1, 2; ¯1, 4; ¯2, 5
        3. 5, 2; 2, ¯1; 0, ¯3; ¯1, ¯4; ¯3, ¯6   **4.** 3, 6; 2, 4; ¯1, ¯2; ¯3, ¯6; ¯4 ¯8

Family Projects

Answer Keys

- Beginning of the Year Inventory 207
- Pretests/Posttests .209
- Midyear Test/Final Test 212
- Reteach Worksheets 214
- Extension Worksheets 222

NOTES

Answer Key
Beginning of the Year Inventory

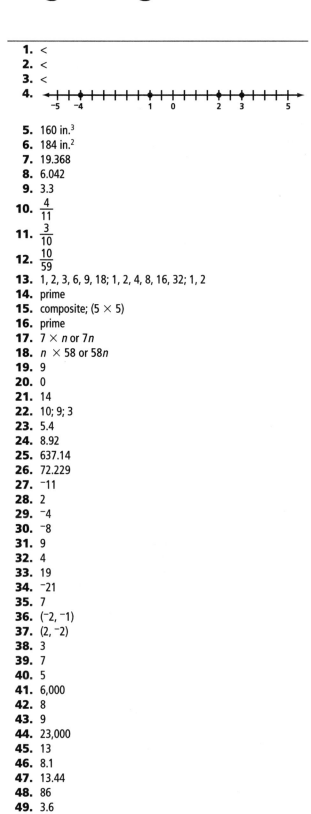

1. <
2. <
3. <
4.
5. 160 in.^{3}
6. 184 in.^{2}
7. 19.368
8. 6.042
9. 3.3
10. $\frac{4}{11}$
11. $\frac{3}{10}$
12. $\frac{10}{59}$
13. 1, 2, 3, 6, 9, 18; 1, 2, 4, 8, 16, 32; 1, 2
14. prime
15. composite; (5 × 5)
16. prime
17. 7 × n or 7n
18. n × 58 or 58n
19. 9
20. 0
21. 14
22. 10; 9; 3
23. 5.4
24. 8.92
25. 637.14
26. 72.229
27. ⁻11
28. 2
29. ⁻4
30. ⁻8
31. 9
32. 4
33. 19
34. ⁻21
35. 7
36. (⁻2, ⁻1)
37. (2, ⁻2)
38. 3
39. 7
40. 5
41. 6,000
42. 8
43. 9
44. 23,000
45. 13
46. 8.1
47. 13.44
48. 86
49. 3.6

50. 0.74
51. 0.02
52. 0.308
53. 2 × 5^2
54. 5 × 2^2
55. 3^2 × 2^2
56. 0.3; $\frac{3}{10}$
57. 0.25; $\frac{1}{4}$
58. 0.66; $\frac{33}{50}$
59. 25%
60. 2%
61. 62.5%
62. 4
63. 7.6
64. 14.5
65. 95
66. 16 students
67. $\frac{1}{5}$
68. $\frac{2}{3}$
69. No, they have the same number.
70. 37
71. 32
72. 36.5
73. 54 ft; 150 ft^2
74. 20 yd; 15 yd^2
75. $1\frac{3}{8}$
76. 24
77. $4\frac{1}{8}$
78. <
79. <
80. 36 R3
81. 5 R11
82. 296 R27
83.

Emergency Vehicles

police cars
fire trucks

84.

Ages of Children at the Park on Sunday

85. $y = 48 \div 8$; $y = 6$
86. $a = 9 \times 2$; $a = 18$
87. 9,620
88. 57,400

Answer Key
Beginning of the Year Inventory

89. 608,000
90. Possible answer: $5 + n = 17$; $n = 12$
91. obtuse
92. right
93. Check students' drawings.
94. Check students' drawings.
95. Check students' number lines; $7\frac{3}{8}$ miles
96. $\frac{7}{10}$
97. $5\frac{1}{2}$
98. $1\frac{2}{5}$
99. $6\frac{1}{10}$
100. 15
101. 19
102. Ordered pairs will vary.
103. 0.08
104. 3.46
105. $\frac{3}{50}$
106. $1\frac{3}{40}$
107. $\frac{2}{3}$
108. $\frac{9}{16}$
109. $4\frac{11}{12}$
110. $3\frac{9}{10}$
111. hundredths
112. tenths
113. tenths
114. =
115. <
116. >
117. 1.6, 0.16, 0.106, 0.016
118. 9
119. 22
120. 6,000,000
121. 3,060,400
122. five thousand, twenty-eight
123. 24%
124. 36

125. $\frac{3}{4}$
126. $\frac{2}{15}$
127. 162
128. 1,812
129. 6,198
130. 17,325
131. 11:45 A.M.
132. Hollis
133. Check students' drawings.
134. Check students' drawings.
135. Check students' drawings.
136. $\frac{4}{15}$
137. 20
138. $\frac{2}{7}$
139. ⁻3
140. 21
141. 1
142. ⁻4
143. April
144. It decreased by $70.
145. 823
146. 3,350
147. 5,143
148. 107,532
149. Yes.
150. No.
151.

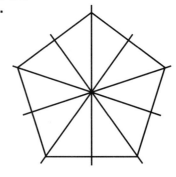

Answer Key • Pretests and Posttests

Unit 1 Pretest

1. 3,040
2. $3,000,000 + 20,000 + 7,000 + 400 + 9$
3. ninety thousand, three hundred forty-two
4. 1,003
5. 119,922
6. 7,371
7. 27 R147
8. 30
9. 23
10. 10
11. 25
12. 125
13. 6
14. 28
15. 55
16. 133
17. mean: 15.4; median: 16; no mode; range: 10
18. mean: increase; median: increase; mode: same; range: decrease
19. $\dfrac{j + 9 + 15}{3} = 14;$ ($j = 18$)

Unit 1 Posttest

1. 9,020
2. $6,000,000 + 800,000 + 10,000 + 60 + 2$
3. thirty-one thousand, sixty-five
4. 1,519
5. 213,537
6. 12,619
7. 18 R313
8. 28
9. 17
10. 18
11. 53
12. 80
13. 11
14. 256
15. 55
16. 105
17. mean: 36.8; median: 34; no mode; range: 25
18. mean: decrease; median: decrease; mode: same; range: decrease
19. $\dfrac{w + 32 + 53}{3} = 43;$ ($w = 44$)

Unit 2 Pretest

1. 0.047
2. 83.602
3. >
4. =
5. <
6. 482
7. 482.2
8. 482.17
9. 30.4, 3.04, 0.34
10. 11.20, 11.02, 10.12
11. 2.647
12. 7.18
13. 122.42
14. $122.22
15. 17.213
16. 24.48
17. 4.232
18. 0.48
19. 21.03
20. 0.047
21. 0.45
22. 0.13
23. 45
24. 3.7769
25. 1.8
26. 5.8
27. 74.09
28. 6.12
29. 16

Unit 2 Posttest

1. 0.105
2. 230.047
3. >
4. =
5. <
6. 94
7. 93.5
8. 93.53
9. 27.3, 2.73, 2.37
10. 0.16, 0.106, 0.016
11. 6.372
12. 3.69
13. 57.56
14. $70.51
15. 6.445
16. 42.3
17. 14.322
18. 0.74
19. 18.06
20. 0.097
21. 0.23
22. 0.13
23. 70
24. ⁻192
25. 2.4
26. 1.04

(Unit 2 Posttest continued)

27. 108.4
28. 17
29. 3.75

Unit 3 Pretest

1. 2, 3, 4, 6, 9
2. 2, 3, 4, 5, 6, 9, 10
3. 10
4. 320
5. $C; 2 \times 3 \times 5$
6. P
7. $C; 2^6$
8. 3; 36
9. 5; 30
10. Possible answers: $\dfrac{2}{5}, \dfrac{8}{20}$
11. Possible answers: $\dfrac{3}{5}, \dfrac{18}{30}$
12. $\dfrac{13}{50}$
13. $3\dfrac{2}{3}$
14. =
15. <
16. >
17. 0.09, $\dfrac{2}{3}$, 0.75, $\dfrac{4}{5}$, 0.85
18. $\dfrac{12}{5}$, 2.75, 3.13, $\dfrac{10}{3}$, 3.6
19. Norridge
20. about twice as many
21. 2

Unit 3 Posttest

1. 2, 3, 4, 6
2. 2, 3, 4, 5, 6, 10
3. 25
4. 72
5. $C; 3^3$
6. $C; 2^3 \times 7$
7. P
8. 1; 144
9. 12; 144
10. Possible answers: $\dfrac{2}{3}, \dfrac{6}{9}$
11. Possible answers: $\dfrac{4}{7}, \dfrac{8}{14}$
12. $1\dfrac{2}{5}$
13. $3\dfrac{3}{4}$
14. <
15. >
16. =
17. 0.55, $\dfrac{7}{12}$, 0.6, $\dfrac{2}{3}$, 0.8
18. 1.45, 1.6, $\dfrac{12}{7}$, 1.77, $\dfrac{9}{5}$
19. Grayslake

(Unit 3 Posttest continued)

20. about the same
21. 6

Unit 4 Pretest

1. $2\dfrac{7}{8}$
2. $\dfrac{19}{20}$
3. $5\dfrac{7}{24}$
4. $5\dfrac{11}{30}$
5. $\dfrac{3}{7}$
6. $1\dfrac{1}{6}$
7. $\dfrac{1}{3}$
8. $12\dfrac{2}{3}$
9. $22\dfrac{2}{5}$
10. $2\dfrac{5}{8}$
11. $7\dfrac{1}{2}$
12. $2\dfrac{5}{9}$
13. $\dfrac{1}{5}$
14. 21
15. 1
16. $1\dfrac{2}{3}$
17. $\dfrac{7}{20}$
18. $\dfrac{7}{9}$
19. $2\dfrac{5}{6}$
20. Possible answer: 5; each value is a multiple of 5.
21. 6

Unit 4 Posttest

1. $1\dfrac{5}{6}$
2. $\dfrac{23}{24}$
3. $4\dfrac{11}{20}$
4. $4\dfrac{13}{30}$
5. $\dfrac{1}{3}$
6. $1\dfrac{1}{4}$
7. $\dfrac{1}{10}$
8. $16\dfrac{4}{5}$
9. 21
10. $3\dfrac{19}{24}$

Answer Keys

Answer Key • Pretests and Posttests

(Unit 4 Posttest continued)

11. $6\frac{1}{3}$
12. $5\frac{1}{4}$
13. $\frac{1}{4}$
14. 25
15. 1
16. $3\frac{1}{5}$
17. $\frac{5}{12}$
18. $1\frac{3}{10}$
19. $1\frac{19}{20}$
20. Possible answer: 25; each value is a multiple of 25.
21. 7

Unit 5 Pretest

1. 3 in.
2. 7 cm
3. 10,560
4. $1\frac{1}{2}$
5. 1,700,000
6. >
7. <
8. =
9. 3 L
10. 1.8 kg
11. 7 pt
12. 0°C
13. 20°F
14. 4 ft 6 in.
15. 10 wk 6 days 6h
16. 2 lb 14 oz
17.

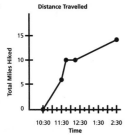

Distance Travelled

18. No; The graph is horizontal between 11:45 and 12:15, showing that no distance was traveled during that time.
19. 14.4 miles per hour

Unit 5 Posttest

1. $4\frac{1}{2}$ in.
2. 11 cm
3. 2,640
4. 35
5. $7\frac{1}{3}$
6. >
7. <
8. <
9. 60 L
10. 2 lb
11. 3.6 L
12. 90°F
13. 90°C
14. 9 ft 11 in.
15. 14 wk 2 days 20 h
16. 4 lb 12 oz
17.

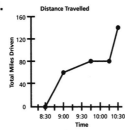

Distance Travelled

18. No; The graph is horizontal between 9:45 and 10:15, showing that no distance was driven during that time.
19. 330

Unit 6 Pretest

1. 3 to 25; 3:25; $\frac{3}{25}$
2. 14 to 3; 14:3; $\frac{14}{3}$
3. 12
4. 12
5. 80
6. $17\frac{1}{2}$
7. $4\frac{1}{2}$
8. $56\frac{1}{4}$
9. $2.64
10. 20 miles
11. 75
12. 8
13. $66\frac{2}{3}$%
14. $12\frac{1}{2}$%
15. $\frac{1}{5}$

(Unit 6 Pretest continued)

16. $\frac{7}{20}$
17. 0.42
18. 0.8
19. 30%
20. 7.5%
21. 300%
22. 70
23.

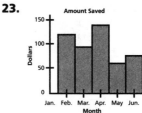

Amount Saved

24. 28%

Unit 6 Posttest

1. 4 to 17; 4:17; $\frac{4}{17}$
2. 9 to 2; 9:2; $\frac{9}{2}$
3. 9
4. 30
5. 8
6. 62.5
7. 37.5
8. $6\frac{1}{4}$
9. $6.00
10. 15 miles
11. 150
12. 24
13. $87\frac{1}{2}$%
14. $16\frac{2}{3}$%
15. $\frac{3}{5}$
16. $\frac{17}{20}$
17. 0.37
18. 0.1
19. 6%
20. 12.5%
21. 400%
22. 85
23.

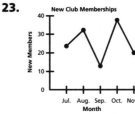

New Club Memberships

24. 16%

Unit 7 Pretest

1.–9. Check students' drawings.
10. rectangle
11. right triangle
12. hexagon
13. regular pentagon
14. parallelogram
15. isosceles
16. 120°, obtuse
17. 80°, acute
18. 90°, right
19. 6 cm
20. 90°
21. 50°
22. 50°
23.–25. Check students' constructions.
26. 20°
27. 20°
28. 160°
29. 20°
30. 160°
31. 5

Unit 7 Posttest

1.–9. Check students' drawings.
10. scalene obtuse triangle
11. square
12. trapezoid
13. regular octagon
14. quadrilateral
15. rhombus
16. 90°, right
17. 120°, obtuse
18. 45°, acute
19. 6 in.
20. 90°
21. 60°
22. 30°
23.–25. Check students' constructions.
26. 110°
27. 55°
28. 110°
29. 55°
30. 70°
31. 8

Unit 8 Pretest

1. 32 mm
2. 16 ft
3. 21.98 in.
4. 9.42 cm
5. 48 cm²

Answer Key • Pretests and Posttests

(Unit 8 Pretest continued)
6. 150 ft^2
7. 15 yd^2
8. 38.25 cm^2
9. 240 cm^3
10. 502.4 in.^{3}
11. 184 in.^{2}
12. 222 yd^2
13. 6 cm
14. reduced by $\frac{1}{4}$
15. 63.585 in.^{2}; $A = \pi r^2$

Unit 8 Posttest

1. 28 yd
2. 24 m
3. 87.92 ft
4. 2.5 cm
5. 168 cm^2
6. 130 in.^{2}
7. $5\frac{1}{4}$ in.^{2}
8. 180 ft^2
9. 216 in.^{3}
10. 18.84 cm^3
11. 208 cm^2
12. 100 ft^2
13. 8 in.
14. $\frac{1}{9}$ of original surface area
15. 50 in.^{2}; $A = \frac{1}{2} bh$
16. cube; 12

Unit 9 Pretest

1. Sally's Cafe
2. April
3. Possible answer: median; Most of the data are clustered near the median.
4. No; The people would all be sports fans.
5. $\frac{1}{36}$
6. about 3 times
7. $\frac{1}{8}$
8. two $12 CDs and one $8 CD
9. $1\frac{1}{3}, 2\frac{1}{3}, 3\frac{1}{3}$

Unit 9 Posttest

1. Westlake
2. 1995
3. Possible answer: median; Most of the data are clustered near the median.
4. No; These students don't ride bikes to school.
5. $\frac{35}{36}$
6. about 97 times
7. $\frac{1}{15}$
8. two $16 (medium) fish and one $24 (large) fish
9. Answers may vary. Possible answer: 1, 2, 3, 20

Unit 10 Pretest

1. >
2. <
3. =
4. >
5.
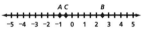

6. 5
7. 4
8. $^-$18
9. 6
10. $^-$26
11. 0
12. 40
13. $^-$3
14. 11
15. 12
16. Add 10 to $^-$5.
17. Possible answer: $n + (n + 4) = 10$; Suki is 7 years old.

Unit 10 Posttest

1. <
2. <
3. =
4. >
5.
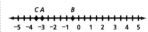

6. 5
7. $^-$4
8. $^-$20
9. 6
10. $^-$23
11. 1
12. $^-$10
13. $^-$8
14. 14
15. 4
16. Add $^-$5 to $^-$8; To combine negative numbers, you add them.
17. Possible answer: $n + (n - 2) = 18$; Kevin is 8 years old.

Unit 11 Pretest

1. x- and y-values and ordered pairs will vary.
2. E
3. C
4. B
5. D
6. A
7. $2\frac{1}{4}, 2.3, 2\frac{3}{8}, 2.5$
8. $0.6, \frac{5}{6}, \frac{7}{8}, 0.9$
9. $^-$18.5
10. 0.09
11.
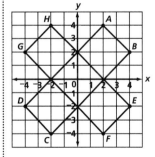

Unit 11 Posttest

1. x- and y- values and ordered pairs will vary.
2. E
3. D
4. B
5. A
6. C
7. $0.08, \frac{1}{12}, \frac{1}{10}, 0.15$
8. $3.1, 3\frac{1}{6}, 3.3, 3\frac{1}{3}$
9. $\frac{7}{10}$
10. $^-4\frac{1}{2}$
11.
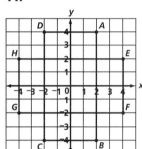

Answer Key • Midyear Test

1.	C		31.	B
2.	F		32.	F
3.	A		33.	D
4.	G		34.	J
5.	A		35.	C
6.	G		36.	H
7.	A		37.	C
8.	G		38.	F
9.	A		39.	B
10.	H		40.	G
11.	B		41.	C
12.	F		42.	J
13.	B		43.	B
14.	J		44.	J
15.	D		45.	C
16.	H		46.	J
17.	B		47.	B
18.	G		48.	H
19.	A		49.	C
20.	J		50.	G
21.	D		51.	C
22.	F		52.	K
23.	C		53.	A
24.	G		54.	H
25.	B		55.	B
26.	H		56.	K
27.	C		57.	B
28.	G		58.	H
29.	C		59.	B
30.	J		60.	J

Answer Key • Final Test

1.	B	31.	B
2.	G	32.	G
3.	B	33.	B
4.	H	34.	J
5.	A	35.	A
6.	G	36.	H
7.	C	37.	C
8.	F	38.	G
9.	B	39.	D
10.	F	40.	H
11.	D	41.	B
12.	J	42.	H
13.	A	43.	A
14.	G	44.	J
15.	C	45.	E
16.	F	46.	F
17.	B	47.	C
18.	H	48.	G
19.	C	49.	C
20.	J	50.	G
21.	B	51.	A
22.	F	52.	G
23.	B	53.	A
24.	H	54.	H
25.	B	55.	B
26.	G	56.	G
27.	D	57.	B
28.	H	58.	F
29.	A	59.	B
30.	G	60.	F

Answer Key • Reteach Worksheets

Reteach 1, page 55

1. 1,000; 8,000
2. 1,000,000; 5,000,000
3. million; thousand; four hundred
4. seven million; six hundred four thousand; one hundred ten
5. 8,000; 40
6. 400,000; 7,000; 500
7. 2,000,000; 800,000; 600
8. 800,000; 40,000; 9,000; 600; 70; 2
9. 200,000 + 40,000 + 9,000 + 500 + 60 + 8
10. 7,000,000 + 800,000 + 20,000 + 2,000 + 600 + 30 + 1
11. 30,000
12. 2,000,000
13. 9,235,634

Reteach 2, page 56

1. millions; <
2. thousands; >
3. millions; 654; >
4. <
5. >
6. <
7. >
8. >
9. <
10. 103,786,562
11. 72,865,132; 98,567,890; 103,786,562
12. 6,873; 9,854; 9,964; 16,498
13. 125,493; 125,567; 125,687; 125,786
14. 1,569,721; 5,693,127; 7,693,721; 9,593,127

Reteach 3, page 57

1. 10^3; 10^4; 10^5; 10^6
2. 10^3
3. 3×10^6
4. 10^3
5. 9×10^3
6. 3×10^4
7. 6×10^4
8. 5×10^5
9. 5×10^6
10. 2×10^5
11. 3×10^6
12. 1×10^5
13. 5; 900,000
14. 400

(Reteach 3 continued)

15. 90,000
16. 7,000
17. 6,000
18. 300,000
19. 2,000,000
20. 200,000
21. 100
22. 80

Reteach 4, page 58

1. 10,000,000,000; 30,000,000,000
2. billion; million; thousand; hundred
3. three hundred fifty-eight million, seven hundred sixty-two thousand, one hundred eight
4. seven hundred seventeen billion, two hundred ninety-eight million, three hundred twenty-one thousand four
5. 12,610,142,506
6. 30,000,000,000; 300,000,000; 8,000,000; 70,000; 50
7. 60,000,000,000 + 4,000,000,000 + 500,000,000 + 10,000,000 + 2,000,000 + 300,000 + 20,000 + 9,000 + 700 + 80 + 3

Reteach 5, page 59

1. the order
2. the grouping
3. 9
4. 0
5. 1
6. 49; 200 + 49 = 249
7. 240 + 60 + 18 = 300 + 18 = 318
8. 13 + 37 + 62 + 38 = 150
9. 24 + 6 + 92 + 8 = 30 + 100 = 130
10. 486
11. 26
12. 24
13. 216
14. 25
15. 34

Reteach 6, page 60

1. subtraction
2. addition
3. subtraction
4. subtraction
5. 5; 4; 4
6. + 2; + 2; 43; 43 − 2 = 41
7. $q + 7 - 7 = 32 - 7$; 25; 25 + 7 = 32
8. $p + 12 - 12 = 40 - 12$; $p = 28$; 28 + 12 = 40
9. $x - 8 + 8 = 15 + 8$; $x = 23$; 23 − 8 = 15
10. $18 - 3 = y + 3 - 3$; $15 = y$, 18 = 15 + 3
11. 10; Yes.
12. 10 − 3 = 7; Yes.
13. 7 − 10 = 13; No.

Reteach 7, page 61

1. the order
2. the grouping
3. 9
4. 1
5. 4
6. 0; zero
7. 11; commutative
8. 2; associative
9. 14; commutative
10. 0; zero
11. 5; associative
12. 49; 10 × 49 = 490
13. 50 × 2 × 76 = 100 × 76 = 7,600
14. 0

Reteach 8, page 62

1. multiplication, addition; multiplication, addition
2. addition, multiplication; multiplication, addition
3. subtraction, division; division, subtraction
4. 100 + 8; 108
5. 100; 108
6. 100; 350
7. 35; 35 + 16 = 51
8. 6; 21 + 9 = 30
9. 6; 26 − 18 = 8
10. 56 − 16 = 40
11. 19 + 3 × 10 = 19 + 30 = 49
12. 6 × 3 = 18
13. 80 + 80 = 160
14. 20 + 15 = 35
15. 14 ÷ 7 × 7 = 2 × 7 = 14

Reteach 9, page 63

1. 525; 75; the mean
2. 69, 70, 71, 74, 74, 83, 84; 74; the median
3. 74; the mode
4. 93
5. 93
6. 91
7. 117
8. 123
9. 117

Reteach 10, page 64

1. division
2. multiplication
3. division
4. multiplication
5. $\frac{64}{4}$; 16; 16
6. 5; 125; $\frac{125}{5} = 25$
7. 12; 6 × 12 = 72
8. 432; $\frac{432}{6} = 72$
9. 12; 12 × 12 = 144
10. $25 \times 50 = \frac{x}{25} \times 25$; $1,250 = x$; $50 = \frac{1,250}{25}$
11. $\frac{17q}{17} = \frac{136}{17}$; $q = 8$; 17 × 8 = 136
12. $\frac{16 \times m}{16} = 64 \times 16$; $m = 1,024$; $\frac{1,024}{16} = 64$
13. $240 \times 15 = \frac{s}{15} \times 15$; $s = 3,600$; $\frac{3,600}{15} = 240$
14. $\frac{8z}{8} = \frac{168}{8}$; $z = 21$; 8 × 21 = 168
15. $\frac{12t}{12} = \frac{1,716}{12}$; $t = 143$; 12 × 143 = 1,716
16. $\frac{f}{21} \times 21 = 231 \times 21$; $f = 4,851$; $\frac{4,851}{21} = 231$

Reteach 11, page 65

1. 0.1; 0.9
2. 0.01; 0.07
3. tenths
4. hundredths
5. five hundred ninety-three and seventy-two hundredths
6. 7; 0.03

Answer Key • Reteach Worksheets

(Reteach 11 continued)
7. 80; 6; 0.3
8. 400; 30; 9; 0.7; 0.02
9. 700 + 90 + 8 + 0.3
10. 8,000 + 900 + 60 + 2
+ 0.7 + 0.04
11. 0.4
12. 0.07
13. 634.82
14. 9,483.64

Reteach 12, page 66
1. nine tenths; <
2. seventy-one hundredths;
>; >
3. sixty-eight hundredths;
0.60; less; less
4. <
5. >
6. <
7. <
8. <
9. >
10. >
11. <
12. <
13. <
14. >
15. <
16. 0.1; 0.6
17. 7.6, 7.32, 7.1, 7.01

Reteach 13, page 67
1. one
2. one
3. two
4. three
5. one
6. two
7. two
8. three
9. 1,719.9
10. 21,491.2
11. 3,207.68
12. 310.380
13. 524.8
14. 750.2
15. 418.88
16. 228.96
17. 1,563.92
18. 1,463.08
19. 22.776
20. 15.344

Reteach 14, page 68
1. 1.23
2. 1.05
3. 2.87

(Reteach 14 continued)
4. 29.6
5. one
6. one
7. two
8. two
9. 2.46; 2.46 × 4 = 9.84
10. 11.15; 11.15 × 7 = 78.05
11. 2.457; 2.457 × 3 = 7.371
12. 18.723; 18.723 × 4 =
74.892
13. one
14. one
15. one
16. one
17. 1.4; 1.4 × 41 = 57.4
18. 3.12; 3.12 × 17 = 53.04
19. 2.236; 2.236 × 43 =
96.148
20. 6.438; 6.438 × 40 =
257.52

Reteach 15, page 69
1. right
2. two; right
3. right
4. 76
5. 35.8
6. 69.24
7. 1,936.7
8. 2,735
9. 6,510
10. 8,253
11. 14,670
12. 9,100
13. left
14. three; left
15. 4.81
16. 8.332
17. 3.7944
18. 0.413
19. 0.0254
20. 0.0047
21. 1.3594
22. 0.0389
23. 0.0018

Reteach 16, page 70
1. subtraction; addition
2. addition; subtraction
3. multiplication; division
4. division; multiplication
5. minus 4.7; p = 4.9; 4.9
6. plus 2.3; plus 2.3; y =
9.2; 9.2 − 2.3 = 6.9
7. minus 4.4; minus 4.4; t =
3.4; 4.4 + 3.4 = 7.8
8. 13.7; 6.3 = 13.7 − 7.4

(Reteach 16 continued)
9. 109.52; 14.8 = $\frac{109.52}{7.4}$
10. 0.21; 5.9 + 0.21 = 6.11
11. 8; 28.8 = 3.6 × 8

Reteach 17, page 71
1. Yes.
2. No.
3. Yes.
4. Yes; No.
5. Yes; Yes.
6. No; No.
7. 15; 3
8. 18; 9
9. 18; 3; 6
10. 2, 3, 6, 9
11. 2, 3, 5, 6, 9, 10
12. 3, 5, 9

Reteach 18, page 72
1. 4; 2
2. 2; 5; 2
3. 3; 6^5
4. 8 × 8 × 8; 3 × 3 ×
3 × 3 × 3
5. 16
6. 3 × 3 × 3 × 3 × 3 =
243
7. 4^2 = 4 × 4 = 16
8. 2 × 2 × 2; 5 × 8 = 40
9. 3 × 3; 12 + 9 = 21
10. 6 × 6; 36 − 10 = 26
11. 3 × 3; 6 × 5 + 9 = 30
+ 9 = 39
12. 5 × 5 × 5; 4 × 125 +
100 = 500 + 100 = 600
13. 9; 10 + 9^2 = 10 + 81 =
91
14. 82
15. 21
16. 151

Reteach 19, page 73
1. 2 × 3
2. 2 × 2
3. 2 × 2
4. 2 × 2 × 2 × 3 or 2^3 × 3^1
5. 6; 3 × 2 × 3 × 2
6. 4; 3 × 3 × 2 × 2
7. 12; 4 × 3; 2 × 2 × 3
8. 18; 2 × 9; 2 × 2 × 3 ×
3
9. 3 × 3 × 2 × 2; 3^2 × 2^2
10. 200 = 100 × 2 = 50 ×
2 × 2 = 25 × 2 × 2 ×
2 = 5 × 5 × 2 × 2 × 2
11. 2^3 × 5^2

Reteach 20, page 74
1. 8; 3
2. 0
3. ends; terminating
4. 0.666
5. 2
6. 6
7. $0.\overline{6}$
8. 0.25
9. 0.8
10. 0.875
11. 0.1875
12. $0.\overline{4}$
13. $0.4\overline{6}$
14. $1.\overline{6}$

Reteach 21, page 75
1. lesser
2. $\frac{3}{6}$
3. right; lesser
4. right; $\frac{10}{6}$, $\frac{10}{6}$, $\frac{6}{3}$, $\frac{6}{3}$, $\frac{10}{6}$
5. <
6. >
7. >
8. <
9. >
10. >
11. >
12. >

Reteach 22, page 76
1. $\frac{1}{2}$; 0; 0
2. 9; 1; $\frac{1}{2}$
3. 3; 20
4. 21; 14$\frac{1}{2}$
5. 2$\frac{1}{2}$; 11$\frac{1}{2}$
6. 28$\frac{1}{2}$; 4; 24$\frac{1}{2}$
7. 10$\frac{1}{2}$; 12; 22$\frac{1}{2}$
8. 9$\frac{1}{2}$; 31$\frac{1}{2}$; 41
9. 4$\frac{1}{2}$; 3; 1$\frac{1}{2}$
10. 15; 3; 18
11. 6; 1$\frac{1}{2}$; 4$\frac{1}{2}$

Answer Key • Reteach Worksheets

Reteach 23, page 77

1.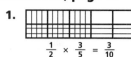

$$\frac{1}{2} \times \frac{3}{5} = \frac{3}{10}$$

2.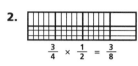

$$\frac{3}{4} \times \frac{1}{2} = \frac{3}{8}$$

3. $\frac{1}{2} \times \frac{3}{5} = \frac{3}{10}$; $\frac{1}{3} \times \frac{1}{2} = \frac{1}{6}$

4. $\frac{2}{5} \times \frac{2}{3} = \frac{4}{15}$

5. $\frac{3}{4} \times \frac{1}{2} = \frac{3}{8}$; $\frac{2}{3} \times \frac{3}{4} = \frac{6}{12} = \frac{1}{2}$

Reteach 24, page 78

1. 1; reciprocals
2. 1
3. $\frac{7}{5}$
4. $\frac{5}{3}$
5. $\frac{2}{9}$
6. $\frac{3}{10}$
7. (D)
8. (C)
9. $\frac{1}{8}$
10. $\frac{4}{1}$ or 4
11. $\frac{1}{15}$
12. $\frac{10}{1}$ or 10
13. $\frac{17}{3}$; $\frac{3}{17}$; $\frac{3}{17}$
14. $\frac{5}{6}$
15. $\frac{9}{20}$
16. $\frac{8}{59}$
17. $\frac{3}{47}$
18. $\frac{1}{3}$
19. $\frac{6}{5}$
20. $\frac{4}{9}$
21. $\frac{1}{13}$

Reteach 25, page 79

1. minus $\frac{1}{3}$; $\frac{1}{3}$
2. plus $\frac{2}{7}$; $\frac{5}{7}$
3. $\frac{3}{6} = \frac{1}{2}$
4. $\frac{1}{27}$
5. $\frac{13}{12} = 1\frac{1}{12}$
6. $\frac{10}{6} = 1\frac{2}{3}$

Reteach 26, page 80

1. 0.5
2. 30
3. 0.7
4. 0.73
5. 80
6. 82
7. 7; 7
8. 7.7
9. 77
10. 3.4 cm
11. 34 mm
12. 3 cm

Reteach 27, page 81

1. eighth; sixteenth
2. half
3. quarter
4. sixteenth
5. $2\frac{3}{8}$ in.
6. $2\frac{5}{16}$ in.
7. $2\frac{1}{2}$ in.
8. 2 in.
9. $1\frac{3}{16}$ in.
10. $\frac{13}{16}$ in.
11. $1\frac{11}{16}$ in.

Reteach 28, page 82

1. 1,000
2. $\frac{1}{100}$; 0.01
3. 1,000; $\frac{1}{1000}$; 0.001
4. 1,000; 6,000
5. 8,000
6. 70,000
7. 150,000
8. 100,000; 700,000
9. 800,000
10. 7,000,000

(Reteach 28 continued)

11. 15,000,000
12. 1,000; 1,000,000; 7,000,000
13. 8,000,000
14. 70,000,000
15. 150,000,000
16. 100; 900
17. 1,000; 9,000
18. 800
19. 8,000
20. 15,000
21. 8,000
22. 70,000
23. 150,000
24. =
25. =
26. >
27. <
28. >
29. >
30. >

Reteach 29, page 83

1. 1,000; $\frac{1}{1000}$
2. $\frac{1}{1,000}$; 0.001
3. 1,000; 1,000; 1,000
4. $\frac{1}{10}$; = 0.1
5. 1,000; 500
6. 300
7. 800
8. 2,000
9. 100; 250
10. 170
11. 60
12. 400
13. 1,000; 4,000
14. 30,000
15. 200,000
16. 500
17. =
18. =
19. >
20. <
21. <
22. =
23. <

Reteach 30, page 84

1. c
2. e
3. b
4. a
5. below; 20
6. 30
7. 25°C

(Reteach 30 continued)

8. ⁻5°C
9. ⁻15°C
10. rise of 10°C
11. fall of 15°C
12. fall of 25°C
13. rise of 20°C

Reteach 31, page 85

1. 1; Pacific
2. 2; 6:00
3. 9:00; 10:00 P.M.
4. 2:00 P.M.
5. add; 2
6. 5

Reteach 32, page 86

1. 12; 48
2. 12; 12
3. 216
4. 51
5. 66
6. 7
7. $9\frac{1}{2}$
8. $68\frac{1}{4}$
9. 3; 3; 21
10. 3; divide by 3
11. 36; 36; 252
12. 36; divide by 36
13. 18
14. 180
15. 25
16. 19
17. 15
18. 15
19. 5,280; 5,280; 21,120
20. 5,280
21. 1,760; 1,760; 7,040
22. 1,760
23. 396,000
24. 176,000

Reteach 33, page 87

1. 8; 56
2. 8; 8
3. 48
4. 28
5. $\frac{3}{4}$
6. 16; 16
7. 16; divide by 16
8. 12
9. 160
10. $4\frac{1}{4}$
11. 18

216

Answer Key • Reteach Worksheets

(Reteach 33 continued)

12. $5\frac{1}{4}$
13. 48
14. 7
15. 96
16. 2
17. 36
18. 1,024
19. 80
20. 144
21. 6
22. 136
23. 2,000; 4,000
24. divide by 2,000; 4.2
25. 6,000
26. 3.2
27. 6.25

Reteach 34, page 88

1a. August
1b. 75
2a. Jan. and Dec.
2b. 58
3a. 70°F
3b. October
4a. 63°F
4b. Yes; November
5a. 61, 63, 66, 74, 74, 70, 63, 58
5b. 66°F

Reteach 35, page 89

1. 24
2. 39; 39
3. 50%
4a. 20
4b. 20%
5a. 2
5b. 8
5c. 8; 2
6. 234
7. 588
8. 1,022
9. 18
10. 165
11. 495

Reteach 36, page 90

1. 6 to 9; 9 to 6
2. $\frac{9}{6}$
3. $\frac{2}{3}$
4. $\frac{1}{5}$
5. $\frac{3}{60} \div \frac{3}{3} = \frac{1}{20}$

(Reteach 36 continued)

6. $\frac{3}{2}$
7. $\frac{30}{1}$
8. $\frac{1}{3}$
9. $\frac{9}{2}$
10. $\frac{16}{5}$
11. $\frac{16}{75}$

Reteach 37, page 91

1. 6
2. 2; 8
3. 3; 3; 21
4. 3; 6; 6
5. 20; 20

Reteach 38, page 92

1. 75; 3; 225; 225 mi
2. $\frac{4.5}{d}$; 1; d; 75; 4.5; 337.5; 337.5 mi
3. 1; 600; 8; 8in.
4. $\frac{m}{1,050}$; 75; m; 1; 1,050; 14; 14 in.

Reteach 39, page 93

1. 25%; 0.25; $125
2. $125; $375; $375
3. 4; 0.06 × 4; $168
4. $1,350 × 12% × 2; $1,350 × 0.12 × 2; $324
5. $1,837.50

Reteach 40, page 94

1. $\frac{25}{100}$; $\frac{1}{4}$
2. 0.35; $\frac{1}{3}$
3. $\frac{1}{2}$
4. $\frac{2}{3}$
5. 3; 12; 12; up; 10.73
6. 50; 50; 5; 50; 10; 10; underestimate; down; 11.96
7. $\frac{2}{3} \times 90 = 60$; overestimate
8. $\frac{1}{4} \times \$8 = \$2$; underestimate

(Reteach 40 continued)

9. $\frac{3}{4} \times 160 = 120$; overestimate

Reteach 41, page 95

1. C, D, E, H, I, K, O, X
2. I, O, X
3.

4.

5. No.
6. Yes.
7. Yes.
8. Yes.

Reteach 42, page 96

1. e
2. a
3. b
4. c
5. d
6. QT
7. PQ
8. QY
9. AB

Reteach 43, page 97

1. acute
2. 110°
3a. 90°
3b. right
4. 150°; obtuse
5. acute
6. 70°; acute
7. 90°; right
8. 135°; obtuse
9. 25°; acute

Reteach 44, page 98

1. APD and CPB
2. 40°
3. CPB
4a. 180°
4b. supplementary
5. 20°
6a. 45°
6b. 45°
6c. 45°

(Reteach 44 continued)

6d. complementary
7. FBE (or ABC)
8. complementary
9. supplementary
10. HBC

Reteach 45, page 99

1. circle O
2. OQ
3a. OQ
3b. radii
4. x
5. XY, XZ, XV, XW
6. YW, VZ
7. YV, VW, WZ, VZ, YW
8. Possible answers: VXY, VXW, WXZ, YXZ
9.–10. Possible answers:

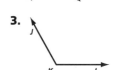

11. central angle

Reteach 46, page 100

1.

2.

3.

4a.–c.

4d. MN ≈ PQ

Answer Key • Reteach Worksheets

Reteach 47, page 101

1.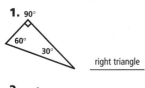

right triangle

2.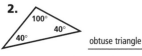

obtuse triangle

3.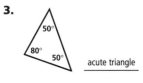

acute triangle

4a.–c.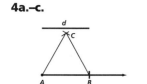

4d. equilateral

Reteach 48, page 102

1a. trapezoid
1b. parallelogram
2a. congruent
2b. right
3a. parallel
3b. congruent
4a. right
4b. congruent, rhombus
5. $314°$; $D = 360° - 314°$ $= 46°$
6. $140°$

Reteach 49, page 103

1. B, C
2a. AB
2b. BC
2c. AC
3. $\frac{8}{6} = \frac{12}{AB}$; $AB = 9$
4. $AC = 13\frac{1}{3}$

Reteach 50, page 104

1. pentagon
2. 6; hexagon
3. eight; 8; octagon
4a. are congruent
4b. regular
5. sides
6. Its 4 angles are not all congruent.
7. square

(Reteach 50 continued)

Name of Regular Polygon	Measure of One Angle	Number of Angles	Sum of the Angle Measures	Pattern for the Sum
equilateral triangle	60°	3	180°	1 × 180°
square	90°	4	360°	2 × 180°
regular pentagon	108°	5	540°	3 × 180°
regular hexagon	120°	6	720°	4 × 180°
regular heptagon	$128\frac{4}{7}°$	7	900°	5 × 180°
regular octagon	135°	8	1,080°	6 × 180°

Reteach 51, page 105

1a. 10 units
1b. 5 square units
2a. 12 units
2b. 5 square units
3a. 14 units
3b. 6 square units
4a. 14 units
4b. 7 square units
5. square unit
6. 3.4 units
7. 10.8 units; 5 square units
8. 14.8 units; 11 square units
9. 13 units; $6\frac{1}{2}$ square units

Reteach 52, page 106

1. 24
2. 5; 24
3. 120
4. 12
5. 27
6. 40
7. 14
8. 14
9. 20

Reteach 53, page 107

1. $P = 4(5) = 20$ units; $A = 5^2 = 25$ units
2. $P = 2(9) + 2(3) = 24$ units; $A = 9 \times 3 = 27$ units^2
3. $P = 4(1.3) = 5.2$ units; $A = (1.3)^2 = 1.69$ units^2
4. $P = 2(4\frac{1}{2}) + 2(\frac{1}{2}) = 10$ units; $A = (4\frac{1}{2})(\frac{1}{2}) = 2\frac{1}{2}$ units^2
5a. $6 + 3 + 5 + 3 + 5 + 6 + 6 = 34$ units
5b. 36 units^2
5c. 15 units^2
5d. $36 + 15 = 51$ units^2
6. False.
7. True.

Reteach 54, page 108

1. $A = \frac{1}{2} \times 15 \times 13 = 97.5$ m^2
2. 60 cm^2
3. $A = 165 \times 12 = 198$ ft^2
4. 78 cm^2

Reteach 55, page 109

1. diameter
2. 3.14; $\frac{22}{7}$
3. 18; 56.52 in.
4. 10.048 ft
5. 1.4; 8.792 cm
6. 35.796 in.
7. 44 ft
8. 528 ft

Reteach 56, page 110

1. $A = 3.14 \times 3^2 = 28.26$ cm^2
2. $A = 3.14(2.3)^2 = 16.6106$ ft^2
3. $r = 9$ in.; $A = 3.14 \times 9^2 = 254.34$ in.^{2}
4. $r = 2.1$ ft; $A = 3.14(2.1)^2 = 13.8474$ in.^{2}
5. $A = 9\frac{5}{8}$ in.^{2}
6. $A = 3,850$ m^2

Reteach 57, page 111

1a. 6; rectangle
1b. bases; congruent
2. 6; square; congruent
3. cube
4. rectangular prism
5. triangular prism

Reteach 58, page 112

1. 6; congruent
2. $6 \times 25 = 150$ cm^2

(Reteach 58 continued)

3a.
Face	Area	cm^2
front	7 × 6	42
back	7 × 6	42
top	5 × 7	35
bottom	5 × 7	35
left	5 × 6	30
right	5 × 6	30
Total		214 cm^2

4. 28 in.^{2}
5. 162 ft^2

Reteach 59, page 113

1. base; height
2. $V = lwh = 5 \times 4 \times 3 = 60$ in.^{3}
3. 64 cm^3
4. 72 m^3
5. 12 ft^3

Reteach 60, page 114

1a.
stem	leaf
8	3 9 7
9	5 5 8 5 1 3 2 3 8 6 9
10	1 7 8 2 4 0 5
11	5 8 6 7

1b.
stem	leaf
8	3 7 9
9	1 2 3 3 5 5 5 6 8 8 9
10	0 1 2 4 5 7 8
11	5 6 7 8

2a.
stem	leaf
1	8 7 8
2	0 5 8 6 0 4 4 1 6 1 2 0 0 0 1 4 0 9 0
3	0 3 6

2b.
stem	leaf
1	7 8 8
2	0 0 0 0 0 0 0 1 1 1 2 4 4 4 5 6 6 8 9
3	0 3 6

Answer Key • Reteach Worksheets

Reteach 61, page 115

1. 16 to 25 years
2. 56 to 65 years
3. There are fewer people that age; fewer people that age drive.
4.

People Who Go to Movies

5. 11–20 years and 21–30 years
6. 22 movies
7. 28 movies
8. 11 to 20 years

Reteach 62, page 116

1.

2	3	5	7	5
3	6	3	3	2
1	4	3	5	3

1a. 3
1b. 3 to 5
2.

102	101	103	101	100	102
102	104	102	103	100	101
101	101	101	105	104	102

2a. 101
2b. 101 to 102
3.

9	5	11	6	11	12
10	13	12	7	7	11
11	9	11	6	7	9

3a. 11
3b. 7 to 11 or 9 to 11

Reteach 63, page 117

1a. 2
1b. 5
1c. $\frac{2}{5}$
2a. 1
2b. 6
2c. $P(5) = \frac{1}{6}$
3. $\frac{2}{8}$ or $\frac{1}{4}$
4. $\frac{5}{6}$
5. $\frac{2}{3}$
6. $\frac{11}{18}$

Reteach 64, page 118

1. 2 points scored
2. Colts and Steelers
3. 8 weeks
4a. Colts
4b. Week 6
4c. 28
5a. Week 2
5b. 24
6. Week 5
7. Week 4
8. 4

Reteach 65, page 119

1. 5, 55, and 60
2. 25 to 40
3. 33.16 or 33.2
4. 31.87 or 31.9
5. 30
6. The median, because the outliers give a misleading value of the mean.

Reteach 66, page 120

1. $50 \times n = 8 \times 800$
   $50n = 6{,}400$
   $n = 128$
   128 students will take the bus.
2. $\frac{35}{140} = \frac{n}{1{,}300}$
   $140 \times n = 35 \times 1{,}300$
   $140n = 45{,}500$
   $n = 325$
   325 students will eat pudding.
3. 786 students will vote for Ed.

Reteach 67, page 121

1. not random
2. random
3. random
4. not random
5. 84
6. 218 or 219
7. 3,461
8. 24,917 or 24,918
9. biased
10. fair

Reteach 68, page 122

1. The intervals on the graph are irregular.
2. The bottom part of the graph is missing.
3. The scales used are different.
4. The bars in the graph are different sizes.

Reteach 69, page 123

1a. 3
b. 4
c. $\frac{3}{4}$
2. $\frac{4}{7}$
3. $\frac{3}{6}$ or $\frac{1}{2}$
4. $\frac{85}{500}$ or $\frac{17}{100}$; $\frac{1}{6}$

Reteach 70, page 124

1.

Outcomes:	1H 1T
	2H 2T
	3H 3T
	4H 4T
	5H 5T
	Total: 10

2. $3 \times 5 = 15$
3. $2 \times 8 = 16$

Reteach 71, page 125

1. 1R, 2R, 3R, 4R, 5R, 6R, 1B, 2B, 3B, 4B, 5B, 6B
2. 3
3. $\frac{1}{4}$
4. $P \text{ (heads)} = \frac{1}{2}$; $P(Z) = \frac{1}{8}$;
   $P \text{ (heads and } Z) = \frac{1}{2} \times \frac{1}{8}$;
   $P \text{ (heads and } Z) = \frac{1}{16}$
5. $P \text{ (star and even number)}$
   $= \frac{1}{2} \times \frac{1}{2}$; P (star and even number) $= \frac{1}{4}$

Reteach 72, page 126

1. I
2. D
3. I
4. I
5. $P \text{ (star)} = \frac{1}{5}$; $P \text{ (circle)} =$
   $\frac{1}{4}$; $P \text{ (star and circle)} = \frac{1}{5}$
   $\times \frac{1}{4}$ or $\frac{1}{20}$
6. $P \text{ (Kordell)} = \frac{1}{5}$;
   $P \text{ (Ashley)} = \frac{1}{4}$;
   $P \text{ (Kordell and Ashley)} =$
   $\frac{1}{5} \times \frac{1}{4}$ or $\frac{1}{20}$

Reteach 73, page 127

1. $5(4) + 3^2$; $5(4) + 9$; $20 + 9$; 29
2. $12 \div (4) + 6$; $3 + 6$; 9
3. 6
4. 16
5. 10
6. 8
7. 17
8. 13

Reteach 74, page 128

1. $^-3$
2. $^+6$ or 6
3. $^-7$
4. $^+2$ or 2
5. $^-6$
6. $^-9$
7. $^+4$ or 4
8. $^+8$ or 8
9. $^-5$
10. $^+7$ or 7

Answer Key • Reteach Worksheets

Reteach 75, page 129

1. <
2. <
3. >
4. <
5. >
6. >
7. <
8. >
9. <
10. >
11. >

Reteach 76, page 130

1. $^-3$
2. $^-2$
3. $^-6$
4. $^-6$
5. $^+6$
6. $^-2$
7. $^+2$
8. $^+2$

Reteach 77, page 131

1. $3 + 6 = 9$
2. $^-2 + ^-5 = ^-7$
3. $^-1 + 8 = 7$
4. $9 + 3 = 12$
5. $^-7 - ^-5 = ^-2$
6. $^-5$
7. $^+5$
8. $^+6$
9. $^-9$
10. $^+7$
11. $^+4$
12. $^-3$
13. $^+7$
14. 0

Reteach 78, page 132

1. positive, $^+32$
2. negative, $^-12$
3. negative, $^-16$
4. positive, $^+6$
5. positive, $^+30$
6. negative, $^-8$
7. negative, $^-15$
8. $^+10$
9. $^-36$
10. $^+42$
11. $^+14$
12. $^-20$
13. $^-27$
14. $^+24$
15. $^-63$
16. $^+72$

Reteach 79, page 133

1. negative, $^-8$
2. positive, $^+5$
3. positive, $^+8$
4. negative, $^-8$
5. positive, $^+8$
6. negative, $^-7$
7. negative, $^-3$
8. $^+6$
9. $^-5$
10. $^+5$
11. $^-5$
12. $^-1$
13. $^-6$
14. $^+8$
15. $^-9$
16. $^+3$

Reteach 80, page 134

1. $3(8 - x) + 22 = 3(8 - 12) + 22 = 3(^-4) + 22 = ^-12 + 22 = 10$
2. $x(16 \div 4) - 7 = ^-5(16 \div 4) - 7$; substitute $= ^-5(4) - 7$; evaluate within parentheses $= ^-20 - 7$ or $^-27$; subtract
3. $^-21$
4. $^-5$
5. $^-1$
6. 24
7. 41
8. 24

Reteach 81, page 135

1. $xy - z^2 = (7)(^-4) - (2)^2$
   $= (7)(^-4) - 4$
   $= ^-28 - 4 = ^-32$
2. $z + x - y = ^-3 + 5 - (^-2)$
   $= ^-3 + 5 + 2$
   $= 2 + 2 = 4$
3. $^-18$
4. 60
5. $^-2$
6. $^-7$
7. $^-9$
8. $^-5$
9. 4
10. 30

Reteach 82, page 136

1. 3; 3; 12; $y = 12$; 3; identity
2. 7; 7; $^-7$; $^-7$; 0 $^-3$; $z = ^-3$; $^-7$; identity
3. $k = ^-22$
4. $x = ^-6$

(Reteach 82 continued)

5. $n = 18$
6. $m = ^-13$
7. $h = 8$
8. $p = ^-33$

Reteach 83, page 137

1. 8
2. 0
3. 8
4. 1
5. (8, 2)
6. (4, 4)
7. (2, 1)
8. (7, 5)
9. G
10. B
11. N
12. K
13.–23.

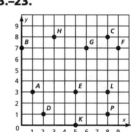

Reteach 84, page 138

1. $^-4$
2. $^-2$
3. $^-2$
4. $^-3$
5. (4, 0)
6. ($^-2$, $^-3$)
7. (1, 2)
8. ($^-3$, 3)
9. N
10. G
11. B
12. K
13.–23.

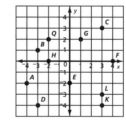

Reteach 85, page 139

1.
x	$^-x + 4$	y
1	$^-1 + 4$	3
2	$^-2 + 4$	2
$^-1$	$1 + 4$	5

2.
x	$^-x - 1$	y
1	$^-1 - 1$	$^-2$
2	$^-2 - 1$	$^-3$
3	$^-3 - 1$	$^-4$

3.
x	$2x - 5$	y
1	$2 \cdot 1 - 5$	$^-3$
2	$2 \cdot 2 - 5$	$^-1$
$^-2$	$2(^-2) - 5$	$^-9$

4.
x	$^-2x + 3$	y
0	$^-2(0) + 3$	3
$^-1$	$^-2(^-1) + 3$	5
1	$^-2(1) + 3$	1

5.
x	y
0	3
$^-1$	2
1	4

6.
x	y
0	3
1	2
3	0

7.
x	y
2	1
0	$^-1$
$^-2$	$^-3$

8.
x	y
0	4
$^-1$	3
$^-2$	2

9.
x	y
1	1
0	$^-1$
$^-1$	$^-3$

10.
x	y
2	$^-3$
$^-1$	3
0	1

11.
x	y
1	$^-1$
2	2
3	5

Answer Key • Reteach Worksheets

(Reteach 85 continued)

12.

x	y
⁻1	⁻4
⁻2	⁻1
⁻3	2

Reteach 86, page 140

1.

x	y
⁻1	⁻4
⁻2	⁻1
⁻3	2

2.

x	y
0	3
⁻1	2
1	4

3.

x	y
1	1
0	⁻1
⁻1	⁻3

4.

x	y
0	3
1	2
3	0

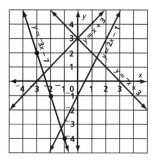

5.–8. Ordered pairs will vary;

x	y
1	⁻1
2	2
3	5

x	y
0	4
⁻1	3
⁻2	2

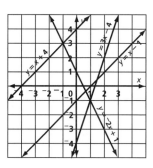

Reteach 87, page 141

1. ⁻17
2. 1
3. $\frac{-6}{1}$
4. 17
5. 7
6. $\frac{61}{12}$
7. ⁻39
8. 8
9. $\frac{-11}{6}$
10. 6; 3
11. 100; $\frac{3}{20}$
12. $\frac{8}{100}$; $\frac{2}{25}$
13. 100
14. ⁻4; ⁻2
15. $\frac{-173}{100}$
16. 3
17. 100; 7
18. $\frac{65}{100}$; $\frac{13}{20}$
19. 135; 27
20. 100; 13
21. $\frac{350}{100}$; $\frac{7}{2}$
22. <
23. <
24. >
25. >
26. <
27. >

Reteach 88, page 142

1. ⁻5
2. 12
3. $\frac{-2}{3}$
4. $\frac{4}{5}$
5. $\frac{-7}{4}$
6. ⁻0.25
7. 1.8
8. $1\frac{1}{6}$
9. $\frac{9}{4}$
10. ⁻5
11. $\frac{1}{6}$
12. $\frac{5}{6}$
13. $\frac{-1}{2}$
14. $\frac{4}{3}$
15. $\frac{-2}{5}$

(Reteach 88 continued)

16. $\frac{-2}{7}$
17. b
18. b
19. b
20. c
21. $\frac{1}{2} - (\frac{3}{4} - 1)$

Reteach 89, page 143

1. $\frac{4}{3}$; $\frac{4}{3}$; 0
2. $\frac{8}{3}$; $\frac{64}{9}$; $\frac{64}{9} = \frac{-67}{9}$
3. $\frac{-1}{6}$
4. $\frac{-1}{4}$
5. $\frac{1}{2}$
6. $\frac{-1}{9}$
7. $\frac{9}{10}$

Answer Key • Extension Worksheets

Extension 1, page 147

1. $30 \times 50 = 1{,}500$
2. $50 \times 90 = 4{,}500$
3. $50 \times 30 = 1{,}500$
4. $400 \times 800 = 320{,}000$
5. $600 \times 800 = 480{,}000$
6. $300 \times 100 = 30{,}000$
7. $10 \times 30 = 300$
8. $40 \times 100 = 4{,}000$
9. $300 \times 900 = 270{,}000$
10. between 20 and 30
11. between 3 and 4
12. between 20 and 25
13. between 2 and 3

Extension 2, page 148

1. 25; 5
2. 49; 7
3. 64; 8
4. 36; 6
5. 100; 10
6. 6
7. 9
8. 11
9. 12
10. 4 and 9; 2 and 3
11. 9 and 16; 3 and 4
12. 36 and 49; 6 and 7
13. 81 and 100; 9 and 10
14. between 7 and 8
15. between 7 and 8
16. between 11 and 12

Extension 3, page 149

1. 7; 3
2. 8.7
3. 10^5
4. 1.9×10^4
5. 2.6×10^5
6. 3.7×10^6
7. 1.45×10^5
8. 4.37×10^6
9. 3.289×10^5
10. 4; 16,000
11. 3,200,000
12. 490,000
13. 714,000

Extension 4, page 150

1. 4; 5
2. 7; 8
3. 8; 9
4. 11; 12
5. 6.8; $6.8 \times 6.8 = 46.24 = 46$
6. 7.9; $7.9 \times 7.9 = 62.41 = 62$

(Extension 4 continued)

7. 9.6; $9.6 \times 9.6 = 92.16 = 92$
8. 10.6; $10.6 \times 10.6 = 112.36 = 112$

Extension 5, page 151

1. No.
2. Yes.
3. No.
4. Yes.
5. Yes.
6. Yes.
7. No.
8. Yes.
9. No.
10. 1, 2, 4, 7, 14, 28
11. $1 + 2 + 4 + 7 + 14 = 28$
12. 1, 2, 4, 8, 16, 31, 62, 124, 248, 496; $1 + 2 + 4 + 8 + 16 + 31 + 62 + 124 + 248 = 496$
13. less than perfect; $1 + 2 + 4 + 8 + 16 + 32 < 64$

Extension 6, page 152

1. $2 \cdot 2 \cdot 3 \cdot 5$; $2 \cdot 2 \cdot 3 \cdot 7$
2. 12
3. 420
4. $2 \cdot 2 \cdot 2 \cdot 3 \cdot 3$; $2 \cdot 2 \cdot 2 \cdot 3 \cdot 5$
5. 24
6. 360
7. 9; 180
8. 36 and 45
9.
10. 6; 180

Extension 7, page 153

1. $\frac{1}{2} + \frac{1}{4} + \frac{1}{8}$;

2. $\frac{1}{2} + \frac{1}{4} + \frac{1}{24}$;

(Extension 7 continued)

3. 6
4. 12
5. 20
6. 30
7. The denominator of the first unit fraction is 1 more than the denominator of the original fraction; the denominator of the second fraction is the product of the denominators of the original fraction and the first fraction in the sum. In terms of a number, $n: \frac{1}{n} = \frac{1}{n+1} + \frac{1}{n(n+1)}$
8. $\frac{1}{10} = \frac{1}{11} + \frac{1}{110}$

Extension 8, page 154

1. $\frac{5}{12}$
2. $\frac{4}{3}$ or $1\frac{1}{3}$
3. $\frac{6}{5}$ or $1\frac{1}{6}$
4. $\frac{1}{49}$
5. $\frac{1}{64}$
6. $\frac{1}{25}$
7. 6
8. 125
9. 81

Extension 9, page 155

1. $\pm\frac{1}{8}$ in.; $10\frac{5}{8}$ in.; $10\frac{7}{8}$ in.
2. $\pm\frac{1}{16}$ in.; $6\frac{5}{16}$ in.; $6\frac{7}{16}$ in.
3. $\pm\frac{1}{20}$ in.; $9\frac{13}{20}$ in.; $9\frac{3}{4}$ in.
4. ± 0.5 mm; 7.5 mm; 8.5 mm
5. ± 0.5 mm; 8.5 mm; 9.5 mm
6. ± 0.5 cm; 12.5 cm; 13.5 cm
7. $1\frac{5}{8}$ in.; $\frac{1}{16}$ in.; $1\frac{9}{16}$ in.; $1\frac{11}{16}$ in.
8. ± 42 mm; 0.5 mm; 41.5 mm; 42.5 mm

Extension 10, page 156

1.

	Allie	Burt	Cindy
Art	no	no	yes
Bill	yes	no	no
Cliff	no	yes	no

Art — Cindy, cat
Bill — Allie, alligator
Cliff — Burt, beaver

2.

	Teacher	Doctor	Tailor
Al Teacher	no	yes	no
Jo Doctor	no	no	yes
Rita Tailor	yes	no	no

Al Teacher — doctor
Jo Doctor — tailor
Rita Tailor — teacher

3.

	Math	Science	French
Ann	yes	no	no
Dan	no	no	yes
Jan	no	yes	no

Ann — Math
Dan — French
Jan — Science

Extension 11, page 157

1. 15.24
2. 3.6
3. 64
4. 6.48
5. 105.12
6. 20.828
7. 5.5
8. 10.0
9. 62.5
10. 18.3
11. 53.5
12. 14.1
13. 33.3
14. 6.1
15. 24

Extension 12, page 158

1.

2. Yes.

222

Answer Key • Extension Worksheets

(Extension 13 continued)

3. 10; 15; 20;

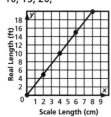

4. 6; 9; 12; 15;

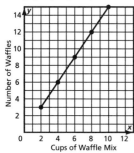

Extension 13, page 159

1. x and t; y and w
2. x and w; y and t
3. x and y; w and t
4. 120°
5. 110°
6. 70°

Extension 14, page 160

1. E
2. F
3. I
4. H
5. G
6. C
7. 2 units left and 1 unit up
8. J; I; F
9. S
10. Q
11. R
12. T
13. M
14. X

Extension 15, page 161

1.

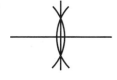

(Extension 15 continued)

2.

3.

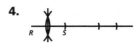

4.

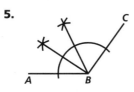

5.

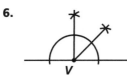

6.

Extension 16, page 162

1. 12.5 m
2. 7 cm
3. 32.4 mm
4. 14.14 m
5. 14 cm
6. 121 m²
7. 17 cm
8a. 17 m
8b. 15 m
9. 50 cm
10. 25 cm
11. $A = 625\pi$ or 1,962.5 cm²

Extension 17, page 163

1a. 5:1
1b. 25:1
2a. 2:3
2b. 4:9
3a. 2:1
3b. 4:1
4. $v = 30$ units³
5. $v = 240$ units³
6. $v = 810$ units³
7. $v = 1,920$ units³

(Extension 17 continued)

8.

Prism	Scale Factor	Ratio of Volumes
I:P	2:1	240:30 or 8:1 or 2³:1³
II:P	3:1	810:30 or 27:1 or 3³:1³
III:P	4:1	1920:30 or 64:1 or 4³:1³

9. The ratio of the volume is the cube of the scale factor ratio.

Extension 18, page 164

1. 7.5 ft²; 1,080 in.²
2. 1 yd²; 9 ft²
3. 1,728 in.²; $1\frac{1}{3}$ yd²
4. 7.065 ft²; 2.355 yd²
5. $v = \frac{2}{3}$ yd³; 18 ft³; $SA = 4\frac{1}{3}$ yd³; 42 ft³
6. $v = 24$ in.³; $\frac{1}{72}$ ft³; $SA = 76$ in.²; $\frac{19}{36}$ ft²
7a. 144 in.²
7b. 1,728 in.³
8a. 9 ft²;
8b. 27 ft³
9. $\frac{1}{144}$ ft²
10. $\frac{8}{9}$ yd²
11. $\frac{1}{4}$ ft²
12. 3 ft²
13. $\frac{1}{1,728}$ ft³
14. $\frac{1}{9}$ yd³

Extension 19, page 165

1. 32
2. 28
3. 27.67
4. 12.14
5. 27
6. 10
7. 16, 27
8. 7
9. 32, 33, 35, 38, or 46
10. 3, 6, 7, 9, 10, 13, or 14

(Extension 19 continued)

11.

Winning Scores	Stem	Losing Scores
9	3	3 4 4 6 8
9 6 6 6 3 2	4	0 0 2 2 5 7
8 8 3	5	8
9 8 0	6	3 8 8
1	7	6
0	8	
2	9	

12. 53
13. 43
14. 57.5
15. 47.75
16. 55.5
17. 42
18. 46
19. 34, 40, 42, 68

Extension 20, page 166

1. Lower Quartile: 30.5
   Median: 48
   Upper Quartile: 64

Stem	Leaf
2	1 4 7 /
3	4
4	0 6 /
5	0 8
6	1 / 7
7	0 2

2. Lower Quartile: 8.5
   Median: 11
   Upper Quartile: 15

Stem	Leaf
0	4 6 7 7 7 8 / 9 9 9 7
1	0 0 / 2 3 3 4 5 5 / 5
2	1 3 4
3	5 8

3. Lower Quartile: 64.5
   Median: 70.5
   Upper Quartile: 77.5

Stem	Leaf	
4	9	
5	3 6 6	lower quartile
6	3 4 / 5 6 7 7 8	
7	0 / 1 1 1 3 4 7 / 8 9	
8	0 3 5	median
9	0	upper quartile

Answer Key • Extension Worksheets

Extension 21, page 167

1.

2.

3.

4.

5.

6.

7.

8.

9.

10.

11.

12.

Extension 22, page 168

1. x; 1; 3
2. $6x$; 6; 18; $6x = 24$; 4
3. x; 3; $^-5$; $x = 8$
4. $2x$; 6; $^-10$; $2x = ^-16$; $^-8$
5. $x - 1 = ^-5$; $x = ^-4$
6. $^-4x + 4 = 20$; $^-4x = 16$; $x = ^-4$
7. $x + 5 = 11$; $x = 6$
8. $^-2x - 10 - 22$; $^-2x = ^-12$; $x = 6$
9. $^-5 = x + 4$; $^-9 = x$
10. $15 = ^-3x - 12$; $27 = ^-3x$; $^-9 = x$

Extension 23, page 169

1. 9, 4, 1, 0, 1, 4, 9
2. $^-9$, $^-4$, $^-1$, 0, $^-1$, $^-4$, $^-9$

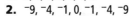

3. 10, 5, 2, 1, 2, 5, 10
4. 18, 8, 2, 0, 2, 8, 18

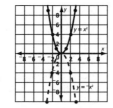

Extension 24, page 170

1. 59
2. 104
3. 24
4. 86
5. 20
6. $^-15$
7. 5
8. $^-10$
9. 62.6
10. 127.4
11. 109.4
12. $^-22$
13. 8.6
14. $^-32.8$
15. $^-4.4$
16. 22.2
17. $^-8.9$
18. $^-23.3$
19. $^-31.7$
20. $^-22.2$